DELLA FATTORIA BREAD

DELLA FATTORIA BREAD

63 FOOLPROOF RECIPES FOR *Yeasted, Enriched & Naturally Leavened Breads*

KATHLEEN WEBER

with Amy Albert & Amy Vogler
Photographs by Ed Anderson

⌘ FOREWORD BY THOMAS KELLER ⌘

ARTISAN

Published by Artisan
A division of Workman Publishing
Company, Inc.
225 Varick Street
New York, NY 10014-4381
artisanbooks.com

Published simultaneously in Canada by
Thomas Allen & Son, Limited.

Library of Congress Cataloging-in-
Publication Data

Weber, Kathleen (Baker)
  Della Fattoria bread / Kathleen Weber;
with Amy Albert and Amy Vogler ;
photographs by Ed Anderson.

pages cm
  Includes an index.
  ISBN 978-1-57965-531-0
1. Bread. 2. Della Fattoria (Bakery) I.
Albert, Amy (Journalist) II. Vogler, Amy.
III. Title.
TX769.W385 2014
641.81'5—dc23   2014004630

Design by Laura Palese

Printed in Singapore
First printing, September 2014

10 9 8 7 6 5 4 3 2 1

TO MY HUSBAND, ED, AND MY CHILDREN, ELISA AND AARON,
who were always willing participants in my escapades

AND TO MY DELLA FATTORIA FAMILY OF BAKERS,
past and present, who have always worked so hard to make the best bread every day

CONTENTS

FOREWORD

BY THOMAS KELLER

———————————

In 1995, about a year after taking over The French Laundry, I started hearing rumblings about a local baker. She was baking bread in a wood-burning oven outside the kitchen door of a family-run ranch in nearby Petaluma. Through the server at our restaurant who first told me about the bread, I asked for a sample.

A few weeks later, on a scorching Yountville summer day, a couple pulled up to The French Laundry in a worn '78 Volvo sedan. Kathleen Weber was holding a bread basket filled with loaves of pain de campagne and pain au levain. She and her husband, Ed, introduced themselves, and I took them on an impromptu tour of the kitchen. We talked about wild yeast and the importance of quality ingredients. We also spoke about their elemental approach to their craft, how they baked their hand-shaped loaves directly on the hearth. I tasted what they'd brought. It was some of the best bread I'd ever tried. We didn't know it then, but breaking bread together marked the start of a beautiful friendship.

That summer, I ordered five loaves a day (a custom bâtard shape rather than a boule). We became the Webers' first fine-dining customer, and a business relationship formed, one that continued for the next eight years. The recipe for pain de campagne dough appears in this book, along with a number of variations, from pumpkin seed and olive to chocolate cherry and Meyer lemon–rosemary. As both our ventures grew, the number of wood-burning ovens and the number of loaves produced increased, until I opened Bouchon Bakery to address the growing needs of The French Laundry and Bouchon Bistro.

During those early years, in the spirit of preserving artisanal tradition, Kathleen and I worked together on developing breads—from a seeded whole wheat reminiscent of a bread I first tasted as a young chef in New York City to a walnut baguette that Kathleen wrapped in craft paper as only a true *boulangère* would. We also tested with mini loaf pans in various shapes. The process was always experimental and convivial, and together we learned from our successes and failures.

As Kathleen told me later, every evening in those early years, Ed would stoke the fire in their lone oven (which he had built for Kathleen's birthday) so she could work into the night. When she learned that well-known personages in the culinary world were dining at The French Laundry, she began to bake with even greater intention, knowing that a gourmand she admired might be enjoying her bread the next day. That commitment to craft lives on in the Webers' son, Aaron, who worked for us at The French Laundry before joining Della Fattoria, the family business.

I believe chefs have a responsibility to make a positive impact, in part by supporting the people around them. That has been a guiding goal since I opened my first restaurant—to help the fishermen and farmers, foragers and gardeners, and, in this case, suppliers whose work is so closely intertwined with mine. I know that what they do enriches what we do, and ensures that our guests enjoy memorable experiences. Kathleen and Ed set out with a great idea and a superior product. The small boost we gave them was the least we could do.

In *Della Fattoria Bread*, you'll learn how to make many of the breads Kathleen serves at her bakery and you'll also find unique and personal recipes such as Grape-Harvest Levain Boule and Weber Family Pizza. But this book is much more than an instructional guide. It is filled with invaluable bread-baking techniques, including starters, along with important information on baking equipment and proper technique. Reading it, you'll see what I have seen throughout the years. You'll come to appreciate Kathleen's fearlessness, a fearlessness that will give you courage to take risks yourself. Kathleen is a baker, but, as she says, she thinks like a cook, drawing on her senses and her experiences in what you might describe as her strategic but instinctive approach to baking bread. Her teachings will rub off on you, informing your decisions as you cook and bake.

Bread. Is there any food richer in symbolism? At once simple but essential, it is, in many ways, like friendship. Kathleen puts it slightly differently: "Bread is our boss," she says, "our art form and our way of life."

And what a life it is.

THOMAS KELLER,
The French Laundry

PREFACE

———————

The hiss of bakers' feet skating over flour-covered floors. The clap and scrape of wooden peels against the oven floor. The calls of "Load up," "Doors off," and "Behind you!" Our ten bakers are scrambling in a space too small to produce more than a thousand loaves of bread, using an oven that, as the bake progresses, cannot be reheated. It's Friday, our busiest day of the week. Our mixer is Lindsey; at five foot two and ninety-five pounds, she's all brains, muscle, and observation. She doesn't miss a thing. She always has a smile, and she loves her dough. She arrives at 6 A.M. to mix, transfer, and fold more than two thousand pounds of it! The rest of the crew starts arriving at 10 A.M. to begin shaping. All these people are smart, really smart: they love to bake, and they love each other.

Isaac is not only a master baker, he is also a master teacher and a team builder. Emerson is our Zen guy. He knows his bread, and he has an energy about him that is steady, focused, and calming. Rachel, full of drama, rolls in on her bike, greets the dogs, and then, shoulders squared, tackles the shaping. Lorenzo, our brainy social director and political commentator, gives his bread the importance it deserves. He is funny and keeps us laughing. Betty, another tiny but mighty one, works with the speed of a machine. She has been with us for many years, and her daughter, like our grandsons, grew up in the bakery. Wesley is long and willowy, and she always knows what's happening everywhere in the room. I know I can count on her. Chad, our math brain, is a little shy. You might mistake him for someone very serious because he is always concentrating, but then his sense of humor will surprise you. Marguerite is Lorenzo's cousin, full of energy and efficiency and always with a smile on her face. Unless it's freezing outside, she arrives in her running shorts ready to move! Charlie, tall and handsome, didn't bake before he came to us, but he was sure that was what he wanted to do. Driven by passion and with an easygoing personality and natural leadership qualities, he quickly became an invaluable member of our team. If it sounds like I love these people, I do. They are my dream crew.

Restaurants always need more bread on the weekends, and so on Fridays we are baking for them and for our rain-or-shine Ferry Plaza Farmers Market in San Francisco. Friday is game night, the busiest night of the week at Della Fattoria.

Our family bakery is attached to our house, on the family ranch on the north side of Petaluma. It is run by the four of us—me; my husband, Ed; our daughter, Elisa; and our son, Aaron—and it is where we bake our wood-fired breads. We also have a café in downtown Petaluma, and we sell our bread throughout the Bay Area.

Della Fattoria grew out of a passion for wood-fired baking, an obsessive quest for lost tradition. We started in 1995 and quickly developed a following: noted chefs who feature our bread in their restaurants, independent food markets that sell our bread, and devoted regulars who visit our stand at the farmers' market every week. In the Bay Area, opinions about who makes the best pain au levain run strong, and we're in it to make the greatest we can. As our bakers have heard me say often, there's no reason to do this work unless you strive to create the best bread in the world. Isaac, our head baker, is committed to the "Old World" way of baking. He reminds his bakers that the dough is alive,

like you and me—it just has a shorter life span.

Late on Friday night, the bakers are still going strong. I marvel at the breads lined up row after row on metal racks. There's a certain way our breads look when they're just pulled from the oven—radiant and golden, as if they're filled with the glow of a candle. The rustic shapes and nut-brown crusts are magic, and the distinct aroma of our bread—roastiness, sweetness, and smoke—is like no other. After all these years, I still feel the thrill of the bake.

I'm lulled to sleep by the racks rolling across the floor and the rock 'n' roll that the bakers play as the sound track for their work. How lucky am I to get to fall asleep and then wake up to the wonderful smell of freshly baked bread?

Ed and I never made a decision to be professional bakers. That came gradually as we started baking for one or two restaurants, and then others began to ask. We never put together a business plan. I was selling women's clothing part-time and began making bread at home because I loved it. If starting a bakery had been a conscious decision, a strategic plan, it would have never happened. Every aspect of making our kind of bread carries some uncertainty: starter that's fueled by wild yeasts, doughs that are pushed to the limit for moisture content, ovens that can't be heated up again once baking begins. Starting down this path was like having a baby: you do it and don't realize what you're in for until you're in it and can't turn back, yet you're propelled forward, caught up in the details and the joy. We invented the business as we went along. We don't cut corners, and we don't make decisions based on efficiency. Bread is our boss, our art form and our way of life.

It's Saturday morning, 3:00 A.M. The alarm sounds and I hear the voices of NPR in the darkness. I drag myself out of bed and put the coffee on. When I bring Ed his wake-up cup, he's quiet, but I can feel his anxiety as he ticks off a farmers' market list in his head. Baskets? Cash box? Paper bags? He slips into the bakery to feed the oven.

Ed grew up on the ranch where we now make our home and our business. We moved here when our kids were small so they could grow up in the country and so Ed could help his parents. Composer, pianist, guitarist, farmer—my husband is a Renaissance man, and there isn't a person in the world he can't comfortably talk to. Ed has also been master of the fire since we began baking. He begins stoking the ovens early so they reach at least 900°F before tapering off for the bake. Baking by wood fire is a constant challenge, and it requires the fire chief to pay attention to all the daily variables, from the weather to how much bread we'll be baking.

By 4 A.M., Ed is starting to load the van. He has it down to a science now, and eventually the van is stuffed with tables, tents, baskets, and beautiful breads: bâtards, baguettes, épis, boules, Pullmans, and what we hope will be enough Meyer Lemon–Rosemary Campagne, our signature bread. Then off he goes: timing is important here; he needs to arrive at Ferry Plaza in time to get a place in line with the other merchants who queue up in their vans and then slowly caravan in so they're set up and ready for the hordes who arrive when the market opens at 8 A.M.

At 5 A.M., I head downtown to the café to help pack up the pastries. As I label and fill bags with cookies, our pastry chefs pull croissants and Danish from the ovens and lift bagels out of boiling water. These talented and dedicated people move around each other effortlessly, carrying trays one-handed over their shoulders, like bricklayers carrying hods of mortar. Their practiced moves are almost as lovely as the pastries, almost as wonderful as the smells that fill the room.

Like a troupe of magicians, our pastry crew has packed up my little SUV, stuffing it with amazing temptations. Surely mine is the best-smelling car on the road. I make the forty-mile drive to the city, crossing the Golden Gate Bridge, a chile-red swoop of steel cabling peeking out of the fog. I'm at Ferry Plaza by 7 A.M. Vendors—many old friends of ours, who have come up in the business like we have—lug sacks of oysters, boxes of produce, and crates of jam into their stalls. Around a corner is Ed, hanging his signature can of flowers on the front of the tent. Our stall's tables are set with red and yellow Provençal tablecloths. Our beloved Kelly and Zac, who have been with us for years, fill huge French laundry baskets with the many loaves that we will sell today.

My cell phone goes off—it's Aaron. He and our daughter are putting on an event at the ranch this evening. Elisa is bursting with creative energy. She manages the ranch gardens and oversees our special events, vacation rentals on the ranch, and our website. She is also a talented photographer, documenting the various goings-on of each week. Aaron, a trained chef, has been manning our hearth ovens since 1997. Soon after we became Della Fattoria in 1995, he joined us, fresh from the kitchens at The French Laundry, The Sonoma Mission Inn, and Daniel Patterson's first restaurant, Babette's,

in Sonoma. These days, Aaron heads up the kitchen at the café, with an easy elegance that makes it all look effortless. He possesses the urgency of a line cook, the precision of a master baker, and an unerring palate. Right now, he is giving me a list of things he needs for the ranch dinner: a little cheese from Cowgirl Creamery and Andante Dairy; some porcini, if they have them, from Gourmet Mushrooms; and some apple balsamic from The Apple Farm.

It's almost opening time. The market doesn't officially start until eight, but some regulars come early. Over the years we've gotten to know our customers, and their lives, their work, how they like to cook. We've watched their kids grow up; we know their grandchildren. They gather at our stall to gossip and tease. Ed is in his element. The line gets longer and the crowd thickens, because the faithful who throng our stand week in and week out know we sell out early.

What an astounding mix they are, from people we otherwise would never have met to those whose work we've long admired. A remarkable array of chefs and home cooks, they all generously share information on cooking methods and tips on what's best at the market today.

The market is still in full swing when I see Zac beginning to load empty baskets into the van and hear Kelly saying, "Sorry, we're out of that." We'll be on our feet until everything is gone. We'll be bone-tired this afternoon when we get home, where we'll rest our weary selves, then resume the rhythm of the week and do it all over again before coming back to the market next Saturday. We could never have imagined this life for ourselves, but I wouldn't trade it for the world.

INTRODUCTION

———————————•———————————

I started baking traditional Italian-style breads while I was working as the manager of a high-end clothing boutique. It was the early 1990s and my kids were independent. Baking turned into an obsessive quest for me, but I was certainly never thinking "career."

Long before Ed and I thought of starting a bakery, some friends gave me a copy of *The Italian Baker* by Carol Field. I had never seen a baking book like it before, one that shared the bakers' personal stories along with regional history. I hadn't ever made rustic traditional bread, yet I was instantly drawn to this way of baking. Immediately I made my first pre-ferment, or *biga*, a starter that is used in many Italian breads. The biga needed to sit overnight, so I had a little time to think about which bread I would make with it.

Pane Pugliese was the recipe I finally chose. I was excited to bake bread not contained in a pan. The dough was wetter than anything I'd worked with before, and it seemed a miracle that such shaggy floppiness turned into the best thing that had ever come out of my oven. In all my years of baking, I had never seen anything like it. The crust was crunchy and crackly; the interior crumb was golden, chewy, and full of lacy holes. The fragrance was out of this world. From that moment on, I baked day and night, reading through *The Italian Baker* as if it were a novel I couldn't put down. I was under the spell.

A good twenty-five years before my pre-ferment revelation, during the sixties and early seventies, I'd started baking as a young bride. Ed and I would

gather with an expanding group of friends to drink cheap wine, smoke cigarettes, play bridge, and talk about the war in Vietnam and the meaning of life. Food was the backdrop for it all. It was the new art form, and we reveled in cooking, experimenting, and feeding our Bohemian tribe. We were in the starving-student stage of our marriage, but my being able to cook and bake meant we could still have great parties. The aroma of baking bread made our house feel like a home and a place where our friends wanted to gather. For very little money, I could create beautiful and delicious loaves that tickled my husband, and that made me very happy. (My nana used to say, "Cookin' lasts, kissin' don't.")

Of course, during the 1960s and '70s not every woman felt that way. For centuries, a woman's day was a very busy one, and every chore that she didn't have to do was time saved. Then women began entering the workforce. Store-bought bread and processed foods (like instant soup and TV dinners) seemed like wonderful time-savers, and baking bread, now thought of as difficult, messy, and time-consuming, fell out of favor. Feminism and baking just didn't go together. For lots of women, the idea of making food to please others carried heavy baggage, as did anything to do with the home arts.

Thankfully, a counterreaction took place, a push against mass-produced food and the industrialization of our food sources.

Julia Child challenged us to cook things our mothers never would have thought of cooking. Alice Waters and Deborah Madison taught us to use beans and vegetables and to make food delicious by keeping it fresh and local. Paula Wolfert traveled through Mediterranean and Middle Eastern countries spending time with home cooks and professional chefs and then shared exotic dishes that many of us had never even seen in restaurants. We began to realize that cooking and baking were something that everyone, not just women, could take pride in. One of the delicious results was the artisanal food revolution that started sweeping the country in the late 1970s and continues to this day.

My passion continued to grow, and I spent years perfecting classic recipes. The baguette that I first learned from Julia Child's *Mastering the Art of French Cooking* would later find its way into my repertoire as Della Fattoria's first baguette. Baking from Julia was knowledge that I hung on to. I was training my senses and teaching myself good instincts. I often baked the bread for Elisa and Aaron's school lunches; those sandwich loaves later morphed into our café Pullman loaf.

After Elisa and Aaron grew up, I moved on to experimenting with rustic Italian breads, reformulating the recipes to use natural starters made from grapes grown on the ranch. That Pane Pugliese, the first Italian-style bread I mastered, with its crunchy, nut-brown crust, large holes, and moist, chewy interior, was a Della Fattoria best seller from the get-go (see page 117).

The transition from home baker to professional was almost a happy accident. I continued making bread—before work, after work, in the middle of the night. Then we built a brick oven on our deck; that was the turning point, and it ended up completely transforming our family's lives.

I gave my breads away every chance I got, and during the early and mid-nineties, I started to develop an underground following of chefs who requested my breads for special events. First Aaron, who was then cooking at The Sonoma Mission Inn, relayed a request from chef Mark Vann for bread for an olive-oil tasting. I baked a couple of breads that we thought would be enough for two days, but all the bread was gone in forty-five minutes. Mark ordered more for the next day, and within a month, we were baking daily for the inn. One of the results of that happy collaboration was our Sausage-Sage Levain Bâtard (page 195).

Our next customer was Thomas Keller, chef and owner of The French Laundry. For him, we developed our Pain de Campagne. From there, word spread, and more restaurants came calling. At the time, it was just Ed and me doing all the baking and running the business. The hours were insane and we were working harder than we ever had before, but it was magical, and we were so amazed by the way our bread was being received that it gave us a kind of superpower.

We were making the very best bread we could, using ancient methods, skimping on nothing, and doing it our way. We intended our bread to complement fine cuisine, and indeed, we found that chefs loved it because it paired so well with food. In the beginning,

they were able to be part of the design. In fact, many of our most popular breads were the results of chef requests. Today we still enjoy working with chefs, and many of them have become role models for us. I have found that the most talented and creative ones seem to be the most generous, natural teachers; they are eager to share their techniques and discoveries. This should come as no surprise: to cook is to nurture, and to share food is an act of generosity.

Over the years, aspiring and professional bakers from all over the world have come to the Weber Ranch to learn our methods and sharpen their craft. We've hosted cooking school externs, and we've had apprentices from Germany, Colombia, Australia, and Japan. Today they train under Aaron's watchful eye. We love sharing our knowledge, and we're determined to make sure the art of artisanal bread baking continues to flourish.

Cookbooks have been the textbooks of my life, from *Joy of Cooking* to *The Silver Palate Cookbook*, from books by Julia Child, Jacques Pépin, Marcella Hazan, Paula Wolfert, Martha Stewart, Alice Waters, Rose Levy Beranbaum, and Flo Braker to Carol Field's *The Italian Baker*. I have been so enriched by them and by the many others that have overcrowded my bookshelves and spilled out into stacks on the floor. Generosity is the common language of good cooks and bakers, and it's my hope that this book will find a way into your kitchen too.

Our aim has always been to be bakers who think like cooks, trusting our instincts and senses. It's these instincts that I want to share with you.

HOW THE BOOK WORKS

Della Fattoria Bread maps my journey from home baker to full-time professional by taking you from simple breads to more complicated ones. By sharing my road map, I hope to inspire and encourage you. Maybe even help you fall as madly in love with baking as I did.

The first chapter is devoted to yeasted breads—easy and straightforward, these are the ideal place to begin if you're new to bread baking. Enriched doughs come next. These are also leavened with yeast, but now, with a little knowledge in your hands, you'll be ready to learn to handle these silky and sometimes slippery, buttery doughs. Next are pre-fermented breads, here leavened with the starter known as a *biga*. Biga was the first type of natural starter I taught myself to work with, thanks to Carol Field's *The Italian Baker*. Naturally leavened breads follow. These breads rely on a starter that you'll learn to feed and care for yourself. The only thing better than the look and taste of a loaf of naturally leavened bread is how proud you'll feel at having made one. Naturally leavened breads are the heart and soul of my baking life and are how Della Fattoria made its name. A chapter on crackers, breadsticks, pizza dough, and flatbreads rounds out the book. Easy to make, these recipes fill the occasional need for immediate gratification.

The recipes in *Della Fattoria Bread* are built upon basic doughs, and they include variations that will allow you to develop an entire bread repertoire. Getting to know a basic bread recipe and then experimenting is how you gain confidence and know-how. Learning to use the time window ("bake for 35 to 40 minutes") in tandem with the doneness test ("or until the top is a rich golden brown") is how you'll get the best possible result each time you bake. It's also how you'll develop baker's instincts.

Each chapter starts with a rundown of the techniques involved and the equipment needed. Recipe ingredient lists take the form of a baker's box, with metric, U.S., and volume weights. Getting familiar with using a baker's box means understanding proportions—one of the biggest assets you can possess as a baker and a cook. There's a complete explanation of the baker's box on page 28.

Some of the sidebars throughout the book offer simple suggestions to make your baking life easier. Others shed light on techniques that might be new to you. Those called Courage in the Kitchen are meant to cheer you on when you're attempting a technique that might be unfamiliar. Photographs of techniques act as a companion to the recipes, guiding you as you master

shaping, braiding, and other skills essential to artisanal bread making.

There will be times when you may have more bread than you need or you may need some inspiration for other ways to serve it. Accompanying some of the bread recipes are ways to use your freshly baked bread or even bread that is a day or two old.

At the end of the book is a list of my favorite mail-order sources for bread-baking ingredients and equipment.

THINK LIKE
A BAKER

INGREDIENTS, EQUIPMENT & PROCESS

———————

Bread requires just a few simple ingredients, but you can't expect to make great bread unless you start with the highest-quality flour, pure water, and salt without additives. That's all there is to it, no exceptions. All flours are not equal, for example.

INGREDIENTS

Flour, water, yeast, salt—the ingredients for making bread are basic, but the importance of seeking out the best ones available was a realization I made early on, and it was one of my most crucial revelations as a baker. Top ingredients make a difference: the volume, color, and flavor of the baked bread will be better in every way. Fine ingredients are available at good grocers and specialty stores, and it's easier than ever before to get them online. For specialty flours and other recommended ingredients, see Sources, page 270.

Flour

In my early years of baking breads with a pre-ferment, I was so in love with the results that I dared to bring some bread to Bernadette Burrell, chef-owner of our favorite hangout in Petaluma, Dempsey's Restaurant and Brewery. We loved Bernadette's food, so her opinion was important to me. She took a look at the bread and said, "You need better flour." I was surprised. The possibility of getting flour someplace other than the supermarket had never even occurred to me, but Bernadette let me order flour from one of her distributors. The difference was stunning, even at first glance.

Much more golden in color than the flour I had been using, Bernadette's flour certainly looked prettier. But what struck me more were the aroma and the feel. Less processed, the flour smelled sweet, and when I picked up a handful and squeezed it lightly, it clung to itself before floating through my fingers. The flour I had been using felt like dust in comparison; it just poured through my fingers.

As my understanding of flour has evolved, so has my appreciation of the effect of *terroir* on the grain, as well as the varieties of wheat used. Much of the commercial flour available today is overprocessed and too dependent on chemical fertilizers and pesticides. Often it's made from dwarf varieties that can more easily tolerate heavy winds, strains of wheat developed for resistance to pests and tolerance to weather damage, and grains higher in protein (gluten) than the grains grown before the 1960s. Half a century ago, food scientists were striving to find hardy wheat that would grow in Third World countries facing huge food shortages. The goal was important, but the unintended consequence has been inferior products and the resultant need to fight for our food quality.

Yes, you should use organic flour. Shop at a store with a brisk turnover so you'll be assured of getting a fresher product. If possible, buy your flour in bulk; this way, you'll actually be able to smell the bin to see if what you're buying is fresh. When fresh, all-purpose flour has a sweet aroma. When the flour is stale, it can smell like cardboard. And when you squeeze a handful of fresh all-purpose flour in your fist, it will hold together briefly before slipping through your fingers.

Whole wheat flour should smell sweet too, and it should also smell nutty. If whole wheat flour is stale, it will smell like rancid oil. Tips on storing flour appear on page 12.

It's worth the effort to find millers who are producing in smaller quantities. Bay State Milling in Woodland, California; Giusto's in South San Francisco; and Central Milling in Logan, Utah (with a subsidiary in Penngrove, California) all offer a terrific product; see Sources, page 270. I also recommend checking your local farmers' market for a flour supplier.

Increasingly, farmers' markets feature a vendor or two who sell local organic wheat. Many bring small portable mills so you can grind your own flour.

TYPES OF FLOUR

All-purpose flour is called for most often in these recipes, but some call for bread, whole wheat, rye, pumpernickel, durum, or semolina flour.

ALL-PURPOSE FLOUR is 11 to 12 percent protein.

BREAD FLOUR is higher in protein, usually 13 to 14 percent. It can make breads too tough, but it is sometimes helpful for boosting the structure of a flour like semolina or used with an ingredient like cooked polenta. We use it in breads such as the Pane Integrale Boule, Seeded Wheat Bread Boule and Bâtard, and Polenta Bâtard.

WHOLE WHEAT FLOUR is ground with the wheat berry intact, so you're getting all the nutrients that the grain provides. Whole wheat flour can be purchased in various grinds: fine, medium, coarse, and extra-fine (also known as whole wheat pastry flour). I like using a medium grind, but I sometimes throw some coarsely ground whole wheat flour or cracked wheat into doughs like our Wheat and Barley Pullman Loaf and Pane Integrale Boule for texture.

RYE FLOUR is ground from the endosperm of the rye berry. Flour labeled medium rye is ground from the entire endosperm. White rye is ground from just the center of the endosperm; cream rye is ground from a larger percentage of the endosperm; and dark rye is ground from the outer layer of the endosperm. Our Pumpernickel Rye Boule and Knäckebröd are both made with rye flour.

PUMPERNICKEL is a dark, flavorful rye flour that includes the germ and bran. It has a more robust texture and flavor than regular rye flour, which feels almost as fine as cornstarch. It gives a delicious and hearty depth to breads such as Aunt Clara's Wheat, White, and Pumpernickel Bread; the Pumpernickel Rye Boule; and the Pane Integrale Boule; and to our Pain au Levain Dough.

DURUM FLOUR is ground from one of the oldest wheat varieties. Its kernels are large and have a beautiful yellow-gold endosperm. When durum is coarsely ground, it's known as semolina (see below). The Pane Durum Boule and Oval Loaves both use durum flour.

SEMOLINA is a coarse durum wheat flour. We use it for our Semolina Oval Loaf. Make sure you don't buy an extra-finely ground semolina made for pasta.

White flour will keep well in an airtight container in a cool area. I use a Cambro container, which you can pick up at a local restaurant supplier or bulk discount store, or see Sources, page 270.

Whole-grain and the other flours listed above should be used as soon as possible, because the germ in the whole grain is full of natural oils and enzymes and the flour will go rancid quickly. These flours are best purchased in small quantities and stored in the refrigerator or freezer.

Water

At the Weber Ranch, we're lucky enough to be situated on a well, so we always have really pure, nonchlorinated water for our breads. At the café, we are on city water, so to get the same results as with our well water, we filter it. With water making up from 70 to 90 percent of a bread recipe, quality can make a huge difference in the final product. Water treatment varies from city to city, so I can't make a blanket statement about what's best for your bread, but I do recommend using bottled or filtered water at least for your natural starter. This way, you'll avoid any potential contamination and be able to create a good, healthy starter. Once you get the starter going, you'll need to experiment. I know many bakers who use tap water with no problems, but if you have unsatisfactory results with your bread, there's a good chance that the water is the culprit.

Yeast

All the breads containing yeast in this book were tested with SAF instant yeast (see Sources, page 270), which is very reliable. Make sure you check the package for the expiration date. Once opened, the yeast should always be tightly sealed and stored in the fridge. I've also used Red Star and Fleischmann's instant yeasts with good results. Though it may sound counterintuitive, I don't recommend using fresh yeast. It has a short shelf life even when refrigerated, and because of that, it is less reliable than instant.

Salt

Many bakers say that salt is salt, but I disagree. Iodized table salt leaves a bitter aftertaste, and I can't recommend it for bread baking. Both fine (not coarse) sea salt and kosher salt are very affordable and easily available.

I love Brittany gray sea salt, which is hand-harvested in France using traditional Celtic methods. I use it for just about everything, including the breads in this book. Gray sea salt tastes great on salads, vegetables,

grilled meats, and popcorn. Less refined than most salts, it has a bright, clean taste with no bitterness. It also retains more of the trace minerals found in seawater, including iron, magnesium, calcium, potassium, manganese, zinc, and iodine. But gray sea salt is expensive, and I admit it's not absolutely necessary in bread baking. The recipes will turn out great with fine sea salt or kosher salt.

You'll read a lot about weighing ingredients throughout this book, starting with The Importance of Weighing, page 20. We always weigh salt because the grains vary in size and therefore in weight. Your scale may not register amounts as small as the equivalent of ¼ or ½ teaspoon in grams, in which case you can use a measuring spoon. For a small amount of salt, the differences shouldn't be significant—but if you start to double and triple recipes, it's even more important to weigh.

Sugar

Very few of our breads call for sugar, but sometimes we add it to yeasted doughs to enhance flavor and browning. Unless otherwise specified, when a recipe calls for sugar, it means granulated cane sugar.

Milk

When a recipe calls for milk, use whole milk. Della's Roll Dough (page 73) calls for powdered milk; there we mean nonfat milk powder.

Olive Oil

Extra virgin olive oil comes from the first pressing and is the most flavorful olive oil. It's perfect for drizzling over a just-baked pizza or over pasta, where you can appreciate the flavor. You might also want to use extra virgin olive oil to brush on the Durum Crackers (page 243) or in the Olive Oil Wreath (page 128), which make the oil one of the star ingredients. Pure olive oil is also fine for baking. Regular olive oil is refined and may include additives.

Cracked Wheat

Coarse and irregular in texture, cracked wheat looks like wheat berries that have been crushed by a rolling pin. We use it for flavor and texture in the Wheat and Barley Pullman Loaf (page 66) and the Pane Integrale Boule (page 209); the kernels are visible in the baked bread.

❧

EQUIPMENT

❧

My grandfather loved to work with wood and refinish furniture, and his tools said a lot about who he was. The handles of his planes and drills and even screwdrivers were wood, and they were all the more beautiful because they were burnished by frequent use and worn to the shape of his hand. His woodworking tools were his pride and joy, and they always held the promise of a new project. Bakers' tools are the same. From our proofing baskets to our ovens, the tools we work with matter. From the time we put on our aprons until we finish for the day, we have an intimate relationship with them. I like the way my bowl scraper feels in my hand, and the way it fits into the curve of a bowl. I love my smooth, well-oiled work board. My handsome mixer and the stone in my oven call me to my workbench, make me feel prepared and happy to get to work, and, most important, help me produce a better product.

There are some tools that are essential for bread making in general and others that are specific to certain types of bread. Each chapter in this book lists the equipment needed for the recipes in that chapter, but here is a list of my essential items, in order of importance. Most are available at well-stocked cooking supply retailers, such as Sur La Table and Williams-Sonoma, but I also recommend seeking out local shops and restaurant supply stores. And you'll find a complete list of sources on page 270.

Hands

Your hands are your most important tool for bread baking. There is no other way to get a real sense of the dough than with your hands. I do use a stand mixer, but with very few exceptions (such as with a sticky dough, like those for the naturally leavened breads or the overnight pizza dough), I always turn the dough out onto a floured board and knead it by hand. Pre-shaping and shaping are always done by hand. Determining when a dough is ready for baking is always done with a finger. The better you become as a baker, the more you'll realize that much of the knowledge you're acquiring is in your hands.

Scale

After your hands, I think a scale is the most important piece of equipment for a baker. The result will be consistency in your baking (see The Importance of Weighing, page 20). I recommend investing in a digital scale that reads from tenths of a gram up to kilograms. Brands like My Weigh (see Sources, page 270) offer high-quality models.

The scales in the My Weigh iBalance series, particularly the 2600 and 5500, are

good choices. Other less-expensive models by My Weigh, as well as the ones made by OXO, are fine choices, but they weigh only to 1 gram. This will be fine for most recipes, including those in this book, but having the option of going to tenths of a gram may become important to you as your baking progresses. Also, before purchasing a scale, consider other kitchen tasks that you will use it for, like weighing big cuts of meat.

Oven

I have a couple of ovens in my home kitchen. When I use my old workhorse, a Magic Chef gas oven from the 1930s, I crank it as high as it will go, knowing that as soon as I open the oven door, a lot of the heat will be lost. (My newer oven has a window and a light, but the old girl has neither, so I have to open the door more often to check on what's baking.) I'm not recommending this as the most energy-efficient way to bake, but my point is this: you've got to get to know your oven.

Every oven is different. And even if it's been professionally calibrated, there can be a temperature fluctuation of as much as fifty degrees while the oven cycles. Because of this variation, it's best to preheat your oven for a full hour before baking. This way, the oven will go through a few cycles before you bake the bread. Once the bread is in the oven, don't keep opening the door to check on it—that's what the window and the light are for.

The recipes in this book were tested in both gas and electric ovens, and the temperatures and times were tested carefully. That said, they should be used as guidelines. If your bread looks and smells as if it's getting too dark, it probably is. If that is the case, tent the bread with foil until

Setting Up Your Oven for Baking Bread

For most breads, I recommend that the rack be placed in the lower third of the oven with a baking stone set on it, but for enriched breads, I recommend the center position. Even breads baked in loaf pans or other vessels will benefit from being baked on the stone. And most will be turned out onto the stone during the final part of baking for more even browning. Depending on your oven, the rack should probably be in the lowest position when baking in a tagine (see Baking in a Clay Pot or Tagine, page 102). Placement will also vary for the pre-fermented and naturally leavened breads, where you want a setup to generate steam (see Creating Steam in the Oven, page 108).

the inside is fully baked, and then the next time you bake that bread, lower the oven temperature by 25 degrees, either when you preheat it or as soon as the bread goes in the oven. If your bread doesn't look browned enough, bake it a bit longer and think about increasing the baking temperature the next time you try the recipe.

The location of the heating element and how the oven cycles vary depending on the oven. In gas ovens, the heating element is typically on the top, and heat comes through panels on the sides. In electric ovens, the heating elements are typically on the top and bottom. In newer models, heating elements are no longer exposed. The placement of

· Creating Your Warm Spot ·

For proofing your dough, you need a warm place in the kitchen to enable the dough to develop. Because baking is a variable process, settling on a specific place will provide consistency. The main consideration is that your warm spot be draft-free. Some possible options include near a radiator, on top of the fridge, or even inside a microwave, with a bowl of warm water. Inside a turned-off gas oven will be problematic, because you'll need to preheat the oven for baking, unless you have a second oven; this would be an easy solution because it's draft-free and the pilot light provides just enough warmth. But for those without a second gas oven, what to do?

This option is my favorite, and it will work if you have none of the above (or even if you have all of them). Purchase a Cambro container from your local restaurant supply or bulk discounter, or see Sources, page 270; a plastic tub or even a large cardboard box will also work. When the dough is transferred from the mixer to a lightly oiled bowl and covered with lightly oiled or sprayed plastic wrap, set it in the container and cover. Then, once your dough is shaped (whether it proofs on the work surface, in the pans they will be baked in, in baskets, or set on linens), invert the container over the dough. Doughs that are proofed in the pans they will be baked in, in baskets, or set on linens also can be put on the counter and covered with the container. It will eliminate drafts and keep the temperature constant, and because the plastic is transparent, you'll be able to monitor the progress. The container will create its own mini-environment—kind of like a greenhouse; you can even put a hot water bottle in it. And when you're not using the Cambro to proof your dough, it is a perfect place to store your bread-making equipment so it's all in one place.

heating elements and how the oven cycles can play a big role in how you set up your oven to bake the bread; see Setting Up Your Oven for Baking Bread, page 16.

Baking/Pizza Stone

Some breads are baked entirely on a baking stone and some are turned out of the baking vessel during the last part of baking to brown on a stone. Aside from rolls that could break apart when turned out of the baking pan, just about every bread I can think of will benefit from some browning time on a baking stone.

Stand Mixer

Most stand mixers come with a dough hook, a paddle, and a whisk attachment and at least one mixing bowl. Most of the recipes in this book call for the paddle or the dough hook. I suggest buying a second bowl for the mixer, especially if you like to make more than one batch of bread on a given day.

Most of the recipes in this book were tested with the KitchenAid Artisan model. Especially if you'll be doubling or tripling these recipes, spring for the Pro model.

Work Surface

The best surfaces for working with most doughs are smooth and cool. Granite, marble, stone, and manufactured stone surfaces are all great; so is stainless steel.

A butcher block countertop or large cutting board is also fine, provided it's well oiled. Brioche dough, in particular, is easier to work with on wood than on stone. If you're working on wood, you'll probably need to add a bit more flour to the work surface to keep the dough from sticking, especially for naturally leavened doughs, which are on the sticky side. Because wood tends to retain traces of the foods prepped on them (onions sliced, garlic chopped), it's ideal to have a designated wood surface that's just for doughs.

The Importance of Weighing

Easier cleanup, more accurate measurements, and better results: there are so many reasons using a kitchen scale will make your baking life easier and more fun. Measuring by weight instead of volume also makes it much easier to reduce or multiply a recipe quickly and accurately. I strongly recommend that you use a scale for all the recipes in this book. If you don't have one, any good cookware store stocks them (or see Sources, page 270). Look for one that is accurate, easy to read, and simple to use.

With a scale in your kitchen, you will no longer need to use measuring spoons and cups. There will be far less to wash, because you can weigh all of the ingredients in the same bowl. And you'll avoid any degree of uncertainty. Flour, for example, is easily compacted, so one person's measured cup won't be the same quantity as somebody else's. With a scale, accuracy is achieved no matter who is doing the weighing.

All of the recipes in this book were tested using gram measurements, and the U.S. measurements were rounded in most cases.

Mixing Bowls

The bowls I use exclusively are bread bowls, crockery bowls that are wide at the top and narrow at the bottom. You'll need a 4½- to 5-quart bowl for the doughs in this book (if you also have a 3-quart, that will be preferable for a few doughs, like the Arborio Rice Bread on page 37, but it's not essential). I sometimes use this bowl for salads too—I make my dressing in the bowl: the tapered shape is great for that.

Will other mixing bowls work? Probably yes. But deep tapered bowls help doughs reach their full height during proofing. Glass bowls like Pyrex also work fine, and many bakers like to use a plastic vessel for proofing. I'd avoid working with metal bowls—I find that metal doesn't hold as consistent a temperature, and consistent temperature is essential for proofing dough.

Cast-Iron Pot

Although some of these recipes call for other pans and pots, such as a Pullman pan, traditional loaf pans, and even clay pots, the workhorse in my kitchen—and in this book—is a 9-inch-diameter, 3½- to 4-quart enameled cast-iron pot. Most of the boules in the book come out beautifully baked in a pot this size. A larger one, like the Pane Durum Boule (page 133), needs a 6-quart pot. For more on cast-iron pots, see Proofing & Baking in a Cast-Iron Pot, page 43.

Cambro Container or Plastic Tub

Elongated loaves like baguettes, épis, and bâtards need to be covered completely once they're shaped. An inverted Cambro container or plastic bus tub (sold at restaurant supply stores; or see Sources, page 270) does the trick. Either one will produce the draft-free environment dough needs for proofing; see Creating Your Warm Spot, page 17. Other loaves can be proofed directly in the vessels they'll be baked in, covered with plastic wrap. But additional protection against drafts never hurts, so if you're in doubt, cover the proofing vessel with an inverted Cambro container or plastic tub.

Plastic Bowl Scraper

For removing dough from the sides of a mixing bowl or releasing a dough from a bowl or a proofing basket, this thin, curved plastic scraper is invaluable. It is a simple, inexpensive tool and way more effective than a silicone spatula.

Bench Scraper (Dough Cutter)

Rectangular with a handle on the top side, a bench scraper can be made of metal or very hard plastic. It is great for dividing and shaping dough. It's also handy for cleanup, doing just what its name says: scraping scraps of dried dough off the bench or work surface.

Kitchen Timer

It's easy to get distracted; to keep track of all the steps of bread making, set a timer. I use the timer on my phone, but you could also use the digital kind that clips onto your apron so that the timer is never out of earshot.

Thermometer

An instant-read probe thermometer, like the Thermapen (see Sources, page 270), is invaluable in the kitchen. I use it for taking the temperature of the water for the dough. A thermometer is also a huge help when learning

how to know when a loaf is baked through (see Is It Baked?, page 58). Knowing how to determine doneness simply by the sound of a baked loaf will come with time.

Plastic Wrap

It may sound odd, but plastic wrap is really important in bread baking. It helps keep dough from drying out and forming a skin during its first proof and, in some instances, during its second. Make sure to oil the plastic wrap lightly or spray it with cooking spray before covering the dough. This prevents the dough from sticking to the plastic wrap and deflating when you remove the wrap. You will have larger pieces to work with if you buy a larger roll from a local warehouse store.

HOME ON THE RANCH

Petaluma, our hometown, was once known as "The Egg Basket of the World." We live on one of its old chicken ranches, and we still have chickens of assorted varieties strutting and clucking and laying colorful eggs every day. We have California Mutant sheep to keep the grass down and entertain us with their antics, and we have an assortment of dogs and cats. We have a boutique vineyard of Pinot Noir grapes that sometimes make it into wine and in other years provide a bonanza for the birds. We have field crops of tomatoes grown especially for the famous BLTs we serve at the café every summer, as well as peppers, potatoes, squash, pumpkins, and raspberries. We have flower gardens to attract birds and bees (and humans too). Giant arrangements of our flowers bring the feel of the ranch to the café.

The Weber Ranch is where our day begins and ends. It is home to the "old folks" (that would be my husband, Ed, and me); our kids, Elisa and Aaron; and their spouses, children, and dogs and cats. Luckily, we all have separate houses, and, thankfully, we all share the workload. This land works as hard as it did when it was producing ten thousand eggs a day. It's where we built our first wood-fired oven in 1994, where our breads are baked every day, and where we host ranch dinners every summer.

We've lived here with our kids since 1969. New furnishings weren't even an option when our children were small. Fortunately, I married a man who just found things he liked to look at and hung them up on the walls—Model A grilles, prints with folk art frames, and other odd bits he picked up at Woody's Junk Store in downtown Santa Rosa. For one of our early wedding anniversaries, Ed bought me an operating-room light from the St. Vincent de Paul thrift shop. When he first brought that oversized monstrosity into the house, I thought I was going to kill him. But after my initial fit, I had

to admit it was absolutely fabulous: all chrome and safety glass, with a tilting arm and wheeled legs for rolling anywhere we needed task lighting, perfect for my knitting. It became the focal point of our living room and set a tone that continues to define our sense of style even today.

We have our own look: original, comfortable, and fun. What we discovered by accident was the satisfaction and comfort of authenticity. When you come to the ranch, you'll see found objects— sewer covers used for stepping-stones, rebar for fencing, and wood repurposed as outdoor tables and seating. You'll see my daughter's wild gardens, my son-in-law's metal sculptures, and gigantic outdoor dining tables made by both of them. And you'll see our red ranch house and the chimney of the ovens. The barn-like house where our son, Aaron, and his family live was once a granary; the home that belongs to Elisa and her family wasn't even originally on our farm. It was a house that was going to be torn down to make way for a new school but instead was dragged here from across town. You'll see my grandsons' bikes and scooters, a plethora of dog toys, and the mandatory rusted-out trucks and junk piles that every rancher needs in case he has to fix something.

When you walk in the back door of our house, you'll see my funny old kitchen with its 1950s yellow-and-blue tile on the counters and backsplash. You'll see doorless cabinets painted mustard yellow, with paprika-colored shelves. The floor is the same blue-and-white linoleum that Ed and his sister used to roller-skate on when they were kids. My 1930s black Magic Chef stove came from a local restaurant that was auctioning off all its old equipment. The range has a tall back with a shelf that holds my forty-year-old collection of orange Le Creuset cast-iron pots. That is the shelf I proof my bread on. The cooktop has four large burners on the left and a big iron flattop on the right. The two 36-inch-wide ovens have seen countless loaves of bread, cookies, pies, and cakes, not to mention roasts and turkeys and casseroles. That stove has been the backdrop for so many memories. Finally, if you're a clean-counter person, you probably won't like my kitchen, because I like everything I have there to be within reach—on the open shelves, hanging, or stacked on the counter.

Looking beyond the kitchen, you'll see the world of my husband, Ed, known to most as Mr. Ed. There's a grand piano, his tube amp, too many guitars to count, shelves full of books, CDs, and a microphone collection. Beyond that is a ham radio station with old-model radios, especially military ones from World War II, which he collects and uses to talk to people all over the world. We both like to be surrounded by the things we love and love to use every day so they become the texture of the room. Who we are becomes very obvious.

In an old farmhouse like ours, the only entry people ever use is the door that leads into the kitchen, my favorite room. It's clear that this is a home where food and cooking dominate. My kitchen is where everyone hangs out and feels most comfortable. It is the place where you can get down to brass tacks. My kitchen is the spot in which we all just get to be with one another—no airs and no pretense.

THE PROCESS

There's a misconception that making bread requires hours and hours of work. Although the process does stretch out, little of it is active time: there's a lot of in-between time when the bread is resting or proofing. While that's happening, you can go about your day.

There are seven basic steps involved in bread baking. You'll notice variations in the steps as the recipes in this book progress from yeasted to enriched to those using a pre-ferment and then to naturally leavened loaves, but the fundamental process is the same.

STEP 1. Organizing

The more organized you are and the cleaner you keep your work area, the better things will go. Because of the stretched-out nature of the process, you may find that bread baking best fits into your schedule if you start it in the morning—maybe during a quiet few minutes before the rest of the household gets going. Or, if you're a night owl, starting in the afternoon might suit you better. In any case, take the time to set everything up first.

Read through the recipe completely at least once, or even two or three times. Then start gathering your materials. Get all of your utensils and equipment out first; make sure that scrapers, timer, and thermometer are close at hand. Then pull out your ingredients and weigh everything out. If you set yourself up nicely, you'll be far less likely to forget things if you get interrupted.

A word about messiness: I've heard people complain that baking can be messy.

They're right. Because I know I'm more efficient in a clean, orderly work space, I've devoted a lot of time and thought to baking in a way that allows me to work with abandon yet satisfies my need for order. If you already bake, you probably feel the same way I do, but if you're new to baking, hear me out: getting into the habit of cleaning up as you go can make the difference between having fun in your kitchen and hating it.

Put a pan of hot soapy water in your sink so that each tool can go into the water when you're finished using it. A silicone sink strainer is a help, because it catches globs of dough and flour—you can then just turn the strainer inside out and empty its contents into the garbage can. Several companies make them, including OXO (see Sources, page 270).

And, again, almost every recipe in this book has some downtime. Even if it's just ten minutes when you're waiting for the dough to relax, that's enough time to wash, dry, and put away your dirty bowls and utensils. Then, when you're finished baking, your kitchen is already clean. I know this isn't rocket science, but developing the habit of keeping your work space tidy ensures that you'll make fewer mistakes and will be able to enjoy both the process and the result.

STEP 2. Mixing & Kneading

Mixing is the very beginning of the development of the dough, when it begins to take on its structure and the flavors start to evolve. Then, when the dough is transferred from the mixing bowl to the work surface for its initial knead, you may find it really sticky. The temptation will be to add more flour.

If you feel you absolutely have to, go ahead—but add as little as possible. Or, if the dough is simply too sticky to turn out on the board for kneading, try kneading it right in the mixing bowl, using your plastic bowl scraper. You can also transfer very sticky doughs directly to the proofing bowl without kneading. As handling dough becomes more familiar, though, working with a sticky dough in its initial stages of development will become less daunting.

STEP 3. First Proof

Once the dough is mixed and kneaded on the work surface, it is transferred to a lightly oiled bowl, where it will proof for 1½ to 3 hours, depending on the dough, in a warm place (see Creating Your Warm Spot, page 17).

This stage is sometimes called bulk fermentation. The flavor of the dough will develop more fully during this period, and the structure will continue to develop. Naturally leavened doughs undergo three folding steps that greatly help the dough structure.

STEP 4. Dividing, Pre-shaping & Shaping

After proofing, the dough is transferred to a floured board, where, if you're making more than one loaf, it is divided with a bench scraper. The dough is then pre-shaped (see Pre-shaping, page 44), gently molded and coerced into shape. The pre-shaped dough rests on the work surface for 10 minutes and then is shaped into a boule, bâtard, baguette, or other shape.

STEP 5. Second Proof

Once it is shaped, the dough is proofed again. This is also called the second fermentation. Sometimes this will be in the same vessel the bread will be baked in, sometimes it'll be in a basket or bowl, and sometimes it'll simply be covered on the work surface. The second proof will take from 1 to 2 hours, depending on the dough.

STEP 6. Baking

When the proofed dough bounces back in response to a light press (see Is the Dough Ready for Baking?, page 39), it is transferred to its baking pan or directly to the baking stone, or simply covered, if it was proofed in the pan it will be baked in, and put in the oven. The dough is sometimes brushed with milk or olive oil, or a combination of the two, and it is sometimes scored. And some breads need steam (see Creating Steam in the Oven, page 108). Once the dough is in the oven, don't open the oven door until it's time to uncover the pan or take it out (see Is It Baked?, page 58).

STEP 7. Cooling

It's essential to cool any bread thoroughly: when a loaf comes out of the oven, it's still baking (see Cooling Bread Completely, page 50). Transfer the bread to a cooling rack and resist the urge to cut into it until it is completely cooled, which usually takes about 3 hours.

BAKER'S TERMS

Like any art or craft, baking has a language all its own. The terms below are the ones most commonly used in bread making; some appear in this book. If they are unfamiliar, they'll take on more meaning once you start baking.

AUTOLYSE (AU-to-lees): The French term for the step of resting dough for a period of at least 15 to 20 minutes after it has been mixed. *Autolyse* literally means self-digestion; it refers to cells being destroyed by enzymes within them. That may sound like a bad thing, but proteins that are well hydrated form stronger gluten chains, and the protease enzyme works to break down some of the gluten, for better extensibility. The beauty of the process is that it happens without mixing, so the dough will have undergone less oxidation, and that helps with color and flavor. All of the naturally leavened breads in this book undergo an autolyse.

BAGUETTE: The classic long, slender French loaf. A true baguette is almost 3 feet long—too big for home ovens. The recipes here are for our baguettes, which, at about half the length, are just as beautiful and impressive looking.

BÂTARD (ba-TAR): A long loaf that's shorter than a baguette, traditionally with tapered ends.

BIGA (BEE-ga): An Italian pre-ferment (see page 100) used to make breads such as Free-form Pane Pugliese (page 117), the Traditional (Sweet) Baguette (page 142), and most of the other pre-fermented breads.

BOULE (bul): The French word for a round loaf, large or small.

CRUMB: The texture and structure of the inside of a baked bread; also referred to as crumb structure.

DE-GAS: The act of pressing air out of a dough, often done after the final rise and before shaping. The dough is turned out onto the work surface and the excess bubbles gently pushed out. If a pre-shaped loaf has rested a little too long and gotten really puffy, it may need a gentle de-gassing before final shaping.

DIMPLING: The technique of pushing your fingertips into a dough to create indentations in it, usually done right before the dough goes into the oven. Dimpling keeps the dough from puffing too much during baking, as with the Pane Toscano Loaves (pages 121).

ÉPI (ay-PEE): A long loaf cut just before baking to resemble the top of a blade of wheat (see Forming an Olive Oil Wreath, page 130). The finished loaf can be pulled apart into dinner-roll-sized pieces.

FOLDING: A technique for building volume and strength in a dough, especially naturally leavened ones. It is a way to develop a stronger dough without overmixing.

HYDRATION RATE: The percentage of water in a dough. For example, a dough made with 10 pounds of flour that has a hydration rate of 80 percent would include 8 pounds of water. Doughs with a high hydration rate produce the kinds of breads I love best—chewy, with a lacy crumb structure.

JUMP (oven jump): Also referred to as kick, bounce, or oven spring, this is the sudden expansion that occurs when the dough meets the high heat of the oven.

KNEADING: After a dough is mixed, it is often kneaded briefly. In these recipes, kneading means just a few short turns by hand on the work surface. When a dough is first mixed, the gluten strands are going in every direction. Further kneading organizes the gluten strands into a structure of matrixes that trap gas and allow the dough to expand. Kneading can also be done in a mixer with the dough hook attachment.

MIXING: The initial blending of the ingredients for a dough.

POOLISH (poo-LEESH): A very wet pre-ferment that is Polish in origin; thus its name in French. Poolish has a one-to-one ratio of flour and water.

PRE-FERMENT: A wet mixture, sometimes called a sponge or sponge starter, consisting of flour, water, and a small amount of yeast, which is allowed to sit for at least 6 hours, or overnight, before it is used. As with an autolyse, it allows more time for the yeast to interact with the starches and proteins in the flour. A pre-ferment contributes to the manageability of the dough and the flavor and shelf life of the bread. See also BIGA and POOLISH.

REST: To let a dough sit undisturbed for a period of time.

RETARD: Many commercial bakeries prolong the fermentation process by chilling their dough. Retarding allows control over when the dough is ready to bake and encourages flavor development.

SCALE: *Scale* is used by bakers as a verb to refer to weighing dough.

SPONGE: A sponge is a mixture of all the water and yeast called for in a recipe and some of the flour. A sponge gives breads better shape, volume, and flavor. The Yeasted Breads (pages 31–67) use a sponge.

STARTER: The breads in this book other than the yeasted and the enriched get their rise from a mixture of flour and water known as a starter. The pre-ferments use a starter called a biga (see page 100) that is allowed to develop overnight. The naturally leavened breads use a natural starter that initially takes 10 days to develop.

☙❧

HOW TO READ A BAKER'S BOX

☙❧

My baking inspiration has always been the old crones with knobby fingers who baked bread just as their mothers had before them, and I'm pretty sure they didn't think too much about the science of it. They thought in terms of proportions. And that is how professional baking recipes are done: baker's percentages.

After the first few tries, reading a baker's box will become second nature. It's also where the freedom begins. You'll now be able to take any bread recipe, translate it into percentages, and modify it to get exactly the amount of bread you want. Doubling a recipe using volume measurements will throw it out of whack because a cup of flour varies greatly depending on the flour itself and who's measuring it—but with weights and percentages, you can increase or decrease the recipe with confidence.

The baker's boxes that accompany the recipes in this book will get you thinking in terms of percentages. Throughout the book, the recipes use weights, leading with grams followed by ounces, but since Americans think more in terms of pounds, here's a box where I've used pounds as an example (see below). The Campagne recipe calls for 10 pounds of flour (I realize that 10 pounds is a big quantity for home baking, but it's a good round number to illustrate how percentages work).

This is useful for baking in quantity, too. Most stand mixers will indicate how many pounds the mixer will tolerate without overheating. So, for example, say you have this recipe for campagne, but you want to make a total amount of 3 pounds of dough. Multiply the original weight of the total flour (10 pounds) times the desired weight (3 pounds). Then divide that number (30 pounds) by the total weight of the original recipe (19.15) and you have your new flour amount (1.57 pounds). That is your new 100 percent.

CAMPAGNE (weights are in pounds)	
All-purpose flour	10.00
TOTAL FLOUR	10.00
Water	7.60
Starter	1.30
Salt	0.25
TOTAL WEIGHT	19.15

CAMPAGNE (weights are in pounds)	
All purpose flour	1.57
Water multiply 1.57 (total flour) × .76 or 76%	1.20
Starter multiply 1.57 × .13 or 13%	0.21
Salt multiply 1.57 × .025 or .025%	0.04
TOTAL WEIGHT	3.02

Breaking down the recipe, you can see that:

Total flour weight is 100%
Water is 76%
Starter is 13%
Salt is .025%

Add all the ingredients up, and you'll get the total weight of the dough.

For more information on baker's percentages, there are many references online, and now there are even apps you can get for your mobile phone. When calculating my daily recipes for the bakers, I use an Excel spreadsheet with the formulas imbedded. This is pretty easy to do and certainly a time-saver.

YEASTED BREADS

——————— ◆ ———————

——————— ◆ ———————

AS A YOUNG BRIDE IN 1965, I HAD AN AGENDA. Ed and I were both attending college, and I was going to be both the perfect student and the perfect homemaker. (Our parents were convinced we were far too young to get married. Proving them wrong was a strong motivator.)

One day Ed came home to our tiny apartment with the news that he had found the ideal house for us, a big old Victorian near downtown Santa Rosa. It looked like a mansion. Word on the street was that the tenants had been evicted. Ed knocked on the landlords' door. Ever the charmer, my husband convinced them to rent the house to us, then and there, furnished with antiques, for eighty dollars a month.

The building was Colorado red marble with Craftsman-style shingles. The black-and-white marble front steps led to a huge front porch with redwood columns. The windows were big and beveled and the floors were parquet. There was a sunroom and a huge dining room furnished with a round claw-foot oak table with eight leaves. Hanging above it was a milk-glass-and-brass chandelier. This became the perfect gathering place for our eclectic array of friends from the college's drama, philosophy, music, and biology departments, and they were the ideal guinea pigs for a novice cook and baker. It was here, with a Wedgewood gas range, that I baked my first bread. The result was nothing that would make me think baking bread would be what I should do for the rest of my life, but served to starving students who were grateful for anything homemade, it was an out-of-the-park home run.

Having all those mouths to feed taught me to be fearless in the kitchen. More important, it taught me that food invites lively conversation and builds strong connections and a sense of community. We would talk into the wee hours of the morning, discussing music, philosophy, and politics, fueled by good food, cheap wine, wonderful friends, and a table you could put your elbows on. The breads I was baking at that time were made with commercial yeast. I still think that working with yeasted doughs is the best way to start baking bread. Yeasted breads require a shorter time investment than naturally fermented breads, creating a better opportunity for skill development. Yeast offers a degree of predictability that is great for confidence building. And *building* is the key word here, because the techniques you are learning (or revisiting) in this chapter will be the foundation for all the recipes that follow.

Baking so involves the senses that there are many aspects of dough handling that defy precise verbal descriptions. For that reason, you need to train your hands, your eyes, and your nose to recognize the characteristics of dough in its various stages of development. For example, I might use a descriptor like *tacky*. You may not know what that really means before you start baking, but the first time you feel a dough in your hands, you will understand that, yes, it feels tacky and, as a matter of fact, it looks tacky too. These are markers—tactile sensations that will guide

you through the bread-baking process. You will be learning a language, and the best way to learn is by doing.

In the chapters that follow, you'll discover the satisfaction of touching a dough and learning how finished dough should feel. You will learn about dividing and shaping the dough, noticing the remarkable changes in texture and volume as you go.

In this chapter, I introduce you to the pre-shaping we use on all our breads and to some beginning shaping techniques. The breads in this chapter are proofed and baked in pans. I think of these as traditional American breads, intended for sandwiches and toast.

These recipes are from my early years of baking, but I have made one change to my old recipes, and that is the addition of a sponge to some of the doughs. The benefit derived from this short step is undeniable. Starting with a sponge makes a difference in flavor and texture.

A sponge is simply a mixture of water, yeast, and flour. Making a sponge will give any yeasted bread an easy boost. The dough will be more extensible and easier to handle. The loaves will rise to their fullest, and they'll bake to their maximum volume. Think of it as taking time to stretch before exercising. When you warm up, you increase your flexibility and you have a more effective workout. It is the same with a sponge. The water starts changing the structure of the flour as it sits, allowing the gluten strands to relax and become more elastic.

To make this version of a sponge, you combine all the yeast and water in the bowl of the mixer, add half the flour called for, and mix briefly, then let the whole thing sit uncovered for 20 to 30 minutes, until bubbly (see photo, page 35). Then you proceed with the recipe. That's all there is to it.

Yeasted breads may not be as complex in flavor as their Old World counterparts, but they have their own tradition in our culture and are just as important. The recipes that follow are as delicious as they are simple and a great way to get your hands in.

TECHNIQUES

In this chapter, you'll start to develop your baker's instincts, learning the feel of the dough in your hands. Though a stand mixer fitted with a dough hook will do the heavy work for you, you need to get your hands onto the dough to test its progress. I always like to finish the kneading by hand, even if it's just a few rotations; I love the sensation of dough under my fingers. When working with a firm or stiffer dough, you'll learn to recognize when it's just *ready*. You'll find that the dough no longer sticks to your fingers. Once a firm dough is completely kneaded, a chemical reaction has taken place. The dough suddenly feels cooler and less tacky. It actually sweats a little, leaving moisture on your hands.

Some doughs, like Aunt Clara's (page 64), will be really sticky when they come out of the mixer but will tighten up after the first proofing and be easier to handle. Other doughs, like the one for the Arborio Rice Bread (page 37), continue to feel sticky, but as you knead them, you will feel the structure of the dough become stronger and more defined underneath. And, finally, the benefits of resting your dough will very quickly be revealed to you. If at any point you get frustrated with the dough, or it seems to be fighting you, cover it with lightly oiled or sprayed plastic wrap or a towel and walk away for ten minutes. When you come back to it, your hands will instantly recognize that in that short amount of time, a big change has taken place. As if by magic, your dough will have been tamed a bit and will be much more willing to yield to your direction.

Proofing and baking in the same vessel (page 38)

Working with a sponge

Judging readiness of dough with the finger test (see Is the Dough Ready for Baking?, page 39)

Pre-shaping (page 44)

Shaping a Boule (page 46)

Shaping a Bâtard (page 52)

Determining when bread is done (see Is It Baked?, page 58)

Shaping rolls (see White or Wheat Sandwich Rolls, page 61)

Shaping an oval loaf (see Oval Herbed Bread, page 62)

EQUIPMENT NEEDED

- Scale
- Stand mixer with paddle and dough hook attachments
- Baking stone
- Thermometer
- Plastic bowl scraper
- Bench scraper
- Plastic wrap
- 3-quart bread bowl (optional)

- 4½- to 5-quart bread bowl
- Two 8½-by-4½-by-2¾-inch loaf pans
- 13-by-4-by-4-inch Pullman pan (lid optional)
- 9-by-13-inch baking pan or quarter sheet pan (9 by 13 by ½ inch)
- Half sheet pan
- 3½- to 4-quart (9-inch) round cast-iron pot

- 3- to 4-quart (9-by-7½-inch) oval cast-iron pot
- Cambro container or plastic tub
- Cooling rack
- Large spatula or peel
- Pastry brush
- Spray bottle
- Parchment paper

ARBORIO RICE BREAD

ᔗ Makes 2 standard loaves ᔗ

Inspired by a recipe by the brilliant British cookbook writer Elizabeth David, this is one of the easiest breads I've ever made. It comes together fast, is mixed entirely by hand in a single bowl, and is baked in two standard loaf pans. Almost no kneading is required.

It's also one of the most unusual yeasted breads I've seen, as the dough calls for rice. I use Arborio rice instead of regular white rice. Arborio is, of course, the rice that gives risotto its creaminess, and, sure enough, those fat, starchy grains give the bread a similarly creamy texture. If you're calculating exact ratios, the weight of the cooked rice will be 520 grams (18.3 ounces/2½ cups plus 2 tablespoons), which is 70 percent of the flour weight.

When toasted, this bread has a remarkably delicate crunch.

RICE

Arborio rice	158 g	5.5 oz	¾ cup
Water	525 g	18.5 oz	2¼ cups

DOUGH MIX

All-purpose flour	735 g	26 oz	5¼ cups
TOTAL FLOUR	735 g	26 oz	5¼ cups
Instant yeast	13 g	0.5 oz	1 Tbsp plus ¾ tsp
Fine gray salt	19 g	0.6 oz	1 Tbsp
Water, at room temperature (65° to 70°F/18° to 21°C)	468 g	16.5 oz	2 cups
TOTAL WEIGHT	1,755 g/1.75 kg	61.9 oz/3.8 lbs	

WASH

14 to 32 grams (0.5 to 1.1 ounces/1 to 2 tablespoons) olive oil or milk, or a combination (see Brushing Yeasted Doughs Before and After Proofing, page 42)

To cook the rice, combine the rice and water in a small saucepan and bring to a boil. Cover, turn the heat down to low, and cook until the water is absorbed and there are little holes across the surface of the rice, 15 to 20 minutes.

Remove the lid and let the rice cool slightly. The rice should still be very warm when incorporated with the other ingredients.

+ Lightly oil or spray a deep 4½- to 5-quart ceramic or glass bread bowl. (The amount of dough for this bread will work well in a 3-quart bread bowl if you have one.)

+ In a large bowl, whisk together the flour, yeast, and salt.

+ When the rice is still very warm but cool enough to touch, mix it into the flour until the mixture has the texture of a gummy meal. Pour in the water and continue to mix with your hands, gently gathering the mixture together, turning it and pressing it with the heels of your hands, until it all comes together. It will be very sticky, similar in texture to a milky biscuit dough; do not be surprised if you have quite a bit sticking to your hands.

+ Using a plastic bowl scraper, get what dough you can off your hands, pressing it back onto the dough, and turn the dough into the bread bowl. Cover the bowl with a lightly oiled or sprayed piece of plastic wrap and place in a warm, draft-free spot (see Creating Your Warm Spot, page 17) until the dough has at least doubled in volume and there are delicate bubbles across the surface, 1½ to 2 hours.

+ Fairly generously oil or spray two 8½-by-4½-by-2¾-inch loaf pans.

+ Flour the work surface. Turn out the dough, using the bowl scraper, and use a bench scraper to divide it in half. With your fingertips, very gently shape each portion into a bâtard (see photos, Shaping a Bâtard, pages 52–53), about 3 by 7 inches. Set in the prepared pans and very gently brush the tops with the wash. (This dough is not brushed again before baking because the loaves will be too fragile once proofed.) Cover the tops with a lightly oiled or sprayed piece of plastic wrap. Set the pans in your warm spot to proof until the dough reaches the tops of the pans, 1½ to 2 hours; remove the plastic wrap.

+ Meanwhile, position a rack in the lower third of the oven, set a baking stone on it, and preheat the oven to 450°F.

+ Place the pans on the stone and immediately lower the oven temperature to 400°F. Bake for 30 to 35 minutes, or until the tops are a rich golden brown. The loaves will be delicate, but they can carefully be taken out of the pans to brown directly on the stone: place the loaves on the stone and let brown for about 3 minutes, to brown the sides and bottom more evenly. To test for doneness, see Is It Baked?, page 58.

+ Transfer the breads to a cooling rack and let cool completely. For storing options, see How to Store Bread, page 51.

Proofing & Baking in the Same Vessel

Aside from pure ease, there's a big advantage to proofing yeasted shaped dough in the same pan or vessel you will bake it in: the finished loaf will have a more appealing form. Yeasted doughs are a bit too delicate for free-form baking, so for the proofing stage, the walls of the pan or pot serve as a kind of safety net, ensuring that the dough holds its shape. (If you're using a cast-iron pot that has a lid, know that the doughs in this chapter don't get any benefit from being baked with the lid on.)

· Is the Dough Ready for Baking? ·

The finger test is the way to tell if your dough is ready to be baked. Gently touch the proofed bread with your fingertip to check for resistance and bounce-back. Be gentle: don't stab it. If the dough is ready, it will feel taut yet responsive and your fingertip will leave a slight impression.

WHITE SANDWICH BREAD DOUGH

⮞ Makes 1.17 kilograms/2.5 pounds ⮜

Calling this recipe "white bread" doesn't do it justice: the texture is more substantial and the flavor is deeper, thanks to the addition of olive oil, and the dough is also smooth and easy to work with. With this one basic yeasted dough, you can make simple white sandwich bread (or a whole wheat variation), cinnamon raisin bread, sandwich rolls, and herb bread.

Instant yeast	8 g	0.28 oz	2¼ tsp
Warm water (100°F/38°C)	472 g	16.6 oz	2 cups
All-purpose flour	630 g	22 oz	4½ cups
TOTAL FLOUR	630 g	22 oz	4½ cups
Fine gray salt	14 g	0.5 oz	2¼ tsp
Granulated sugar	9 g	0.3 oz	2¼ tsp
Extra virgin olive oil	40 g	1.4 oz	3 Tbsp
TOTAL WEIGHT	1,173 g/1.17 kg	41 oz/2.5 lbs	

Lightly oil or spray a deep 4½- to 5-quart ceramic or glass bread bowl.

‣ For the sponge: Put the yeast, water, and half of the flour in the bowl of a stand mixer fitted with the paddle attachment. Pulse a few times on the lowest setting (to keep the flour from flying out of the bowl), then mix on low speed just to combine, about 1 minute. It is OK if there are some small lumps of flour. Let sit at room temperature until there are bubbles across the top, 20 to 30 minutes.

‣ Meanwhile, in a medium bowl, whisk together the remaining flour, salt, and sugar.

‣ Once the surface of the sponge is bubbly, pour the olive oil over the top, and mix on the lowest setting for just a few seconds to incorporate. Add the dry ingredients and pulse a few times on the lowest setting, then mix on low speed for about 1 minute to combine.

‣ Remove the paddle attachment, scraping any dough from the paddle back into the bowl, and scrape down the sides of the bowl with a plastic bowl scraper. Fit the mixer with the dough hook and mix on low speed for 6 minutes. (If making Cinnamon-Raisin Bread, page 56, add the raisins at this point; if making Oval Herbed Bread, page 62, add the herbs here.)

‣ Flour the work surface. Using the bowl scraper, turn out the dough and knead a few times. The dough will be smooth but somewhat tacky. Place it in the bread bowl. Cover the bowl with a lightly oiled or sprayed piece of plastic wrap and place in a warm, draft-free spot (see Creating Your Warm Spot, page 17) to proof until the dough is very puffy, 1½ to 2 hours.

+ At this point, the dough is ready to be pre-shaped and shaped for a White Boule (page 42), White Pullman Loaf (page 49), or Oval Herbed Bread (page 62) or divided, pre-shaped, and shaped for traditional loaves (see page 50), Cinnamon-Raisin Bread (page 56), or White or Wheat Sandwich Rolls (page 61).

· Variation ·
WHOLE WHEAT SANDWICH BREAD DOUGH

Substituting whole wheat flour for some of the all-purpose flour adds depth and subtle nuttiness. The color is a deeper brown and the bread takes on an appealing, earthy look. Substitute 140 grams (4.9 ounces/1 cup) whole wheat flour for 140 grams (4.9 ounces/1 cup) of the all-purpose flour.

Courage in the Kitchen
∾ GETTING THE FEEL OF THE DOUGH ∾

Handling a dough is the only way to learn how it feels and looks—the sheen, the tautness, the springiness. A dough like White Sandwich Bread Dough, for example, will be shaggy, but pretty easy to work with even when it comes off the mixer. One like Aunt Clara's Wheat, White & Pumpernickel (page 64) will be sticky off the mixer but will relax after its first proof and become much less tacky.

Every dough is different, and the only way to really learn is by hands-on experience. The more you work with the dough, the easier it gets, and this is how you'll develop wisdom in your hands. It's hard to overstate the pure pleasure of handling dough. I like to lift the dough on and off the kneading surface several times before it goes into the bowl for its rise. Then, after it is kneaded, I slide the tips of my fingers underneath it and gently lift it off and set it back onto the board, ever so slightly pulling my fingertips in opposite directions to check for elasticity. I do this at each step: before I divide, after dividing, before shaping, and after shaping. I also like to tap the top of the dough. Every baker I know feels the same way—you see that dough sitting there as cute as a baby's bottom, and it's just irresistible. You have to touch it. That's a good thing, because each touch provides information. With every touch, you're building your baker's bank of knowledge and instincts.

WHITE BOULE

White Sandwich Bread Dough is the ideal dough to learn to pre-shape and shape with. And a boule proofed and baked in a cast-iron pot is the perfect loaf to get you excited about making great bread at home.

White Sandwich Bread Dough (page 40)

32 to 64 grams (1.1 to 2.2 ounces/2 to 4 tablespoons) olive oil or milk, or a combination, for the wash (see Brushing Yeasted Doughs Before and After Proofing, below)

Flour the work surface and turn out the dough, using a plastic bowl scraper. Press out the dough, gather the edges, and roll to pre-shape (see photos, Pre-shaping, page 45). Let sit for 10 minutes.

 ⁕ Fairly generously oil or spray the bottom and sides of a 3½- to 4-quart round cast-iron pot. Using your hands and a bench scraper, shape the dough into a boule (see photos, Shaping a Boule, pages 46–47), and place seam side down in the pot.

 ⁕ Brush the top of the dough with some of the wash. Reserve the remaining wash. Cover the pot with a lightly oiled or sprayed piece of plastic wrap and set in your warm spot to proof until very puffy again, 1½ to 2 hours.

When the dough is very gently pressed with your fingertip, the impression should remain.

 ⁕ Meanwhile, position a rack in the lower third of the oven, set a baking stone on it, and preheat the oven to 375°F.

 ⁕ Remove the plastic wrap and gently brush the top of the loaf again with the wash. Place the pot on the stone and bake, uncovered, for about 50 minutes, or until the top is golden brown. Carefully remove the loaf from the pot and put it on the baking stone for 5 to 10 minutes to brown the sides and bottom more evenly. To test for doneness, see Is It Baked?, page 58.

 ⁕ Transfer the bread to a cooling rack and let cool completely. For storing options, see How to Store Bread, page 51.

Courage in the Kitchen

ભ્ BRUSHING YEASTED DOUGHS BEFORE AND AFTER PROOFING ભ્

I recommend brushing yeasted doughs with olive oil or milk, or a combination. In most recipes, I instruct you to do this twice: the first brushing keeps the loaf from developing a skin on top as it proofs, and the second brushing gives the bread a full-on sheen. Although olive oil and milk is my preferred mixture, an egg beaten with a little water, which is a more traditional wash, will give the bread the shiny look you may be more accustomed to.

· Proofing & Baking in a Cast-Iron Pot ·

I t's a baker's boon: making a boule or an oval loaf and proofing it in the same vessel you'll bake it in. Enter the cast-iron pot, which can be used for any of the boules in this book. There are fewer steps involved than with a clay pot or with free-form baking, and the results are equally beautiful. The pot holds the dough's shape as it proofs and bakes, particularly for yeasted breads (see Proofing and Baking in the Same Vessel, page 38). And with pre-fermented and naturally leavened doughs, which are baked with the lid on, the pot creates the perfect moist environment.

After the dough is shaped, place it seam side down in a fairly generously oiled cast-iron pot. Yeasted loaves are brushed with a wash at this point. Cover the pot with a lightly oiled piece of plastic wrap. (I prefer plastic wrap to the pot's lid here because the seal is better and you can see the dough as it rises.) Let the dough proof until it is just below or at the rim of the pot, depending on the recipe's instructions.

Remove the plastic wrap, brush the dough again if using a wash, and score the top if the recipe calls for it. Yeasted doughs are baked with the lid off. For pre-fermented or naturally leavened doughs, cover the pot with the lid and bake according to the recipe.

· Pre-shaping ·

Patience will reward you in baking. Much of handling dough is about stretching and relaxing it. Pre-shaping is a good example.

Most doughs can't go directly from the proofing stage to being shaped into their final form. That's why we use a step called the pre-shape, which makes it easier to coax the dough into its final shape. All the recipes in this book that call for pre-shaping use the same technique, no matter what final form they take.

To understand the benefits of pre-shaping, try this. Pat any dough out into a flat round, then try to make it larger. The dough will resist. This is because when dough is handled, the gluten tightens up. But if you wait ten minutes, the dough will stretch easily into a larger round.

Taking ten minutes to let the dough relax applies anytime you have a problem and need to reshape a dough. Give it a few minutes to pull itself together, and start again. Forcing dough is a waste of your time. In our bakery, we call it respecting the dough: treat your dough gently and with patience.

This is the pre-shape that is used for all our loaves.

Throughout the pre-shaping and shaping steps, add flour only as needed to keep the dough from sticking to the work surface, and brush off any flour on the dough that will be folded over or under, to avoid "baker's graves" (see Avoiding Baker's Graves, page 111).

After the dough is turned out onto the work surface, it will naturally start to spread, more or less, depending on how slack it is. Using your fingertips, help the dough along by pressing it to about 1 inch thick. The size and shape will vary depending on the amount of dough and is not really important.

NOTE ON USING A BENCH SCRAPER: Although I think your hands are the best tool for getting a feel for and working with dough, sometimes a bench scraper is a tremendous help for pre-shaping and shaping. Particularly if it is a sticky dough, the bench scraper will help you get under and move the dough without having to add too much flour to the work surface. Hold it in one hand and use it to gently guide the dough where it needs to go.

OPPOSITE: (1–3) Gather the edges of the dough, bringing them together in the center to make a circular bundle. (4) Turn the dough over to be seam side down. (5–6) With your hands (or with a hand and a bench scraper; see Note), roll and push the ball against the work surface in a circular motion to tighten the seal. For a baguette or a demi-baguette, where the final loaf will be longer, rather than rolling the dough in a circular motion, place your hands at the top of the dough and bring the bundle toward you, forming an elongated oval.

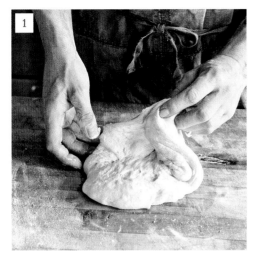

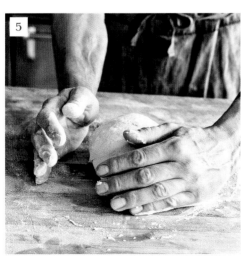

· Shaping a Boule ·

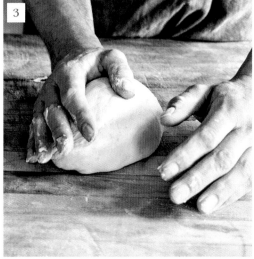

(1) Turn the pre-shaped loaf over to be seam side up. (2) Place your hand under the dough and fold half over onto the other half. (3) All in one motion, move the dough to be seam side down, pressing it against the work surface, beginning to tighten the seal.

(4–6) With your hands (or with a hand and a bench scraper; see Note, page 44), roll the ball against the work surface, in a circular motion, gently lifting and lowering as you do, to tighten the seal. For an oval loaf, as you roll the ball, rock and push the dough into more of an oval shape than a circle.

WHITE PULLMAN LOAF (AKA SAM'S AFTER-SCHOOL BREAD)

∾ Makes 1 Pullman loaf ∾

The square white slices that you'll get from this loaf have a certain nostalgic appeal, but the comparison stops there. This sandwich bread has flavor, character, and substance. In other words, it's a world away from its mass-produced 1950s forerunner. For making sandwich bread, a Pullman pan should be your go-to baking vessel. Pullman pans come in different sizes. I like to use one that measures 13 by 4 by 4 inches. The pan can be used with or without the lid. For a flat top, you proof and bake the bread with the lid on. If you prefer a loaf that's more rounded on top, leave the lid off.

Having literally cut his teeth on Della Fattoria épis, our youngest grandson, Sam, knows his bread. As a two-year-old, he would steal into the bakery, help himself to a baguette, and head out to the garden. I can still picture him: curly blond hair, nose nearly touching a flower while he examined a little bug or drop of water on a blade of grass. He would be talking to himself with the baguette tucked under his arm, a water pistol in one hand and a tiny Lego soldier in the other. By the time he got back to the house, he would have pulled all the bread from the inside of the crust, leaving a hollowed-out shell. Some he would have eaten himself, some he would have shared with the dogs and chickens.

Sam has always been pretty particular about what he eats. As he got older, his preferred after-school snack was a peanut butter and jelly sandwich on "regular bread." By that he meant soft white yeasted bread, and I agreed with him. The sweetness of the yeast dough makes it a great partner for peanut butter and jelly. Calling this "white bread" is somewhat misleading. Although the nostalgic element can't be denied, the result is not your everyday white bread—it has a much more distinctive flavor and texture, and it's anything but bland.

White or Whole Wheat Sandwich Bread Dough
(pages 40–41)

32 to 64 grams (1.1 to 2.2 ounces/2 to 4 tablespoons) olive oil or milk, or a combination, for the wash (see Brushing Yeasted Doughs Before and After Proofing, page 42)

recipe continues

Flour the work surface and turn out the dough, using a plastic bowl scraper. Press out the dough, gather the edges, and roll to pre-shape (see photos, Pre-shaping, page 45). Let sit for 10 minutes.

+ Fairly generously oil or spray a 13-by-4-by-4-inch Pullman pan, and the underside of the lid if using it. Using your hands and a bench scraper, shape the dough into a bâtard (see photos, Shaping a Bâtard, pages 52–53), about 3 by 13 inches. Set in the pan and, with your hands still under the dough, gently stretch it as needed to distribute it evenly in the pan. Brush the top with some of the wash. Reserve the remaining wash if making a loaf with a rounded top.

+ *For a loaf with a flat top*, slide on the lid, leaving about an inch open to check on the height of the rising dough. Lightly oil or spray a small piece of plastic wrap and put it over the hole. *For a loaf with a rounded top*, oil or spray a large piece of plastic wrap and cover the pan with it.

+ Set the pan in your warm spot to proof until very puffy again, 1½ to 2 hours. When the dough is gently pressed with your fingertip the impression should remain.

+ Meanwhile, position a rack in the lower third of the oven, set a baking stone on it, and preheat the oven to 375°F.

+ *If baking with the lid*, remove the plastic wrap and slide the lid closed. Place the pan on the stone and bake for 20 minutes. Carefully remove the lid and bake about 5 minutes to brown the top. Carefully take the bread out of the pan to brown directly on the stone. Put the loaf on the stone and brown for about 5 minutes. To test for doneness, see Is It Baked?, page 58.

+ *If baking without the lid*, remove the plastic wrap and gently brush the top again

Cooling Bread Completely

When bread first comes out of the oven, it's actually still cooking in its own heat. The loaf needs to rest on a rack with air circulating around it to cool. Cooling time depends on the temperature of your kitchen, of course, but generally, breads need 3 hours to cool completely.

Cooling is essential because bread is delicate when it comes out of the oven. Still-warm bread won't slice well: it will squish, ruining the beautiful shape and texture you worked so hard for. A thoroughly cooled baked loaf is worth the wait.

with the wash. Bake for about 30 minutes, until the top is golden brown. Then carefully take the bread out of the pan to brown the sides: put the loaf on the stone and let brown for about 5 minutes. To test for doneness, see Is It Baked?, page 58.

+ Transfer the bread to a cooling rack and let cool completely. For storing options, see How to Store Bread, opposite.

· Note ·
ON BAKING IN TWO TRADITIONAL LOAF PANS

Turn the dough out onto the work surface, divide it into 2 equal pieces, and pre-shape (see photos, Pre-shaping, page 45). Let sit for 10 minutes.

Fairly generously oil or spray two 8½-by-4½-by-2¾-inch loaf pans. Shape each piece of dough into a bâtard, put in the pans as opposite, and brush the tops with the wash. Reserve the remaining wash. Cover the tops with a lightly oiled or sprayed piece of plastic wrap and place in your warm spot to proof for 1½ to 2 hours, or until the dough reaches the tops of the pans. When the dough is gently pressed with your fingertip, the impression should remain.

Meanwhile, position a rack in the lower third of the oven, set a baking stone on it, and preheat the oven to 375°F.

Remove the plastic wrap and gently brush the top of the loaves again with the wash. Bake for about 20 minutes, until the tops are golden brown. Carefully take the bread out of the pans to brown directly on the stone: put the loaves on the stone and let brown for about 5 minutes. To test for doneness, see Is It Baked?, page 58.

Transfer the bread to a cooling rack and let cool completely. For storing options, see How to Store Bread, below.

How to Store Bread

I store my bread on a cutting board, cut side down, covered with a clean dish towel, where it will keep for days. Many of my friends, however, are "clean counter" types and can't stand to have anything sitting out. If that's you, buy a well-vented bread box. The vents are important: in an airtight box, breads with high hydration (like the ones in this book) will get soggy and eventually moldy, because the crust will absorb moisture from the crumb. Never use a plastic bag to store bread.

If you leave a loaf of bread out on the counter, lightly covered, it will never mold. It will eventually get hard, of course. However, you can revive hard bread by sprinkling it liberally with water and then heating it at the same temperature it was baked at for 5 to 10 minutes.

If you know you won't be able to eat your bread in the next couple of days, freeze it. Freezing is the exception to the airtight rule. According to my friend Harold McGee, the extraordinary food science writer, teacher, and author of *On Food and Cooking*, the trick is to wrap the bread twice. There are several options. You can wrap it first in foil and then in a plastic bag. Or use plastic wrap first and then a plastic bag. We have customers who leave the bread in the Della Fattoria paper bag, wrap it in foil or a plastic bag, and freeze it that way.

To defrost the bread, unwrap it and leave it on the counter at room temperature. My friend Jon Paul cuts the bread while it's still partially frozen. He says it's easier to slice that way.

· Shaping a Bâtard ·

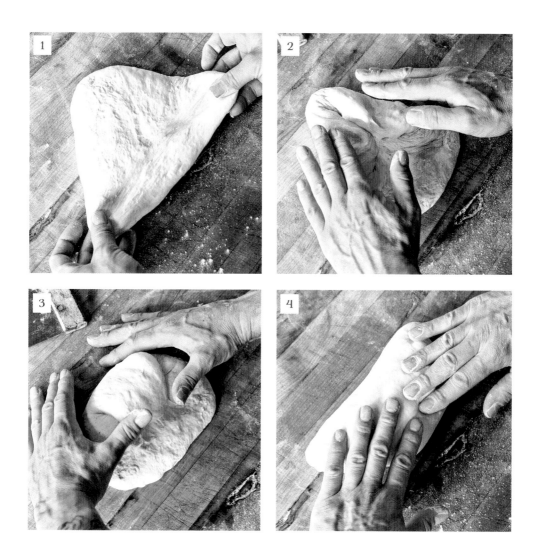

(1) Turn the pre-shaped loaf over to be seam side up and stretch the bottom corners out so the dough is in a triangular shape. (2) Fold the top corners inward, as if wrapping a present. (3) Fold the top of the dough over, bringing it toward the center, creating a thicker piece of dough in what will be the center of the loaf. (4–5) Position your hands under the dough, folding it over so the ends meet in front of you, and then gently rock so the seam is underneath. (6–8) Turn the dough to be seam side up, pull the ends out, and fold them in. Again, position your hands under the dough, fold it over so the ends meet in front of you. (9–10) Use the heel of your hand to seal the edge and gently rock so the seam is underneath. If at any point the dough begins to stick to the work surface, it can be gently loosened with a bench scraper and dusted lightly with flour.

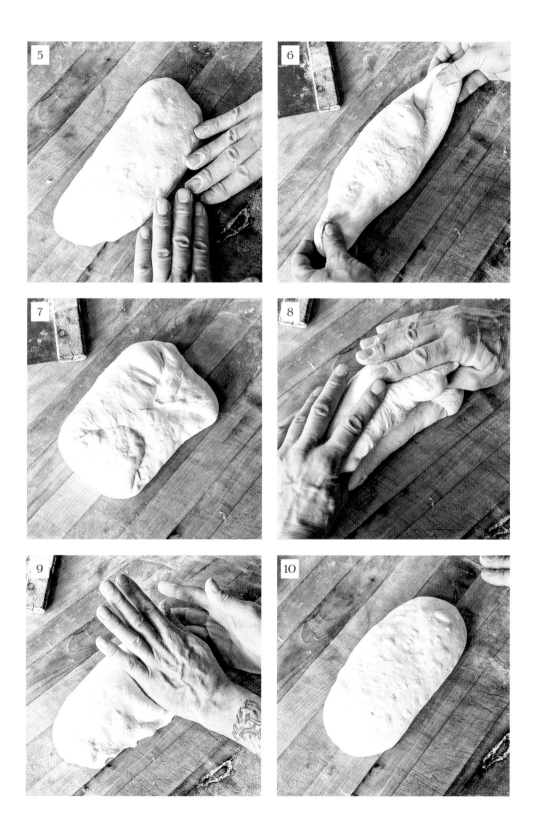

PIMENTO CHEESE PINWHEELS

∾ Makes 25 to 35 small sandwiches ∾

Whenever my mom, Thelma, hosted her bridge club, she'd use white sandwich bread with the crusts cut off to make little round cocktail sandwiches, called pinwheels. (My friends and I used to eat the trimmings, and we'd get the leftovers after bridge club too). Pinwheels are fun to make and delicious, especially with this pimento cheddar spread as the filling. It's also great spread on crostini and baked (see Note).

For 25 to 35 sandwiches, you'll need half a loaf of white Pullman bread and this recipe for the pimento cheese—but if you're like me, you'll want to make a lot of these. They're great finger food for a large gathering or to share with your neighbors. To double the quantity, simply use the full Pullman loaf and double the recipe for the cheese.

I call for Sriracha hot sauce here, but you can use any hot sauce you like—or leave the heat out altogether. The spread is quite addictive. It's a delicious filling for sandwiches, tastes great on toast, and is a good dip for celery sticks and other fresh vegetables.

Pimento Cheese (makes about 2 cups)

2½ cups lightly packed grated extra-sharp cheddar cheese, preferably half white and half orange

¾ cup mayonnaise, preferably homemade

⅓ cup coarsely chopped drained piquillo peppers (see Sources, page 270)

¼ teaspoon Sriracha, or to taste (optional)

Kosher salt and freshly ground black pepper

½ White Pullman Loaf (page 49)

For the pimento cheese: With a fork, mix the cheese and mayonnaise in a medium bowl until combined but not completely smooth (the cheese should still stay in shreds). Add the peppers and season with the Sriracha, if using, and salt and pepper to taste.

+ As good as this spread is, don't be tempted to eat it all now. Cover and refrigerate for at least 2 hours, or preferably overnight. The flavor will get better and better.

+ When ready to make the pinwheels, let the cheese come to room temperature (or the bread might tear when you spread it).

+ Cut the crust off the bread. Cut the loaf lengthwise into ¼- to ⅜-inch-thick slices. You should have 6 to 7 rectangular slices, about 6 by 4 inches.

+ Lay a 12-by-8-inch piece of plastic wrap on the work surface and place one slice of bread on top. Unless the bread is very pliable, lightly spritz the slice of bread with water. Carefully spread about ¼ cup of the cheese on the bread. Starting with one of the long ends, roll the bread up jelly-roll style, using the plastic to wrap it snugly. Wrap it securely in a second piece of plastic wrap. Repeat with the remaining slices of bread and filling.

+ Transfer the rolls, seam side down, to the fridge. Let sit for at least 1 hour, or preferably 2 hours; the rolls can be refrigerated for up to a day.

+ To serve, remove the plastic wrap, trim the ends of the rolls (snack on the trimmings), and slice into ¾-inch-thick coins.

· Note ·
ON CROSTINI

While the pinwheels are fun and nostalgic, I find this mixture the most irresistible when spread on crostini and baked in a hot oven until golden brown and fragrant. Wait until your guests arrive before putting them in the oven, or they won't make it to the table.

I like them on a sliced toasted baguette, but the white Pullman will be every bit as delicious, with a more delicate crunch.

Spread the cheese mixture on cooled toast and put under the broiler to melt the cheese.

CINNAMON-RAISIN BREAD

⤫ Makes 2 standard loaves ⤫

A swirl of cinnamon sugar and raisins plumped in hot water or brandy make a cinnamon bread that tastes delicious, toasted or not. The bread can be put together in a couple of ways. Traditionally, the cinnamon sugar and butter are swirled through the loaf, but the bread can also be shaped as a pull-apart loaf by rolling individual balls of dough in butter and then the cinnamon sugar and arranging them in the pan; see the variation on page 58. This both distributes the cinnamon sugar throughout and gives the exterior extra caramelized topping.

Raisins	320 g	11.3 oz	2 cups plus 2 Tbsp
Brandy or water	240 g	8.5 oz	1 cup
White Sandwich Bread Dough (page 40), just mixed and still in the mixer bowl			
Granulated sugar	100 g	3.5 oz	½ cup
Ground cinnamon	12 g	0.4 oz	1½ Tbsp
Unsalted butter, melted and cooled to tepid	57 g	2 oz	4 Tbsp

14 to 32 grams (0.5 to 1.1 ounces/1 to 2 tablespoons) olive oil or milk, or a combination, for the wash (see Brushing Yeasted Doughs Before and After Proofing, page 42)

To plump the raisins, put them in a small bowl. Bring the liquid to a boil, pour it over the raisins, and let sit for at least 30 minutes, or, if using brandy, as long as overnight. Drain.

⁺ Once the dough is mixed, add the plumped raisins and mix for an additional 30 seconds to 1 minute to evenly distribute them. Then proceed as directed, giving the dough its first proof.

⁺ Fairly generously oil or spray two 8½-by-4½-by-2¾-inch loaf pans.

⁺ Combine the sugar and cinnamon in a small bowl. Reserve about 2 tablespoons of the cinnamon sugar for the top of the loaves.

⁺ Flour the work surface. Turn out the dough, using a plastic bowl scraper, and divide in half, using a bench scraper. Using your fingertips, press each piece of dough into a 9-by-7-inch rectangle. Brush the top of each with half of the melted butter and sprinkle half of the cinnamon sugar over the top. Roll up each piece of dough tightly from one of the short ends, ending with the seam underneath. Set seam side down in the pans. Brush the loaves with the wash and sprinkle with the reserved cinnamon sugar.

⁺ Cover the tops of the pans with a lightly oiled or sprayed piece of plastic wrap. Set the

pans in your warm spot to proof until the dough reaches the tops of the pans, 1½ to 2 hours; remove the plastic wrap. When the dough is very gently pressed with your fingertip, the impression should remain.

+ Meanwhile, position a rack in the lower third of the oven, set a baking stone on it, and preheat the oven to 375°F.

+ Place the pans on the stone and bake for about 35 minutes, rotating them from front to back and side to side halfway through baking, or until the top is a rich golden brown. To test for doneness, see Is It Baked?, page 58, but keep in mind that because of the sticky surface of the bread, it is best to go with color and temperature to know when it is done.

+ Transfer the pans to a cooling rack and let the bread cool for 5 to 10 minutes. Loosen the bread from the sides of the pans if necessary, remove from the pans, and let cool completely on the rack. For storing options, see How to Store Bread, page 51.

· Variation ·
PULL-APART CINNAMON-RAISIN LOAF

After the dough has risen, scale (divide) the dough into 28 equal pieces (about 45 grams/ 1.6 ounces each).

+ Prepare the pans as directed on page 56. Roll one piece of dough into a ball, dip into the melted butter and then the cinnamon sugar, and place in one of the pans. Continue in this manner, placing 10 balls in 2 rows of 5 in the pan. Arrange 4 more balls down the center of the bottom balls, nestling them in between. Repeat with the remaining dough balls in the second pan. Cover, let rise, and bake as described above.

Courage in the Kitchen
ᴄᴐ IS IT BAKED? ᴄᴐ

There are a few ways to check doneness to make sure your bread is fully baked.

COLOR: About 10 minutes before the timer goes off, check for color. Depending on the bread, you're looking for anything from golden to mahogany.

AROMA: If you smell burning, check the bottom of the loaf. If it is burning, turn the bread on its side to finish baking.

SOUND: Tap the loaf on the bottom— it should sound hollow. If it doesn't, it needs more time.

TEMPERATURE: If you're still unsure as to whether or not the loaf is fully baked, insert an instant-read thermometer into the center. Generally, it should register between 200° and 210°F. For enriched breads—those that contain milk, eggs, or butter—look for a reading of 180° to 190°F.

EARLY DAYS

Working where you live can be very convenient. On the other hand, things that you once thought were private no longer are.

One winter during an icy-cold rainstorm, I was padding around the house trying to stay warm in my husband's thick socks, slippers, sweatpants, and an old bathrobe. The dogs barked, and there was a knock on the back door. Had my daughter been locked out of her house? No. Standing in the doorway was an elegant couple who had eaten at The French Laundry the previous night. They liked the bread and were determined to go to the source.

How did they find us? I'll never know; we weren't even listed in the phone book then. Our bread wasn't in any stores yet, so there were no bags with any information on them. But there they stood, and what I remember most was the elegant velvet shoes this lovely lady had destroyed walking down our muddy driveway. All they wanted was a loaf of seeded wheat bread. All I wanted was to drop through a hole in the floor—I was so embarrassed. I somehow recovered long enough to remember my manners, and I was able to carry on a conversation as if this were a completely normal situation. I took them to have a look at our wood oven, and off they went with a couple of loaves of bread.

That was my first encounter with really serious foodies. They're a tenacious breed. In that moment, I understood that our lives were forever changed. As the couple walked back to their car, I mused that the only thing that had been missing were chickens clucking at my feet. I was going to need to revise my at-home wear, and fast. No one should ever have seen me in that bathrobe.

WHITE OR WHEAT SANDWICH ROLLS

∽ Makes 12 rolls ∽

Hearty sandwiches like Sloppy Joes or pulled pork will taste great made with these white or wheat sandwich rolls. Poppy seeds, sesame seeds, fennel seeds, or dehydrated onions—or a combination—make good toppings, but you could omit them.

5 to 10 grams (0.17 to 0.35 ounce/about 1 tablespoon) sesame, poppy, or fennel seeds or dehydrated onions, or a combination (optional)

32 to 64 grams (1.1 to 2.2 ounces/2 to 4 tablespoons) olive oil or milk, or a combination, for the wash

White or Whole Wheat Sandwich Bread Dough (page 40)

Fairly generously oil or spray a 9-by-13-inch baking pan or a quarter sheet pan. Line with parchment paper and lightly oil or spray the paper.

⁜ If using them, spread the sesame, poppy, or fennel seeds and/or dehydrated onions on a dinner plate. Set a ramekin or small bowl of the wash next to it.

⁜ Flour the work surface. Turn out the dough, using a plastic bowl scraper, and, using a bench scraper, scale (divide) the dough into 12 equal pieces (about 96 grams/ 3.4 ounces each). Cup your fingers around one piece at a time (or, once you become proficient, one piece in each hand) and roll it against the work surface to form a ball (see photos, Shaping Rolls, page 77).

⁜ Dip the top of each ball in the wash, letting any excess run back into the ramekin, then dip into the seeds, if using. Place seam side down in the prepared pan, in 3 rows of 4 rolls each. (If not using the seeds, brush the tops of the rolls with the wash.)

⁜ Set the pan in your warm spot, cover with a Cambro container or a plastic tub, and let proof until doubled in size, 1½ to 2 hours. When the dough is gently pressed with your fingertip, the impression should remain.

⁜ Meanwhile, position a rack in the lower third of the oven, set a baking stone on it, and preheat the oven to 375°F.

⁜ Place the pan on the stone and bake the rolls for 35 to 40 minutes, or until the tops are a rich golden brown. To test for doneness, see Is It Baked?, page 58.

⁜ Transfer the pan to a cooling rack and let the rolls cool completely. For storing options, see How to Store Bread, page 51.

OVAL HERBED BREAD

❧ Makes 1 large oval loaf ❧

Rosemary and thyme, those stars of the herb garden, work magic here, transforming white or wheat dough into herb bread. Try with soups, especially tomato, or for a sophisticated grilled cheese sandwich. If you like, the dough can be braided (see photos, Braiding Brioche, pages 92–93). And the pan can be dusted with semolina to add some crunch to the bread. The braid is perfect for a large gathering and looks fantastic as a centerpiece on the table.

White or Whole Wheat Sandwich Bread Dough (pages 40–41), just mixed and still in the mixer bowl

4 to 8 grams/0.2 to 0.3 ounce/1½ to 2½ tablespoons finely chopped rosemary or thyme, or your favorite herb, or a combination of herbs

32 to 64 grams (1.1 to 2.2 ounces/2 to 4 tablespoons) olive oil or milk, or a combination, for the wash (see Brushing Yeasted Doughs Before and After Proofing, page 42)

Once the dough is mixed, add the herbs and mix for about 30 seconds, until evenly distributed. Then proceed as directed, giving the dough its first proof.

+ Flour the work surface and turn out the dough, using a plastic bowl scraper. Press out the dough, gather the edges, and roll to pre-shape (see photos, Pre-shaping, page 45). Let sit for 10 minutes.

+ Fairly generously oil or spray the bottom and sides of a 3- to 4-quart oval cast-iron pot. Using your hands and the bench scraper, shape the dough into an oval (see photos, Shaping a Boule, pages 46–47), and place seam side down in the pot.

+ Brush the top of the dough with some of the wash. Reserve the remaining wash. Cover the pot with a lightly oiled or sprayed piece of plastic wrap and set in your warm spot to proof until very puffy again, 1½ to 2 hours. When the dough is gently pressed with your fingertip, the impression should remain.

+ Meanwhile, position a rack in the lower third of the oven, set a baking stone on it, and preheat the oven to 375°F.

+ Remove the plastic wrap and gently brush the top of the loaf again with the wash. Place the pot on the stone and bake, uncovered, for about 50 minutes, or until the top is golden brown. Carefully remove the loaf from the pot and put it on the baking stone for 5 to 10 minutes to brown the sides and bottom more evenly. To test for doneness, see Is It Baked?, page 58.

+ Transfer the bread to a cooling rack and let cool completely. For storing options, see How to Store Bread, page 51.

AUNT CLARA'S WHEAT, WHITE & PUMPERNICKEL BREAD

⁓ Makes 1 large boule ⁓

My husband's aunt Clara was a wonderful home baker and one of my very first mentors. She was a farmer's wife, and she was home every day at 3 P.M. to prepare Uncle Otto's cake and coffee. This bread was her specialty. She'd never write the recipe down; "a third, a third, a third" was how she used to describe it.

Though Aunt Clara used regular rye flour for this bread, I've changed the rye to pumpernickel. Pumpernickel—dark, flavorful rye flour that has the germ and bran included—has a more robust texture and flavor than regular rye. I love the hearty depth the bread gets from the pumpernickel flour, but regular rye flour will also give a good result (see Note). The dough is a bit sticky coming off the mixer, but it will become more manageable as it develops.

All-purpose flour	224 g	7.9 oz	1½ cups plus 1½ Tbsp
Pumpernickel flour	224 g	7.9 oz	1½ cups plus 1½ Tbsp
Whole wheat flour	224 g	7.9 oz	1½ cups plus 1½ Tbsp
TOTAL FLOUR	672 g	23.7 oz	4¾ cups plus ½ Tbsp
Instant yeast	12 g	0.4 oz	1 Tbsp plus ½ tsp
Warm water (100°F/38°C)	442 g	15.6 oz	1¾ cups plus 2 Tbsp
Fine gray salt	16 g	0.6 oz	2¾ tsp
Extra virgin olive oil	108 g	3.8 oz	½ cup
TOTAL WEIGHT	1,250 g/1.25 kg	44.1 oz/2.7 lbs	

32 to 64 grams (1.1 to 2.2 ounces/2 to 4 tablespoons) olive oil or milk, or a combination, for the wash (see Brushing Yeasted Doughs Before and After Proofing, page 42)

Lightly oil or spray a deep 4½- to 5-quart ceramic or glass bread bowl. Combine the flours in a medium bowl.

✦ For the sponge: Put the yeast, water, and half of the flour mixture in the bowl of a stand mixer fitted with the paddle attachment. Pulse a few times on the lowest setting (to keep the flour from flying out of the bowl), then mix on low speed just to combine, about 1 minute. It is OK if there are some small lumps of flour. Let sit at room temperature until there are bubbles across the top, 20 to 30 minutes.

✦ Meanwhile, in a medium bowl, whisk the remaining flour mixture with the salt.

◆ Once the surface of the sponge is bubbly, pour the olive oil over the top, and mix on the lowest setting for just a few seconds to incorporate. Add the dry ingredients and pulse a few times on the lowest setting, then mix on low speed for about 1 minute to combine.

◆ Remove the paddle attachment, scraping any dough from the paddle back into the bowl, and scrape down the sides of the bowl with a plastic bowl scraper. Fit the mixer with the dough hook, and mix on low speed for 6 minutes.

◆ Flour the work surface. Using the bowl scraper, turn out the dough and knead a few times. The dough will be sticky. Place in the bread bowl. Cover the bowl with a lightly oiled or sprayed piece of plastic wrap and place in a warm, draft-free spot (see Creating Your Warm Spot, page 17) to proof until the dough is very puffy, 1½ to 2 hours.

◆ Flour the work surface and turn out the dough, using the bowl scraper. Press out the dough, gather the edges, and roll to pre-shape (see photos, Pre-shaping, page 45). Let sit for 10 minutes.

◆ Fairly generously oil or spray the bottom and sides of a 3½- to 4-quart round cast-iron pot. Using your hands and a bench scraper, shape the dough into a boule (see photos, Shaping a Boule, pages 46–47), and place it seam side down in the pot.

◆ Brush the top of the dough with some of the wash. Reserve the remaining wash. Cover the pot with a lightly oiled or sprayed piece of plastic wrap and set in your warm spot to proof until very puffy again, 1½ to 2 hours. When the dough is gently pressed with your fingertip, the impression should remain.

◆ Meanwhile, position a rack in the lower third of the oven, set a baking stone on it, and preheat the oven to 375°F.

◆ Remove the plastic wrap and gently brush the top of the loaf again with the wash. Place the pot on the stone and bake, uncovered, for about 50 minutes, or until the top is golden brown. Carefully remove the loaf from the pot and put it on the baking stone for 5 to 10 minutes to brown the sides and bottom more evenly. To test for doneness, see Is It Baked?, page 58.

◆ Transfer the bread to a cooling rack and let cool completely. For storing options, see How to Store Bread, page 51.

· Note ·
ON SUBSTITUTING RYE FLOUR FOR PUMPERNICKEL

If you want to use rye flour instead of pumpernickel in this recipe, be sure that the amount of rye is equal to the pumpernickel by weight, not by volume. While pumpernickel, for example, weighs 140 grams (4.9 ounces) per cup, rye is only 100 grams (3.5 ounces) per cup. Variations like these are further proof of why it's always better to weigh ingredients rather than measure with cups and spoons.

WHEAT & BARLEY PULLMAN LOAF

≈ Makes 1 Pullman loaf ≈

Here's an easy bread with a satisfying texture and a mellow sweetness, thanks to the blend of all purpose-flour, whole wheat flour, cracked wheat, and quick-cooking barley. I'm especially partial to the flavor that the barley flakes add and encourage you to use them (see Note), but rolled oats also work well. The bread is caramel-colored and its flavor has hints of caramel too.

All-purpose flour	381 g	13.4 oz	2½ cups plus 3½ Tbsp
Whole wheat flour	190 g	6.7 oz	1¼ cups plus 2 Tbsp
TOTAL FLOUR	571 g	20.1 oz	4 cups
Instant yeast	11 g	0.4 oz	1 Tbsp plus ¼ tsp
Warm water (100°F/38°C)	476 g	16.8 oz	2 cups
Cracked wheat	32 g	1.1 oz	2 Tbsp plus 1 tsp
Instant barley (see Note)	32 g	1.1 oz	3½ Tbsp
Granulated sugar	25 g	0.9 oz	2 Tbsp
Fine gray salt	15 g	0.5 oz	2½ tsp
TOTAL WEIGHT	1,162 g/1.16 kg	40.9 oz/2.5 lbs	

32 to 64 grams (1.1 to 2.2 ounces/2 to 4 tablespoons) olive oil or milk, or a combination, for the wash (see Brushing Yeasted Doughs Before and After Proofing, page 42)

18 grams (0.6 ounce/1 tablespoon plus 1 teaspoon) cracked wheat for the top (optional)

Lightly oil or spray a deep 4½- to 5-quart ceramic or glass bread bowl. Combine the flours in a medium bowl.

⁺ For the sponge: Put the yeast, water, and half of the flour mixture in the bowl of a stand mixer fitted with the paddle attachment. Pulse a few times on the lowest setting (to keep the flour from flying out of the bowl), then mix on low speed just to combine, about 1 minute. It is OK if there are some small lumps of flour. Let sit at room temperature until

there are bubbles across the top, 20 to 30 minutes.

⁺ Meanwhile, in the medium bowl, whisk together the remaining flour mixture, the cracked wheat, barley, sugar, and salt.

⁺ Once the surface of the sponge is bubbly, add the dry ingredients to the mixer and pulse a few times on the lowest setting, then mix on low speed for about 1 minute to combine.

⁺ Remove the paddle attachment, scraping any dough from the paddle back into the bowl, and scrape down the sides of the bowl with a plastic bowl scraper. Fit the mixer with the dough hook, and mix on low speed for 6 minutes.

+ Flour the work surface. Using the bowl scraper, turn out the dough and knead a few times. The dough will be tacky. Place in the bread bowl. Cover the bowl with a lightly oiled or sprayed piece of plastic wrap and place in a warm, draft-free spot (see Creating Your Warm Spot, page 17) to proof until the dough is very puffy, 1½ to 2 hours.

+ Flour the work surface and turn out the dough, using the bowl scraper. Press out the dough, gather the edges, and roll to pre-shape (see photos, Pre-shaping, page 45). Let sit for 10 minutes.

+ Spread the cracked wheat, if using, on a small tray. Fairly generously oil or spray a 13-by-4-by-4-inch Pullman pan, and the underside of the lid if using it. Using your hands and a bench scraper, shape the dough into a bâtard (see photos, Shaping a Bâtard, pages 52–53), about 3 by 13 inches. If topping with cracked wheat, moisten the top of the bâtard with a damp towel, and then roll in the cracked wheat. Set in the pan and, with your hands still under the dough, gently stretch it as needed to distribute it evenly in the pan. Brush the top with some of the wash. Reserve the remaining wash if making a loaf with a rounded top.

+ *For a loaf with a flat top*, slide on the lid, leaving about an inch open to check on the height of the rising dough. Lightly oil or spray a small piece of plastic wrap and put it over the hole. *For a loaf with a rounded top*, oil or spray a large piece of plastic wrap and cover the pan with it.

+ Set the pan in your warm spot to proof until the dough is very puffy again, 1½ to

2 hours. When the dough is gently pressed with your fingertip, the impression should remain.

+ Meanwhile, position a rack in the lower third of the oven, set a baking stone on it, and preheat the oven to 375°F.

+ *If baking with the lid*, remove the plastic wrap, open the lid, sprinkle with the cracked wheat, and close the lid. Place the pan on the stone and bake for 30 minutes. Carefully remove the lid and bake for about 5 minutes to brown the top. Carefully take the bread out of the pan to brown directly on the stone. Put the loaf on the stone and brown for about 5 minutes. To test for doneness, see Is It Baked?, page 58.

+ *If baking without the lid*, the loaf can be scored (see photo, Scoring Dough, page 107). Remove the plastic wrap and gently brush the top again with the wash. Bake for 35 minutes, until the top is golden brown. Then carefully take the bread out of the pan, put the loaf bottom side down on the stone, and brown for 5 to 10 minutes. To test for doneness, see Is It Baked?, page 58.

+ Transfer the bread to a cooling rack and let cool completely. For storing options, see How to Store Bread, page 51.

· Note ·
ON INSTANT BARLEY

Although it's available at many natural foods grocers, instant barley can be a little difficult to find (see Sources, page 270). But this recipe also works very well made with old-fashioned rolled oats instead. Substitute an equal amount (32 grams/1.1 ounces/¼ cup plus 2½ tablespoons).

ENRICHED BREADS

ARRIVING AT OUR CAFÉ IN DOWNTOWN PETALUMA early in the morning, I'm treated to an incredible combination of scents: freshly ground coffee, the most welcoming wake-up smell in the world, and the irresistible aroma of pastries just out of the oven. It's so seductive and cheering that even the anticipation makes me smile. This is the power of baking.

My grandmother died when I was five, but my grandfather, happily, was remarried a few years later to his cousin's widow, a Swedish woman known to me as Grandma Mary. I was in awe of her—she kept a fantastic house. The first thing you noticed was the smell: cardamom and butter, with a hint of citrus. Then there was the white kitchen with blue-and-white dishes, a combination of cozy and crisp. She poached an egg in milk every morning for my grandfather, drizzled it with butter, and served it on zwieback. She was convinced it would cure his stomach ulcer, though this clearly was not the doctor's suggestion. But if it wasn't her food that kept him well, the love that went into it sure did.

I often think about her when I bake, because she had a quality that has been mostly drilled out of American women. She had faith in ritual and was devoted to taking care of her family and her home. Homemaking was a pleasure for her, and she loved to do special little things for my grandfather that she knew would make him happy. That's the place I want to be in when I bake. How I get there is thinking about who will be eating my baked goods and how that will feel to them—like a gift, I hope.

If I ever wanted to sell my house, I would bake sticky buns before the open houses, no doubt about it. They give off an intoxicating aroma that makes you want to linger, at least until they come out of the oven, and then I wouldn't hesitate to serve them up on a beautiful platter. Baked goods like these say "home" more than anything else I can think of.

I love the enriched breads in this chapter: the tenderness of the crumb; the rich, buttery flavor; the aroma; and the mouthfeel are incomparable. However, I'm not a girl with a lot of discipline, nor am I thin, so enriched breads are rather dangerous territory for me personally. (I've always been afraid that if I delved too deeply into enriched breads, I would have to buy a new wardrobe!) But any baker should be able to make a good dinner roll and a burger bun. And every baker needs a go-to brioche recipe. So we make enriched breads (with a pinch of discipline).

All the breads in this chapter are easy to shape—and a distinct departure from slack, wet bread doughs. What's more, working with dough that's enriched with butter is a heavenly tactile experience. I think it's because the butter, along with milk powder, helps make the dough soft and supple. The dough feels silky, elastic, and sticky all at the same time. If you use fresh farm eggs—we do, because we live on an egg ranch—the doughs will also take on an irresistible golden color.

Though the addition of butter makes working with these recipes a different experience from the others in the book, the trick to the doughs is simple. Although the butter should be at room temperature when it's added, it needs to stay cool as you're working the dough with your hands. If you notice the butter starting to melt or ooze, immediately put the dough in the fridge to cool down for 15 minutes or so, then resume working with it. This takes patience, but you'll be rewarded with delicious and beautiful breads to be proud of.

Enriched doughs include butter, milk powder, eggs, and/or sugar. I like to brush the doughs with egg loosened with cream, half-and-half, or whole milk. Some of these recipes call for slightly more expensive ingredients than do the breads in the other chapters. So think of them as special-occasion breads. The recipe on page 80 is special indeed—it's a gift from award-winning baker Rose Levy Beranbaum. We've been friends from the moment we met and couldn't stop talking about bread. I hope you read this chapter and feel the same enthusiasm.

Managing buttery doughs is all about making sure the dough stays sufficiently cool so that the butter doesn't ooze out of the dough as you're working it with your hands. In this chapter, you will learn how to incorporate the butter into the other ingredients in a way that makes the dough stable. As with other baked goods, the order in which the ingredients are added is important; it is all done for a reason, so follow the directions carefully. These recipes also include more ingredients, so don't skip the *mise en place:* having your ingredients all weighed out and at the right temperature will be a huge factor in your recipe's success.

Shaping dinner, hamburger, and hot dog rolls (page 76)
Braiding dough (page 80)

⤳ EQUIPMENT NEEDED ⤳

* Scale
* Stand mixer with whisk, paddle, and dough hook attachments
* Baking stone
* Thermometer
* Plastic bowl scraper
* Bench scraper
* Plastic wrap
* Gallon-size resealable plastic storage bags (preferably the heavier freezer type)
* 3-quart bread bowl (optional)
* 4½- to 5-quart bread bowl
* Two 8½-by-4½-by-2¾-inch loaf pans
* 13-by-4-by-4-inch Pullman pan (lid optional)
* Quarter sheet pan (9 by 13 by ½ inch)
* Half sheet pan or cookie sheet (with no sides)
* Two 8-inch cake rounds
* Cambro container or plastic tub
* Cooling rack
* Large spatula or peel
* Pastry brush
* Parchment paper or 2 silicone baking mats

DELLA'S ROLL DOUGH

✆ Makes 974 grams/2.1 pounds ✆

Whenever I see a batch of this smooth, loose dough sitting in its container at the bakery, it's almost impossible for me not to stop whatever I'm doing, touch the dough, and shape it into rolls. We use this dough to make our dinner rolls (page 76), as well as hamburger and hot dog rolls (see page 74). I am especially tickled with the hot dog recipe. I love the irony of elevating such a simple food into something divine, though these couldn't be easier to make.

All-purpose flour	500 g	17.6 oz	3½ cups plus 1 Tbsp
TOTAL FLOUR	500 g	17.6 oz	3½ cups plus 1 Tbsp
Granulated sugar	30 g	1 oz	2½ Tbsp
Nonfat milk powder	26 g	0.9 oz	3 Tbsp
Instant yeast	5 g	0.2 oz	1½ tsp
Fine gray salt	10 g	0.3 oz	1¾ tsp
Warm water, (100°F/38°C)	270 g	9.5 oz	1 cup plus 2½ Tbsp
Egg, at room temperature lightly beaten	58 g	2 oz	1 to 2 large (3½ Tbsp)
Unsalted butter, at room temperature	75 g	2.6 oz	5 Tbsp
TOTAL WEIGHT	974 g	34 oz/2.1 lbs	

Lightly oil or spray a deep 4½- to 5-quart ceramic or glass bread bowl. (The amount of dough in this recipe will work well in a 3-quart bread bowl if you have one.)

✦ Combine the flour, sugar, milk powder, instant yeast, and salt in the bowl of a stand mixer fitted with the dough hook. With the mixer running on the lowest speed, add the water, followed by the egg, and finally the butter. Increase the speed to low and mix for 7 minutes.

✦ Flour the work surface. Using a plastic bowl scraper, turn out the dough and knead a few times. This is a very smooth but loose dough. Place it in the bread bowl. Cover the bowl with a lightly oiled or sprayed piece of plastic wrap and place in a warm, draft-free spot (see Creating Your Warm Spot, page 17) to proof until the dough is very puffy and about doubled, 1½ to 2 hours.

✦ The dough is ready to be divided, pre-shaped, and shaped for Hamburger or Hot Dog Rolls (page 74) or Dinner Rolls (page 76).

HAMBURGER OR HOT DOG ROLLS

∽ Makes 8 generously sized hamburger or hot dog rolls ∽

Because these rolls are larger than the Dinner Rolls on page 76, the dough gets the additional step of a pre-shape, which helps them maintain their shape.

Della's Roll Dough (page 73)

32 to 64 grams (1.1 to 2.2 ounces/2 to 4 tablespoons) egg yolk loosened with heavy cream, half-and-half, or whole milk for the wash (see Brushing Enriched Doughs Before and After Proofing, page 86)

5 to 10 grams (0.17 to 0.35 ounce/about 1 tablespoon) sesame, poppy, or fennel seeds or dehydrated onions, or a combination (optional)

For hamburger rolls, lightly oil or spray a half sheet pan, line with parchment paper, and lightly oil or spray the paper. *For hot dog rolls*, lightly oil or spray a quarter sheet pan, line with parchment paper, and lightly oil or spray the paper.

✦ Flour the work surface. Turn out the dough, using a plastic bowl scraper, and, using a bench scraper, scale (divide) the dough into 8 equal pieces (about 120 grams/ 4 ounces each). Pre-shape each piece (see photos, Pre-shaping, page 45). Let sit for 10 minutes.

✦ *For hamburger rolls:* Cup your fingers around one piece of dough at a time (or, once you become proficient, one piece in each hand) and roll it against the work surface to form a ball (see photos, Shaping Rolls, page 77), then press into a round about 4 inches across. Place seam side down on the

prepared sheet pan, in 2 rows of 4 rolls each. With flattened fingers or the palm of your hand, press the tops again to flatten them into disks. Brush the tops with the wash and sprinkle with the seeds, if using.

✦ *For hot dog rolls:* Shape each piece into a small bâtard (see photos, Shaping a Bâtard, pages 52–53), about 1¾ by 5½ inches. Arrange on the quarter sheet pan in 2 rows of 4 buns each; the rolls will be touching. Brush the tops with the wash and sprinkle with the seeds, if using.

✦ Set the pan in your warm spot, cover with a Cambro container or a plastic tub, and let proof until puffy, 1½ to 2 hours. When the dough is gently pressed with your fingertip, the impression should remain.

✦ Meanwhile, position a rack in the center of the oven, set a baking stone on it, and preheat the oven to 375°F.

✦ Place the pan on the stone and bake the rolls for about 25 minutes, or until the tops are a rich golden brown. To test for doneness, see Is It Baked?, page 58.

✦ Transfer the pan to a cooling rack and let the rolls cool completely. For storing options, see How to Store Bread, page 51.

DINNER ROLLS

∾ Makes 16 rolls ∾

Our rich, buttery dinner rolls are a hugely popular item at the café, especially during the holidays. Any extra rolls that you have are perfect for making mini ham or turkey sandwiches with your leftovers the next day. In fact, I'd suggest making extra to ensure that you have enough.

5 to 10 grams (0.17 to 0.35 ounce/about 1 tablespoon) sesame, poppy, or fennel seeds or dehydrated onions, or a combination (optional)

32 to 64 grams (1.1 to 2.2 ounces/2 to 4 tablespoons) egg yolk loosened with heavy cream, half-and-half, or whole milk for the wash (see Brushing Enriched Doughs Before and After Proofing, page 86)

Della's Roll Dough (page 73)

Lightly oil or spray a quarter sheet pan or a 9-by-13-inch baking dish. Line with parchment paper and lightly oil or spray the paper.

+ If using them, spread the sesame, poppy, or fennel seeds and/or dehydrated onions on a dinner plate. Set a ramekin or small bowl of the wash next to it.

+ Flour the work surface. Turn out the dough, using a plastic bowl scraper, and, using a bench scraper, scale (divide) the dough into 16 equal pieces (about 56 grams/2 ounces each). Cup your fingers around one piece at a time (or, once you become proficient, one piece in each hand) and roll it against the work surface to form a ball (see photos, Shaping Rolls, opposite).

+ Dip the top of each ball in the wash, letting any excess run back into the ramekin, then dip into the seeds. Place seam side down

on the prepared pan, in 4 rows of 4 rolls each. (If not using the seeds, brush the tops of the rolls with the wash.)

+ Set the pan in your warm spot, cover with a Cambro container or a plastic tub, and let proof until doubled in size, 1½ to 2 hours. When the dough is gently pressed with your fingertip, the impression should remain.

+ Meanwhile, position a rack in the center of the oven, set a baking stone on it, and preheat the oven to 375°F.

+ Place the pan on the stone and bake the rolls for 20 to 25 minutes, or until the tops are a rich golden brown. To test for doneness, see Is It Baked?, page 58.

+ Transfer the pan to a cooling rack and let the rolls cool completely. For storing options, see How to Store Bread, page 51.

· Shaping Rolls ·

For all rolls, scale (divide) the dough as instructed in the recipes. As noted in the recipe, hamburger and hot dog rolls will be pre-shaped (see photos, Pre-Shaping, page 45) and then shaped following the instructions below.

FOR DINNER ROLLS & HAMBURGER ROLLS

(1) Cup your fingers around one piece at a time, roll against the work surface to form a ball, and set on the prepared pan.

(2) Once you become proficient, cup one piece in each hand and roll against the work surface.

FOR HOT DOG ROLLS

Shaping hot dog rolls is similar to making a bâtard (see photos, Shaping a Bâtard, pages 52–53).

(3–5) Turn the pre-shaped loaf seam side up and pat into a rectangle. Position your hands under the dough, folding it over so the ends meet in front of you. Use the heel of your hand to seal the edge and gently rock so the seam is underneath.

HOT DOGS
with Aaron's Spicy Slaw
∽ Serves 6 ∽

At the Weber Ranch, our favorite hot dog toppers are my son's spicy slaw or sauerkraut with pickled jalapeños. The slaw is also perfect for burgers.

Spicy Slaw (makes about 6 cups)

6 cups thinly sliced Napa cabbage

⅓ cup shredded carrots

2 tablespoons thinly sliced scallions (white and light green portions)

1 to 2 tablespoons minced jalapeño

2 tablespoons coarsely chopped cilantro, plus a few leaves for garnish (optional)

Extra virgin olive oil

½ lime

Kosher salt and freshly ground black pepper

6 hot dogs, preferably grilled

6 Hot Dog Rolls (page 74), split, preferably brushed with a little mayonnaise and grilled or toasted

Sliced pickled jalapeños (optional)

For the slaw: In a large bowl, combine the cabbage, carrots, scallions, jalapeño, and cilantro, if using. Drizzle with olive oil and squeeze the lime over the top. Season to taste with salt and pepper. Garnish with jalapeño rings and cilantro leaves, if you like.

⁎ To serve, nestle each hot dog in a roll and top with some slaw and a few slices of pickled jalapeño, if using.

ROSE'S OVERNIGHT BRIOCHE DOUGH

❧ *Makes 1.17 kilograms/2.5 pounds* ❧

This foolproof brioche recipe is a gift from my brilliant friend Rose Levy Beranbaum, though I've changed a few things over the years. I was introduced to Rose years ago. As a longtime admirer and fully aware of her status as a baking authority, I was expecting someone far more serious. But Rose is as light as her delicate cakes—warm and lovely, always with a smile on her lips and a giggle in her voice.

While she was working on *The Bread Bible*, Rose approached us about including our Seeded Wheat Bread (pages 211–215). Needless to say, we were honored by her request. When the book was released, the first thing I baked was the one thing I had been resisting for years: brioche. Although I had looked at many recipes, there was something besides the calories that put me off—and maybe I thought brioche was beyond my capabilities. But the minute I read Rose's recipe, I gathered my ingredients and baked brioche. I fell in love with the look and feel of the dough, which is remarkable; I know of nothing else like it. And to this day, Rose's brioche is the only one I've ever made. It looks like golden satin and is the softest, most elastic dough I have ever worked with. This dough does take time. There are multiple resting periods required, including overnight in the fridge. But the dough can be made up to 2 days in advance.

Thank you, Rose, for many years of wonderful baking, and for allowing me to include your recipe in this book.

SPONGE

All-purpose flour	142 g	5 oz	1 cup
TOTAL FLOUR	142 g	5 oz	1 cup
Granulated sugar	25 g	0.9 oz	2 Tbsp
Instant yeast	1.5 g	0.05 oz	½ tsp
Water, at room temperature (65° to 70°F/18° to 21°C)	59 g	2 oz	¼ cup
Eggs, lightly beaten and cold	116 g	4 oz	2 to 3 large (¼ cup plus 3 Tbsp)

DOUGH MIX

All-purpose flour	312 g	11 oz	2¼ cups
TOTAL FLOUR	312 g	11 oz	2¼ cups
Granulated sugar	50 g	1.7 oz	¼ cup
Instant yeast	8 g	0.3 oz	2¼ tsp
Fine gray salt	6 g	0.2 oz	1 tsp
Eggs, lightly beaten and cold	226 g	8 oz	4 to 5 large (¾ cup plus 2 Tbsp)
Unsalted butter, cut into ¼-inch pieces, at room temperature	226 g	8 oz	16 Tbsp
TOTAL WEIGHT	1,172 g/1.17 kg	41 oz/2.5 lbs	

Lightly oil or spray a deep 4½- to 5-quart ceramic or glass bread bowl.

 + For the sponge: Combine the flour, sugar, and yeast in the bowl of a stand mixer fitted with the whisk attachment. Add the water and eggs and pulse a few times on the lowest setting (to keep the flour from flying out of the bowl), then mix on low speed just to combine, about 1 minute. It is OK if there are some small lumps. Cover with plastic wrap and let sit at room temperature for 15 minutes (because of the small amount of yeast, there will not be a lot of bubbling at this point).

 + In a medium bowl, whisk together the flour, sugar, yeast, and salt for the dough mix. Pour over the sponge, but do not mix. Cover the bowl with a lightly oiled or sprayed piece of plastic wrap and place in a warm, draft-free spot (see Creating Your Warm Spot, page 17) until the sponge has bubbled up into the flour mixture, 1½ to 2 hours. There will be large cracks in the flour mixture and bits of the sponge may be visible around the edges and/or in some spot(s) of the cracks.

 + Return the bowl to the mixer, fitted with the dough hook. Add the eggs and mix on low speed just until the flour has been moistened

by the eggs; there will be some uncoated flour around the edges. Scrape down the sides of the bowl, increase the speed to medium-low, and mix for 2 minutes. Stop, scrape down the hook and the sides, and then mix on medium-low speed for 5 minutes. Scrape down the hook and the sides and let the dough sit at room temperature, uncovered, for 10 minutes.

 + Mix the dough on medium-low speed until it pulls away from the sides of the bowl and begins to gather around the hook, about 3 minutes. Add the butter a couple pieces at a time, waiting until each addition is incorporated before adding the next. Mix until the dough pulls away from the sides of the bowl again and gathers around the hook.

 + Using a plastic bowl scraper, transfer the dough to the prepared bowl. (It doesn't have to be kneaded on the work surface.) Cover the bowl with a lightly oiled or sprayed piece of plastic wrap and set in your warm spot to proof until the dough is very puffy and doubled in size, 1½ to 2 hours. The dough will still be a little sticky. Using the bowl scraper, gently release the dough from the edges of the bowl and, with wet fingertips, dimple the dough to deflate it. (This is the recipe step that often says to "punch down" the dough; this dough does not need to be deflated violently.) Cover again and refrigerate until firmed up a bit, about 1 hour.

♦ Fold over the top edge (about 2 inches) of a gallon-size resealable freezer bag and set it beside your work surface.

♦ Flour the work surface and use the bowl scraper to turn out the dough. The dough will naturally spread to about 1 inch in thickness. As it does, with your fingertips, press it into a rectangle. Starting at the right short side, stretch the dough over itself about two-thirds, brushing off any excess flour, to make the first fold. Then, starting from the left short side, stretch the dough about two-thirds over itself, brushing off any excess flour, to make the second fold (as if you were folding a letter). Repeat the folds from the top and then the bottom, brushing off excess flour. Lift the dough into the bag, unfold the top of the bag, press out any excess air, and seal. Refrigerate the dough for at least 8 hours, or up to 2 days.

♦ The dough is ready to be pre-shaped and shaped for a Brioche Pullman Loaf or two traditional loaves (page 85), rolled out for Sticky Buns (page 89), or divided, pre-shaped, and braided for the Brioche Braid (page 91).

Courage in the Kitchen

∽ BUTTERY DOUGHS AND FLOUR ON THE WORK SURFACE ∽

For the slack, sticky enriched doughs in this chapter, you want to use just a bit more flour on your work surfaces than for other doughs. It should still be just a thin blanket of flour, but you need to use enough so that when you run your finger across the work surface, you leave a distinct trail.

If the dough is sticking, check the work surface for stray bits of dough that might be causing the sticking. Then scrape the surface clean with a bench scraper, reflour it, and start again.

· Weighing & Using Farm-Fresh Eggs ·

Using farm-fresh eggs will make enriched dough even more golden, but eggs vary in size, so it's a good idea to make sure each one measures 56 grams/2 ounces. If weighing eggs (which is preferable), crack them into a bowl and lightly beat them with a fork. Then any excess can be poured off and reserved for another use.

The volume measurements corresponding to the number of eggs given in the baker's boxes are based on the average size of store-bought large eggs, which will work just fine. But for consistent results, crack the eggs into a bowl and weigh them as described above.

BRIOCHE PULLMAN LOAF

Makes 1 Pullman loaf

Brioche dough can be stiff, especially if you are working with it when it's cold, as in this recipe. The pre-shaping and shaping techniques won't differ from those of other recipes made in a loaf pan, but the process will feel different because this is a cold, buttery dough.

This brioche loaf is baked in a Pullman pan. For bread with a flat top, bake the loaf with the lid on, which will give you square slices; for a loaf with a rounded top, bake it with the lid off, which will give you more traditional looking slices. To make 2 standard loaves of brioche, see the Note.

Rose's Overnight Brioche Dough (page 80)

32 to 64 grams (1.1 to 2.2 ounces/2 to 4 tablespoons) egg yolk loosened with heavy cream, half-and-half, or whole milk for the wash (see Brushing Enriched Doughs Before and After Proofing, page 86)

Flour the work surface. Remove the dough from the refrigerator and, with a plastic bowl scraper, scrape it onto the work surface. Press into a rectangle about 1 inch thick and pre-shape it (see photos, Pre-shaping, page 45). Let sit for 10 minutes.

✦ Fairly generously oil or spray a 13-by-4-by-4-inch Pullman pan, and the underside of the lid if using it. Using your hands and a bench scraper, shape the dough into a bâtard (see photos, Shaping a Bâtard, pages 52–53), about 3 by 13 inches. Set in the pan and brush the top with the wash. Refrigerate the remaining wash if making a loaf with a rounded top.

✦ *For a loaf with a flat top,* slide on the lid, leaving about an inch open to check on the height of the rising dough. Lightly oil or spray a small piece of plastic wrap and put it over the hole. *For a loaf with a rounded top,* oil or spray a large piece of plastic wrap and cover the pan with it.

✦ Set the pan in your warm spot to proof until the dough is about ½ inch from the top of the pan if baking with the lid or at the top edge if not baking with the lid, 2 to 3 hours. When the dough is gently pressed with your fingertip, the impression should remain.

✦ Meanwhile, position a rack in the center of the oven, set a baking stone on it, and preheat the oven to 350°F.

✦ *If baking with the lid,* remove the plastic wrap and slide the lid closed. Place the pan on the stone and bake for 25 minutes. Carefully remove the lid and bake for 5 to 10 minutes, to brown the top. To test for doneness, see Is It Baked?, page 58.

✦ *If baking without the lid,* remove the plastic wrap and gently brush the top again with the wash. Place the pan on the stone and bake for 30 minutes, or until the top is golden brown. To test for doneness, see Is It Baked?, page 58.

✦ Transfer the pan to a cooling rack and let cool for about 10 minutes. Carefully turn the bread out onto the rack and let cool completely. For storing options, see How to Store Bread, page 51.

· Note ·
ON BAKING IN TWO STANDARD LOAF PANS

Flour the work surface. Remove the dough from the refrigerator, and, using a bench scraper, divide the dough into 2 equal pieces. Press each piece into a 1-inch-thick rectangle. Let rest for 10 minutes.

Fairly generously oil or spray two 8½-by-4½-by-2¾-inch loaf pans. Shape each piece of dough into a bâtard, put in the pans as above, and brush the tops with the wash. Refrigerate the remaining wash. Cover the tops with a lightly oiled or sprayed piece of plastic wrap and set in your warm spot to proof for about 2 hours, until the dough has reached the tops of the pans.

Meanwhile, position a rack in the center of the oven, set a baking stone on it, and preheat the oven to 350°F.

Remove the plastic wrap and gently brush the tops of the loaves again with the wash. Place the pans on the stone and bake for about 25 minutes, until the tops are golden brown. To test for doneness, see Is It Baked?, page 58.

Transfer the pans to a cooling rack and let cool for about 10 minutes. Carefully turn the bread out onto the rack and let cool completely. For storing options, see How to Store Bread, page 51.

Courage in the Kitchen
∾ BRUSHING ENRICHED DOUGHS BEFORE AND AFTER PROOFING

As with yeasted doughs (see page 42), I usually like to brush enriched doughs twice, once before and once after proofing. The first brushing keeps the loaf from developing a skin on top as it proofs, while the second one gives it a sheen. There are a couple of exceptions: brioche baked in a Pullman pan with the lid on is only brushed before proofing, and rolls dipped in seeds are dipped in the wash only before proofing.

For the wash, I start with an egg yolk and loosen it with heavy cream, half-and-half, or whole milk.

HAVE A CHEF TO DINNER

When we first started baking bread for The French Laundry, we invited Thomas Keller to dinner at the ranch. I was nervous that he wouldn't accept our invitation, but once he did, I was *really* nervous about what we would serve. It was late autumn and I wanted to make an Alsatian dish called *Baeckeoffe*. I tested it out on the family and, frankly, it wasn't a hit; it was suggested that I make cassoulet instead.

The very best cassoulet I'd ever tasted was made by our friend Daniel Patterson, chef-owner of Babette's in Sonoma. No problem, said Daniel when I asked him for the cassoulet recipe; I could

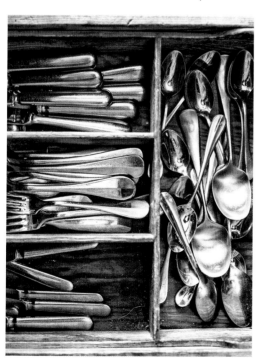

pick it up the next day when I delivered his bread. A short time later, he called back. "Kathleen, I don't think you have time to do this," he said. "You need to make lamb, pork, and beef stock. Then the meat has to be cooked in a certain order. You need to have the right sausages and beans." A good cassoulet may be peasant fare, but it's a complicated undertaking. Daniel proposed that if I brought him my pots, he would make the cassoulet, and I could just add the bread crumbs and heat it up. Talk about kindness! It was an offer I couldn't refuse.

The big day came: we served a simple salad, our toasted Pain au Levain, the cassoulet, Meyer lemon ice cream, and homemade cookies for dessert. Thomas brought a beautiful French wine, and there we were: Thomas and my entire family sitting at the table. The thing about Thomas is that despite his formidable reputation, he's genuinely gracious and generous. He took one bite of the cassoulet, and his eyes went around the table.

"Who made this?" he asked. It never occurred to me that he would ask that very obvious question. All eyes were on me. What could I say?

"Daniel," I said softly.

Thomas knew exactly who I meant, and he laughed. "Why didn't you just say you made it?" he asked.

The tension was broken. We all laughed until we cried, and it was a night to remember. It was the last time I invited a chef to dinner and had another chef cook the food!

STICKY BUNS

꽁 Makes 12 sticky buns 꽁

A dozen sticky buns, baked in two cake rounds, will use half the brioche dough. With the other half, you can make a loaf of Brioche (page 85), or you can make more sticky buns. If you do opt for more buns, you'll probably be reusing the cake rounds from the first batch: make sure they are completely cool and clean before starting the second batch. And if you are making two batches, be sure to stash the rest of the dough in the fridge so it stays cool.

I love pecans in the sticky buns filling and on top, but the soaked raisins from the Cinnamon-Raisin Bread (page 56) are delicious too, or you can leave out the nuts and raisins completely.

BROWN SUGAR-HONEY TOPPING

Brown sugar (light or dark)	168 g	6 oz	¾ cup packed plus 2 Tbsp
Unsalted butter, cut into ½-inch pieces	96 g	3.3 oz	6⅔ Tbsp
Honey	32 g	1.1 oz	1½ Tbsp
Heavy cream	62 g	2.2 oz	¼ cup
Coarsely chopped toasted pecans (see Note; optional)	55 g	1.9 oz	½ cup
Soaked raisins (see page 56; optional)	80 g	2.8 oz	½ cup

FILLING

Brown sugar (light or dark)	70 g	2.5 oz	¼ cup plus 2 Tbsp packed
Ground cinnamon	9 g	0.3 oz	1 Tbsp
1 egg, lightly beaten			
Coarsely chopped toasted pecans (see Note; optional)	55 g	1.9 oz	½ cup

½ recipe Rose's Overnight Brioche Dough (page 80)

Fairly generously oil or spray two 8-inch cake rounds.

⁕ For the topping: Combine the brown sugar, butter, and honey in a small deep saucepan and bring to a simmer over medium heat, stirring as the butter melts. Continue to heat until the mixture reaches 244°F/117.7°C, 3 to 5 minutes.

⁕ Remove the pan from the heat and pour in the cream; it will bubble up. Place back over the heat, stirring to combine, and heat until the mixture returns to 244°F/117.7°C, 2 to 3 minutes. Let cool for a few minutes: it is easiest to pour the topping into the pans while still hot.

 + Pour about half of the topping into each cake round. Sprinkle the pecans or raisins, if using, into the cake rounds.

 + For the buns: Combine the brown sugar and cinnamon for the filling in a small cup.

 + Flour the work surface. Remove the dough from the refrigerator and, with a plastic bowl scraper, scrape it onto the work surface. Roll the dough into a 12-by-14-inch rectangle (a short side should be facing you). Leaving a 1-inch border, brush the dough with the egg. Sprinkle the sugar and cinnamon and then the chopped pecans, if using, over the egg wash. Roll up the dough tightly from the end closest to you, ending with the seam underneath.

 + Cut the dough into 12 equal portions with a bench scraper and set 6 cut side down into each round, 5 around the edge, and 1 in the center. Press on the tops gently to flatten them slightly. They will not be touching at this point. Set in your warm spot, cover with a Cambro container or a plastic tub, and let proof until the buns are about doubled in size and the sides are touching, about 1½ hours.

 + Meanwhile, position a rack in the center of the oven and preheat the oven to 350°F. Because there is a possibility that some of the topping will bubble up while baking, I like to position a rack directly under the center one and put a half sheet pan on it to catch any overflow. Set parchment paper or 2 silicone baking mats on sheet pans or on your work surface.

 + Bake the sticky buns for 10 minutes. Cover loosely with aluminum foil (even if the buns don't look too brown, because that can happen quickly) and bake for another 20 minutes. Remove the foil and bake for 5 minutes more, or until the buns are golden brown with no undercooked portions visible in the center rings.

 + Carefully invert the pans onto the parchment or silicone mats. Any topping that pools on the parchment or remains in the pans can be spread on the buns while it is still hot. Let cool completely.

 + The sticky buns are best eaten the day they are made, but they can be stored in a large storage bag or in a covered container for up to 3 days. They also freeze well if wrapped individually first in plastic wrap and then in foil (see How to Store Bread, page 51). If you like your sticky buns warm, put them on a silicone-lined baking sheet and pop them into a 350°F oven for a few minutes.

· Note ·
ON TOASTING PECANS

If you are making the buns with pecans on top and in the filling, you will need a total of 1 cup (110 grams/3.8 ounces) nuts. I always like to start with whole pecans rather than pieces. To toast the nuts, spread them on a sheet pan and bake in a preheated 325°F oven until just beginning to darken, about 5 minutes. Remove from the oven, pour onto a plate, and let cool completely before using.

BRIOCHE BRAID

⁓ Makes 1 large braided loaf ⁓

Brioche happens to be the perfect dough for making this delicious and beautiful bread. The challah traditionally made for the Jewish Sabbath does not contain butter, but I take the liberty of making it with a dough that contains butter, which gives it a satiny, supple texture that is ideal for braiding. Leftover slices are cause to rejoice—it makes wonderful French toast or bread pudding.

The Oval Herbed Bread (page 62) can also be made as a braided loaf using the same technique. For a bit of extra crunch, sprinkle the pan with some semolina flour.

Rose's Overnight Brioche Dough (page 80)

32 to 64 grams (1.1 to 2.2 ounces/2 to 4 tablespoons) egg yolk loosened with heavy cream, half-and-half, or whole milk for the wash (see Brushing Enriched Doughs Before and After Proofing, page 86)

Lightly oil or spray the back of a half sheet pan, line with parchment paper, and lightly oil or spray the paper or line with a silicone baking mat.

+ Flour the work surface. Remove the dough from the refrigerator and, with a plastic bowl scraper, scrape it onto the work surface. Using a bench scraper, scale (divide) the dough into 6 equal pieces.

+ Follow the steps for Braiding Brioche, pages 92–93.

+ Brush the loaf with some of the wash. Reserve the remaining wash.

+ Set the pan in your warm spot, cover with a Cambro container or a plastic tub, and let proof until expanded, 2 to 3 hours. When the dough is gently pressed with your fingertip, the impression should remain.

+ Meanwhile, position a rack in the lower third of the oven, set a baking stone on it, and preheat the oven to 350°F.

+ Gently brush the top of the braid with the remaining wash. Set the pan on the stone and bake for 35 to 40 minutes, or until the top is a rich golden brown. To test for doneness, see Is It Baked?, page 58.

+ Carefully slide the bread from the pan, loosening it with a spatula if needed, onto a cooling rack and let cool completely. For storing options, see How to Store Bread, page 51.

· Braiding Brioche ·

The most important thing to remember while braiding is over two, under one, over two.

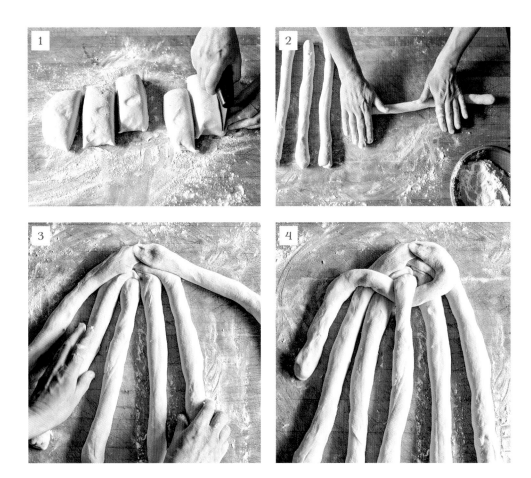

(1) Divide the dough into 6 equal pieces. (2) Working from the center outward, roll each piece into a rope about 1½ by 12 inches. (3) Pinch the ends of the ropes together. They should be tight enough to hold but loose enough that they can be separated and rebraided later. (4) Starting with the rope at the far right, go over two ropes, under one rope, and then over two again. Bring the end of that rope down so it is now the piece farthest to the left. (5) Always starting with the rope at the far right, continue going over two, under one, over two. Occasionally, shift the braid so the ropes are directly in front of you. (6) As you reach the bottom, the pieces may need to be stretched a bit to finish the braid. (7) Bring the ends together and tuck them under the loaf. (8–9) Turn the braid around so what was the top is now in front of you at the bottom of the braid. Undo the braid and redo from right to left, over two, under one, over two, to make a tighter braid. Bring the ends together and tuck them under the loaf. (10) Compact the braid by gently pushing in on the sides and then from top to bottom. Set on the back of the prepared pan.

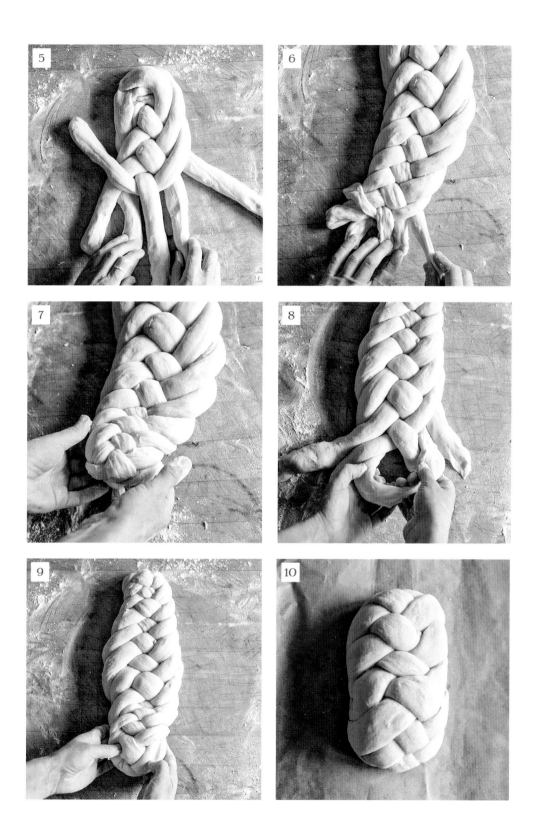

PRE-FERMENTED BREADS

A PRE-FERMENT IS ALSO KNOWN AS A STARTER. It's similar to a sponge (see page 33), but it develops overnight; it goes by various other names, including *poolish* and *biga*. Biga is the Italian version and what we use for the breads in this chapter. Biga is a mixture of flour, water, and a small amount of yeast combined either by hand or in a mixer and left out overnight at room temperature. It more than doubles in volume and becomes very bubbly and effervescent. The effect on the bread is profound in terms of texture, flavor, and extended shelf life.

Pre-fermented breads are the breads that catapulted me from being a casual baker to a baker possessed. Baking rustic, crusty, free-form loaves touched me in an unexpected way. I've always joked that we Webers are Petaluma peasants: completely connected to the land we live on, the sheep and chickens we raise, the gardens that produce much of our food, and our home and hearth. But, equally important, through our land, we have a strong connection with the past, and a frankly sentimental respect for self-reliance.

My mother-in-law was a frugal old girl, and if I ever whined about the cost of living, her predictable answer was, "As long as you can bake a loaf of bread and cook a pot of beans, you'll never starve." Well, I can cook a mean pot of beans (see page 123), but the yeasted pan breads that I had been baking were not crusty or sturdy enough to be a proper companion to a pot of beans, a bowl of soup, or a hearty beef stew.

Then along came Carol Field's *The Italian Baker*. My reaction was pure "Eureka—this is it." Here was the peasant bread that lived in history books and fairy tales. Here

was why bread is part of every meal in Italy. Here was the kind of bread worth going to war for. And so I did. My kitchen became a jumbled zone of just-baked loaves, doughs in progress, doughs in the oven, and doughs in the refrigerator.

As my baking knowledge progressed, so did my work space. My daughter found a large piece of marble that had once been on the front of her friend Erno's tattoo parlor in San Francisco. We piled into the truck and headed for the city to drag it home. The slab was scrubbed and sanded and placed on top of our kitchen table so I would have a beautiful cool marble surface to shape on. Ed found a 20-quart Hobart mixer behind a local restaurant. He paid $200, brought it home, took it apart, painted it all tractor red, and somehow put it back together again. My 5-pound bags of flour turned into 50-pound sacks, and I had them all over the place. There was flour on the floor, in the air, and on every surface. I was in hog heaven.

This was also around the time when Ed and his friends started researching plans for building a wood-fired oven. Alan Scott was

the happiness that went into its building was reproduced in every loaf of bread.

While you may not have a wood-fired brick oven in your backyard, with these recipes, you have the opportunity to bake incredible bread and be part of the large community of artisanal home bakers. This baking tradition, with roots so far into the past, connects us with the bakers who have gone before. Those of us who feel a surge of adrenaline just planning the baking day and an unspeakable thrill when that first crusty, chewy, fragrant, crackling loaf comes out of the oven know that we are part of something bigger than ourselves. Making bread so delicious out of such ordinary ingredients feels like spinning straw into gold. We are bread wizards.

But before you go forward with these breads, I want to emphasize what a miracle it is that we have traditional bread recipes to bake from at all. When she was writing *The Italian Baker*, Carol Field spent time with small bakers in Italy, convincing them to teach her their regional styles. Her work is something I'm grateful for every day. The sad truth is that while we were industrializing our bread manufacturing here in the United States, it was happening in Italy too. When Ed and I were finally able to take a trip to Italy in 2000, we found that the really delicious bread came from very small towns that still had a village baker baking bread in a wood-fired oven. I dedicate this chapter to you. So thank you, Carol.

the oven designer of choice in those days, and he lived nearby. Ed bought plans from Alan, and we went out to see his oven. The idea of building a wood-fired oven still felt like a pretty big mystery, so Alan suggested we host an oven-building workshop. He charged each attendee $200 to participate and insisted that everyone bring food to share. For two weekends, our entire family and a gaggle of amateurs happily mixed mortar, sawed bricks, and slapped them together, all the while drinking wine, eating delicious food, and fending off yellow jackets. It was complete chaos, and in the end, amazingly, I had a beautiful brick wood-fired oven. I felt that all

There isn't a tool in the world that can give you as much information about the dough and what it needs as your hands.

This chapter builds on what you learned in the yeasted and enriched bread chapters about familiarizing yourself with the feel of the dough through pre-shaping and shaping. You'll use new shaping techniques and different ways of proofing the dough, including using proofing baskets and *couches* (proofing linens). You'll learn how to use different vessels to bake in and how to handle a peel. You can try some free-form baking too—setting the loaf directly on a heated baking stone.

Take a moment to notice what the dough feels like in each of its stages: when it's just coming together in the mixer, as it starts to develop tension and structure; before and after you shape it; and when it's ready to go into the oven.

The breads in this chapter are rustic, but they'll help you acquire additional skills to refine your shaping techniques. Notice that while the recipes that follow call for very similar ingredients, simply changing the proportions of those ingredients and using different techniques can produce widely varied results.

Making a biga and a milk starter (pages 100 and 110) and working with them

Proofing in a bowl lined with a linen or in a basket with or without a linen (page 114)

Using a linen for proofing long loaves (page 140)

Forming a wreath (page 130)

Shaping a baguette (page 146)

Dimpling the dough (see Pane Pugliese, page 117, and Pane Toscano Loaves, page 121)

Using a transfer peel (page 145)

Scoring with a bench scraper (see Pane Durum Oval Loaves, page 135)

Additional scoring techniques (see individual recipes)

Cutting for épis (see Forming an Olive Oil Wreath, page 130)

Turning out and baking directly on a stone (see Pane Como Rounded Loaves, page 110, and Free-form Pane Pugliese, page 117)

Baking in a clay pot or tagine (page 102)

✄ EQUIPMENT NEEDED ✄

- Scale
- Stand mixer with paddle and dough hook attachments
- Baking stones
- Thermometer
- Plastic bowl scraper
- Bench scraper
- Plastic wrap
- Liquid measuring cup, preferably with a lid (optional)
- 4½- to 5-quart bread bowl
- Two 9-inch-wide bread baskets (bannetons) or 9-inch bowls
- 12-inch-wide bread basket (banneton)

- Baker's linen (couche) or linen dish towels
- Quarter sheet pan (9 by 13 by ½ inch)
- Half sheet pan
- Cookie sheet (with no sides) or a pizza pan (optional)
- 14-inch cast-iron baking pan
- 3½- to 4-quart (9-inch) round cast-iron pot
- 3½- to 4-quart round clay pot (about 6 inches in diameter) or 10- to 11-inch tagine
- 2-quart round clay pot, 7 to 8 inches in diameter (optional)

- 6-quart (10-inch) round cast-iron pot
- Cambro container or plastic tub
- Transfer peel
- Peel
- Scissors
- Lame or razor blade
- 10-inch cast-iron skillet
- 9-inch perforated pie plate or collapsible steamer basket
- Ball bearings or a piece of chain link (optional)
- Cooling rack

BIGA

Makes 209 grams/7.3 ounces (small batch); 417 grams/14.7 ounces (medium batch); or 835 grams/29.4 ounces (large batch)

A biga starter is used for all of the doughs in this chapter except the Pane Como Round Loaves (page 110), which calls for a milk starter. Biga is a simple mixture of flour, water, and yeast, left at room temperature overnight or for up to eighteen hours. It is best to make it and use it rather than try to maintain it by feeding it (for more on that technique, see the Firm Starter, page 156, in the naturally leavened breads chapter).

You can make a single small batch if you plan on baking only on one day, but I encourage you to make a larger batch and use it for a few recipes over the course of several days. The biga can be refrigerated in a sealed container for up to three days. It can be used straight out of the fridge, but if you do, be sure that the water in the bread recipe is warmer (90°F/32°C).

A small batch is enough to make the Pane Toscano Loaves (page 121), Olive Oil Wreath (page 128), or Traditional (Sweet) Baguette (page 142). You'll need a medium batch for the Country Wheat Boule (page 104) or Free-form Pane Pugliese (page 117), and a large batch to make the Pane Durum Dough (page 132).

Here's another example of why a scale is really essential in baking. The more the biga is handled—even just transferring it from the bowl to measuring cups—the more it will lose volume. If you do have to measure it rather than weigh it, use damp hands and a damp measuring spoon or cup.

FOR A SMALL BATCH

All-purpose flour	125 g	4.4 oz	¾ cup plus 2½ Tbsp
Instant yeast	1.5 g	0.04 oz	½ tsp
Water at 75° to 80°F/24° to 27°C	83 g	2.9 oz	¼ cup plus 1½ Tbsp
TOTAL WEIGHT	209 g	7.3 oz	

FOR A MEDIUM BATCH

All-purpose flour	250 g	8.8 oz	1¾ cups plus 1 Tbsp
Instant yeast	2.5 g	0.08 oz	¾ tsp
Water at 75° to 80°F/24° to 27°C	165 g	5.8 oz	½ cup plus 3 Tbsp
TOTAL WEIGHT	417 g	14.7 oz	

All-purpose flour	500 g	17.6 oz	3½ cups plus 1 Tbsp
Instant yeast	5 g	0.17 oz	1½ tsp
Water at 75° to 80°F/24° to 27°C	330 g	11.6 oz	1¼ cups plus 2½ Tbsp
TOTAL WEIGHT	835 g	29.4 oz	

In the bowl of a stand mixer fitted with the paddle attachment, combine the flour, yeast, and water and mix on the lowest speed for about 1 minute to combine. The mixture will be sticky. Remove the paddle attachment and, with damp hands, scrape any of the biga from the paddle back into the bowl. Transfer the biga to a very lightly oiled or sprayed liquid measuring cup, storage container, or a bowl and cover with a lid or a lightly oiled or sprayed piece of plastic wrap. Let sit at room temperature overnight, or for up to 18 hours.

✦ To use the biga, with damp hands, pinch off the amount you need for the dough you are making. Any remaining biga can be refrigerated for up to 3 days to use in other doughs.

Courage in the Kitchen
☙ KEEP YOUR HANDS DAMP ❧

The best way to handle just-mixed dough is with damp hands. Keeping a bowl of water nearby for dipping your hands into will make removing dough from the mixer attachments or bowl much easier. It makes pinching off a given amount of biga or starter easier too. And folding the doughs in the naturally leavened breads chapter will be trouble-free when your hands are damp.

Likewise, dipping your plastic bowl scraper in water, and letting any excess run off, will help when scraping down the sides of the mixer bowl and loosening the dough from the mixing or proofing bowl.

If dough does stick to your hands, the best way to remove it is to put a little flour on your hands and rub them together. Don't add water: this will make the dough that's on your hands even more gluey.

· Baking in a Clay Pot or Tagine ·

Clay pots hold heat and trap moisture, creating the perfect environment for baking bread (for more on steam in the oven, see page 108). Like baking in cast iron (see Proofing & Baking in a Cast-Iron Pot, page 43), baking in a clay pot is a way to bake a crusty artisan loaf.

The pot should be flameproof and have a lid. (Unless you want to experiment with shapes; see Taking Liberties: Baking in Other Vessels, page 119.) Also, be sure the pot's glaze is lead-free. And be mindful of the shape: the diameter can't be smaller at the top than it is at the bottom or you won't be able to get the bread out. One of my favorite shapes for baking is a tagine, the tapered clay pot from North Africa. The shallow bottom of the tagine allows the bread to rise above its sides, so that when you remove the lid, there is more exposed surface area for browning. One cautionary note: if your boule is too large, it will take on the shape of the top part of the tagine, creating a "conehead"—kind of cute, but a bit of a surprise if you're not expecting it. Keep in mind that the dough will about double in bulk as it proofs, so the lid needs to be big enough to fit over the top once it does.

Good cookery stores carry *cazuelas*, clay cookers from Spain, and La Chamba brand pots from Colombia, as well as Emile Henry and Le Creuset (see Sources, page 270). Other resources for clay pots can be found online. But clay pots aren't solely used to bake bread—your investment will extend to stovetop cooking (see Toscano Trenchers with Kathleen's Pot of Beans, page 123, and Lamb Tagine, page 259). I use clay pots for everything: soups, beans, Bolognese and other sauces, risotto, and sautéed veggies. Their handcrafted beauty makes them the ultimate stove-to-table pots.

You'll need to season a clay pot the first time you use it. And if you go for a month or more without using the pot, it'll need to be seasoned again. Clay pots are often glazed but sometimes not, so it is important to check the manufacturer's instructions on how to best use and care for one. The seasoning method in Step 1 below has worked well for me.

1   To season a clay pot, wash it with water and dry it. Brush on a generous coating of olive oil. Fill the pot three-quarters full with water and set it in the oven. Turn the oven to 225°F and leave your pot in the oven for a couple of hours. I like to do this at night: after the pot has been in the oven for an hour, I turn the oven off and go to bed. The pot will be seasoned and ready to go in the morning. Dump out the water and dry the pot thoroughly.

2   Thirty minutes before you plan to bake your bread, put about 1 inch of water in your pot and heat over very low heat on your stovetop. Or an hour before you plan to bake your bread, fill your pot about three-quarters full with fresh cold water, put on the lid, and put it in the oven. Turn your oven to 400° to 450°F (the temperature to which you will be preheating the oven), set the pot on a baking stone on a rack in the lower third or the bottom of the oven (depending on the height of the clay pot), and let the pot heat up with the oven. If your sink is not close to your oven, set a large pot on the stovetop so there's a place nearby to dump out the hot water. Have a towel, oil, and a brush ready so you can prepare the pot quickly. Also have a lame or razor blade ready for scoring.

3   When you're ready to put the dough in, armed with hefty pot holders, carefully remove the pot from the oven and pour out the water into the pot on the stove (or the sink)—go slowly, so you don't get burned from the steam. Quickly dry the pot and generously brush it with olive oil, making sure to cover it completely. Turn your dough into the hot pot and score the top. Cover with the (hot) lid and put it on the baking stone in the oven.

4   After the bread has baked for 20 to 30 minutes (as instructed in the recipe), remove the lid. I must warn you that what you see will look like a naked wet bird—very disappointing. Not to worry. Finish the baking uncovered. All that moisture on top will help turn your ugly duckling into a swan. The crust will turn brown and shiny, and it will glow (and so will you).

5   For the last few minutes in the oven, turn the bread out onto the baking stone to ensure even browning. When you remove your clay pot from the oven, be sure to set it on a rack covered with a towel or on a warm surface such as your stovetop (if it's over your oven). Putting a heated clay pot on a cool surface will cause thermal cracking and ruin it.

COUNTRY WHEAT BOULE

Makes 1 large boule

With just enough whole wheat to add dimension and sweetness to the flavor, this bread comes out both chewy and airy, with a perfect crust and a good rustic texture. I let the boule proof on the work surface and then bake it in a clay pot or tagine, but it can also be made in a cast-iron pot (see Note). Thick slices of this loaf are perfect for dunking into soups or stews.

Biga (page 100)	140 g	4.9 oz	½ cup plus 1½ Tbsp
Water at 75° to 80°F/24° to 27°C	504 g	17.8 oz	2 cups plus 2½ Tbsp
Instant yeast	8.5 g	0.3 oz	2½ tsp
All-purpose flour	462 g	16.3 oz	3¼ cups plus 1 Tbsp
Whole wheat flour	238 g	8.4 oz	1½ cups plus 3 Tbsp
TOTAL FLOUR	700 g	24.7 oz	5 cups
Fine gray salt	14 g	0.5 oz	2¼ tsp
TOTAL WEIGHT	1,366 g/1.36 kg	48 oz/3 lbs	

Lightly oil or spray a deep 4½- to 5-quart ceramic or glass bread bowl.

✦ Put the biga in the bowl of a stand mixer fitted with the paddle attachment. Add the water and yeast and mix on low speed until the starter is broken up and the mixture appears frothy, about 30 seconds.

✦ In a medium bowl, whisk together the flours and salt. Add to the biga mixture and pulse a few times on the lowest setting (to keep the flour from flying out of the bowl), then mix on low speed for 3 minutes to combine.

✦ Remove the paddle attachment, scraping any dough from the paddle back into the bowl, and scrape down the sides of the bowl with a plastic bowl scraper. Fit the mixer with the dough hook and mix on low speed for 5 minutes. The dough may try to crawl up the stem of the dough hook; if it does, turn off the machine, scrape the dough down, and continue to knead.

✦ Flour the work surface. Using the bowl scraper, turn out the dough and knead a few times. It will be sticky. Place it in the bread bowl. Cover the bowl with a lightly oiled or sprayed piece of plastic wrap and place in a warm, draft-free spot (see Creating Your Warm Spot, page 17) to proof until the dough is very puffy and has tripled in size, 2½ to 3 hours.

✦ Flour the work surface and turn out the dough, using the bowl scraper. Press out the dough, gather the edges, and roll to pre-shape (see photos, Pre-shaping, page 45). Let sit for 10 minutes.

recipe continues

+ Using your hands and a bench scraper, shape the dough into a boule (see photos, Shaping a Boule, pages 46–47).

+ Clean a spot on the work surface and sprinkle with flour. Place the boule seam side down on that spot. Dust the top with flour and cover with a clean linen dish towel or piece of linen (see About Couches or Proofing Linens, page 140) and then cover with a Cambro container or a plastic tub. Let rise until very puffy, about 45 minutes. When the dough is gently pressed with your fingertip, the impression should remain.

+ Meanwhile, position a rack in the lower third of the oven and set a baking stone on it. Fill a 3½- to 4-quart clay pot or the bottom of a 10- to 11-inch tagine (or see Taking Liberties: Baking in Other Vessels, page 119) with water, place on the stone, and preheat the oven to 450°F.

+ Carefully pour out the water from the clay pot or tagine, dry it, and fairly generously oil or spray it. Using the bench scraper, lift the dough into the clay pot or tagine and score the dough in an asterisk pattern (see Scoring Dough, page 107). Put the lid on, if using, and set on the baking stone. Reduce the oven temperature to 400°F and bake for 25 minutes.

+ Take off the lid and bake the bread for about 15 minutes longer, or until the top is golden brown. Carefully remove the loaf from the pot or tagine and put it on the baking stone for about 10 minutes to brown the sides and bottom more evenly and ensure that the bread is baked through. To test for doneness, see Is It Baked?, page 58.

+ Transfer the bread to a cooling rack and let cool completely. For storing options, see How to Store Bread, page 51.

· Note ·
ON BAKING IN A CAST-IRON POT

Once you've shaped it, place the boule seam side down in a lightly oiled or sprayed 3½- to 4-quart (9-inch) round cast-iron pot. Cover with a lightly oiled or sprayed piece of plastic wrap. Let proof until very puffy, then score in an asterisk pattern. Put the covered pot on the baking stone in the preheated 450°F oven, reduce the heat to 400°F, and bake for 25 minutes. Take off the lid and bake for about 20 minutes more, or until the top is golden brown. Carefully remove the loaf from the pot, place it on the baking stone, and bake for 10 to 15 minutes.

· Scoring Dough ·

Dough expands naturally—that's what it wants to do. As the crust is forming, the inner dough is pushing against it. Scoring the dough with a lame or a razor blade, besides creating a beautiful pattern, dictates how the dough expands, ensuring a well-formed loaf.

The scoring step is a fast and easy one: simply insert the tip (about the first ⅛ inch of the blade) into the dough on a sharp angle and quickly run it across the surface. This will create a slash that will probably grow to ½ to ⅔ inch deep as the loaf bakes. But there are variables to consider. If the dough is slightly overproofed, especially if it's a wet dough, scoring should be done with a very light hand. Firm doughs can be scored more aggressively. Tapping the dough lightly with your fingertips before scoring will let you determine how fragile it is; the more fragile, the easier you need to go with the blade.

Dough that hasn't been scored or hasn't been scored deeply enough will pop out in all directions, creating a misshapen loaf with an unattractive surface. If you see a loaf of bread with ugly rips in the sides, the problem may well have been no scoring, or scores that were too shallow.

· Creating Steam in the Oven ·

Having moisture surrounding the dough during the initial moments of the bake is crucial for making great bread. Keeping the crust from forming too early is what allows the loaf to expand rapidly and maintain its shape. Bakers call this expansion "oven jump."

Baking in a very hot oven will allow the dough to expand as much as possible. But—and this is a big but—the initial blast of heat from the oven will also seal the crust and prevent further expansion unless you keep the outer shell supple, using plenty of water during the first minutes of the bake. Though spritzing with a spray bottle is often recommended, I don't like that method. Opening the oven door lowers the temperature, and spraying water spews flour all over the oven. Spritzing also requires you to stay close to the oven, bottle in hand, for the first fifteen minutes of baking.

Professional ovens are steam-injected, but here's an easy way to make your own steam system at home. I found the instructions for the setup on the San Francisco Baking Institute's website and have added some modifications.

1 Purchase a 9-inch perforated pie plate (see Sources, page 270) or sacrifice a metal pie pan by drilling holes about an inch apart all over the bottom. The edges of the pie plate must sit on the rim of a 10-inch cast-iron skillet so the pie pan sits above the bottom of the skillet. Another option is to use a collapsible steamer basket. You probably already have one, and if not, you can find one in most grocery or hardware stores. Because the basket is collapsible (and you'll be filling it with ice), you'll have to be a bit more careful moving it around, but I like it because the feet on the basket means it can just sit in the skillet, rather than have to rest on the rim of the pan. For even more steam, you can put a handful of solid noncoated metal pieces (such as ball bearings) in the skillet, creating more surface area, and more steam, but this is not essential— you'll get nicely browned bread without them.

2 Position an oven rack on the lowest rung and set the skillet on the rack. Or, if your oven element isn't on the bottom of the oven, go ahead and set the skillet on the bottom of the oven. Position a second oven rack on the rung above the pan. Set the baking stone on this rack. The rack with the baking stone needs to be as close as possible to the skillet, but with enough clearance so you can pull out the skillet and push it back in once you've added the pie plate or steamer basket filled with ice.

3 Preheat the oven as specified in the recipe.

4 Just before the dough is ready to be transferred to the oven, scoop ice cubes into the pie plate or steamer basket and set in a bowl to catch any water.

When I am using a peel to get the dough onto the stone, I like to position the dough on the peel first and have it very close to the oven. Because of the peel, my arms and hands can stay far enough away from any steam that will start to generate. Once the dough is on the peel, working as quickly as you can, open the oven door and—carefully, because it will be very hot and heavy—slide the cast-iron skillet out, set the pie plate or steamer basket filled with ice over or in it, and slide the skillet back in. Transfer the dough to the stone, then close the door and don't open it again until specified in the recipe. You can turn on the light and check through the window, if you like.

When I am transferring dough directly to the stone from a proofing basket or bowl, I turn the dough out onto the stone first and then create the steam, as above.

After the bread is baked and you've turned off the oven, leave the skillet in the oven to cool. There may be residual water, and even some rust in the bottom of the skillet—which makes a good case for buying a skillet and pie plate or steamer basket that you'll use just for a steam contraption. If you do plan to use your skillet again for cooking, any rust will need to be rinsed out thoroughly and the skillet reseasoned.

Note that not all breads benefit from steam. Those that use only commercial yeast will have reached their maximum height by the time they're ready to bake. They won't expand much more in the oven, so they don't need steam. Although enriched breads will continue to expand a bit more, they are more delicate, and steam could damage them. But wet doughs like those for the pre-fermented breads in this chapter benefit greatly from the addition of steam, and naturally leavened breads *require* steam. Wet doughs start out in the oven pretty flat, and those first few minutes of steam make the desired expansion possible. Without steam, naturally leavened breads will come out flat as a pancake and gray as an old bone.

PANE COMO ROUND LOAVES

꒰ Makes 2 medium round loaves ꒱

Pane Como, from Lombardy in northern Italy, is as beautiful as it is delicious, and it takes on a subtle sweetness from the milk. Baking this bread will fill you with confidence, because the milk starter couldn't be simpler to make. Many Italian breads, such as those from Tuscany, are perfect topped with olive oil, but Pane Como, from one of Italy's prime dairy regions, lends itself more to butter. It makes great sandwiches, French toast, and table bread.

You'll notice that the recipe calls for diastatic malt powder, which helps the bread expand to its fullest in the oven. The powder also encourages browning and flavor. Full of active enzymes, it adds a subtle sweetness without using another browning and sweetening agent such as sugar, and it accelerates the proofing process as well. The powder is made from sprouted wheat, dried and ground.

MILK STARTER

Warm water (100°F/38°C)	81 g	2.9 oz	¼ cup plus 1½ Tbsp
Whole milk	115 g	4 oz	¼ cup plus 3 Tbsp
All-purpose flour	135 g	4.7 oz	¾ cup plus 3½ Tbsp
Instant yeast	8 g	0.3 oz	2¼ tsp
Diastatic malt powder (see Sources, page 270)	8 g	0.3 oz	2½ tsp
TOTAL WEIGHT	347 g	12.2 oz	

DOUGH MIX

Water at 75° to 80°F/24° to 27°C	364 g	12.8 oz	1½ cups plus 1 Tbsp
All-purpose flour	650 g	22.9 oz	4½ cups plus 1 Tbsp
TOTAL FLOUR	650 g	22.9 oz	4½ cups plus 1 Tbsp
Fine gray salt	16 g	0.6 oz	2¾ tsp
TOTAL WEIGHT	1,377 g/1.37 kg	48 oz/3 lbs	

For the milk starter: In the bowl of a stand mixer fitted with the paddle attachment, combine the water and milk. (The water is warm only to take the chill off the milk; if the milk is not cold, the water can be at room temperature, 65° to 70°F/18° to 21°C.)

Add the flour, yeast, and malt and mix on the lowest speed for about 1 minute to combine. The mixture will be sticky. Remove the paddle attachment and, with damp hands, scrape any starter from the paddle back into the bowl. Cover the bowl with a lightly oiled or sprayed piece of plastic wrap and let sit at room temperature overnight.

+ Lightly oil or spray a deep 4½- to 5-quart ceramic or glass bread bowl.

+ The milk starter will be very bubbly. Remove the plastic wrap and pour the water into the bowl. Fit the mixer with the paddle attachment, return the bowl to the stand, and pulse a few times on the lowest speed to begin to break up the starter.

+ In a medium bowl, whisk together the flour and salt. Add to the starter mixture and pulse a few times on the lowest setting (to keep the flour from flying out of the bowl), then mix on low speed for 3 minutes to combine.

+ Remove the paddle attachment, scraping any dough from the paddle back into the bowl, and scrape down the sides of the bowl with a plastic bowl scraper. Fit the mixer with the dough hook and mix on low speed for 5 minutes. The dough may try to crawl up the stem of the dough hook; if it does, turn off the machine, scrape the dough down, and continue to mix.

+ Flour the work surface. Using the bowl scraper, turn out the dough and knead a few times. It will be slightly sticky. Place it in the bread bowl. Cover the bowl with a lightly oiled or sprayed piece of plastic wrap and place in a warm, draft-free spot (see Creating Your Warm Spot, page 17) to proof until the dough is very puffy and has at least doubled in size, 1½ to 2 hours. The surface will look very bubbly.

+ Flour the work surface and turn out the dough, using the bowl scraper. Divide the dough in half, using a bench scraper. Working with one piece at a time, press out the dough, gather the edges, and roll to pre-shape (see photos, Pre-shaping, page 45). Let sit for 10 minutes.

+ The dough can be shaped and put into two floured 9-inch baskets; two 9-inch bowls, lined with a floured linen dish towel (see About Proofing Baskets, page 114); or one of each. Dust the baskets or linen-lined bowls with flour or a mixture of flour and wheat bran (see To Prevent Sticking, Use Flour and Wheat Bran, page 113).

Courage in the Kitchen
ꙮ AVOIDING BAKER'S GRAVES ꙮ

The unsightly holes in bread known as baker's graves result when flour is trapped inside the dough as you work it on a floured surface. Having enough flour on your work surface is important, of course, so the dough won't stick, but it's also crucial not to use too much flour, or you could end up with baker's graves. (Flour on the outside of a loaf, on the other hand, is fine.) If as you are shaping the dough you see you've gotten flour where you shouldn't have, dust off the flour with a soft-bristled brush. Then wipe any remaining flour off the dough with a damp cloth and let it rest for a minute. Note that baker's graves are not the same as the lacy air holes in the dough—those are a good thing (see Why Air Holes?, page 233).

✦ Using your hands and the bench scraper, shape the dough into a boule (see photos, Shaping a Boule, pages 46–47). Dust the top with flour or the flour-bran mixture and place seam side up in one of the bowls or baskets. If using a basket, cover with a clean linen dish towel; if using a lined bowl, fold the linen over the top. Repeat with the second piece of dough.

✦ Set in your warm spot until the dough is very puffy again and the top reaches the top of the baskets or bowls, 1 to 1½ hours. When the dough is gently pressed with your fingertip, the impression should remain.

✦ Meanwhile, position a rack on the lowest rung of the oven and set a cast-iron skillet on it (see Creating Steam in the Oven, page 108, for more on the steam setup). Position a rack above it, set a baking stone on the rack, and preheat the oven to 400°F.

✦ There are two options for baking: The dough can be turned out directly onto the baking stone or turned out onto a peel and then transferred to the stone. If it is turned out directly onto the stone, it is likely to spread out a bit more and not be quite as evenly round as when using a peel. Depending on the desired look of the finished loaf and/or your comfort level with having to pull out the oven rack with a hot stone on it (see the next paragraph), you might prefer using a peel.

✦ *If turning the dough out onto the stone,* first carefully pull the rack with the stone far enough out that you can invert the baskets and/or bowls directly over the stone. If using an unlined basket, invert the basket and then, if necessary, use the bowl scraper to gently ease the dough onto the stone. If using a lined bowl, use the linen to ease the dough onto the stone. As soon as both breads are on the stone, quickly score them in a tic-tac-toe pattern (see Scoring Dough, page 107) and push the rack back in. Then carefully (the handle will be hot) pull the cast-iron skillet out, set the pie plate or steamer basket of ice over or in it, slide it back in, and close the oven door.

✦ *If using a peel,* dust the peel with flour or the flour-bran mixture and turn the bowls or baskets out onto the peel. (Depending on your comfort level and the size of the peel, you may want to do this one at a time. There will be more heat loss from the oven, but getting used to a peel can take a couple of tries.) Brush off any excess flour. Carefully (the handle will be hot) pull the cast-iron skillet out, set the pie plate or steamer basket of ice over or in it, and slide it back in. Score the loaves in a tic-tac-toe pattern and transfer to the baking stone.

✦ Bake the loaves for 45 to 50 minutes, or until golden brown. To test for doneness, see Is It Baked?, page 58. The loaves should release easily from the stone, but it will be easier to remove them using a peel. Transfer the bread to a cooling rack and let cool completely. For storing options, see How to Store Bread, page 51.

Courage in the Kitchen

Some of the pre-fermented (and all the naturally leavened) doughs are stickier than the others in this book. Getting them out of a proofing basket or a linen-lined bowl, or off a proofing cloth, can be tricky if these haven't been properly floured. Using equal parts all-purpose flour and wheat bran rather than just flour will be enormously helpful in preventing sticking. First, dust the basket or cloth generously. Don't worry about using too much; any excess will come off when the dough is turned out. Also, dust the tops and sides of the shaped loaves with the flour and wheat bran mixture before you put them in to proof; pay special attention to the sides of the loaves to keep them from sticking as the dough rises.

When a loaf is turned out of a basket or bowl, any excess flour can be brushed off the loaf or the peel. When you are making a bread like Pane Como Round Loaves (page 110) or Free-form Pane Pugliese (page 117), where there is an option of turning the dough out directly onto the stone, and you are concerned there may be too much of the mixture, turn the bread out onto a peel first instead.

Some of the flour and wheat bran mixture can also be sprinkled onto the peel so the loaves slide onto the baking stone more easily. Although you may be tempted to use the mixture when pre-shaping and shaping dough, I don't recommend it. At those stages in the dough's development, the wheat bran can stick to the surface and even become incorporated into the dough. It doesn't dust off as easily as flour.

· About Proofing Baskets ·

Using an unlined basket for proofing dough will result in an impression in the finished loaf that's really striking. You can use a lined basket, but your dough will not have the distinctive pattern of the basket. Different baskets leave different patterns, and these can be a way of leaving your own personal signature on the finished loaf.

In a perfect world, I'd learn how to weave my own baskets. That being said, I'm especially fond of the beautiful baskets I have that were crafted from Sonoma grapevine cuttings. Their irregular open pattern leaves a lovely imprint in the finished bread. Look for woven baskets without handles. The basket you use doesn't have to be round.

If you're in an area where Native Americans live, you may find someone selling tribal baskets that are very beautiful. They'll be expensive (think of the time and work put into them), but you'll have them for a lifetime. I've also used baskets from Rwanda, Uganda, and other parts of Africa that are wide and shallow with a distinct coil pattern. These would be perfect for proofing the Free-form Pane Pugliese (page 117). A gorgeous selection of fair-trade baskets is available at Baskets of Africa (see Sources, page 270).

As long as you keep them clean and dry, proofing baskets will last forever. When you proof very wet dough in an unlined basket, be sure to flour the basket very generously—you may need to do it twice (see To Prevent Sticking, Use Flour and Wheat Bran, page 113). When you turn the dough out of the basket, some of the moisture will have been transferred to the basket, and little blobs of dough may be stuck on it. Just leave the basket out in a well-ventilated area to dry completely. When it is dry, go over it with a small brush (I use the small round ones for dishwashing). Once all the flour has been loosened, give the basket a couple of gentle whacks to shake out the rest of the dough and flour. It's fine to rinse proofing baskets with water—just put them in the sun or another warm place to dry completely before you store them.

If a basket becomes misshapen, it can be pushed back into shape by getting it wet and then molding it into its original form. Sometimes it will need something set in it to help hold the shape while it dries (such as a large ball). But sometimes a misshapen basket can add its own charm to a bread's final form.

If you don't have a proofing basket, no worries. You can use a ceramic bowl or other appropriately shaped vessel for proofing dough. I've proofed dough in everything from colanders to flowerpots. Line the bowl with a linen dish towel, draping it over the sides; make sure to flour the towel heavily. Put the dough into the bowl and fold the edges of the dish towel over the dough.

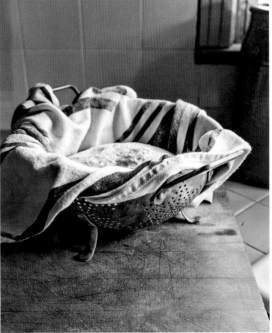

FREE-FORM PANE PUGLIESE

⤳ Makes 1 large wheel ⤳

Pugliese is made in the shape of a wheel. While this loaf is rustic and primitive-looking as can be, it seems very extravagant, in the same way that a wheel of cheese feels abundant.

For a long time, this was my bring-to bread for parties. The beauty in this oversized—and often lopsided—loaf is that it begs to be shared; it's a break-bread-together kind of bread. In fact, I once took it to a picnic in a big beautiful basket lined with a linen towel, but I forgot the knife. Naturally, the menfolk came to the rescue, heroes with their pocketknives—they might as well have tried to cut down a tree. It didn't take long before one exasperated (and brave) man broke the ice by ripping into the thing with his bare hands. That's all it took to change an ordinary picnic into a much more delightful and memorable event.

Traditionally this bread is baked directly on a stone, but it can be baked in a cast-iron pot or a clay pot or tagine. See the Variation and Taking Liberties: Baking in Other Vessels, page 119.

Biga (page 100)	148 g	5.2 oz	½ cup plus 2 Tbsp
Water at 75° to 80°F/24° to 27°C	526 g	18.5 oz	2¼ cups
Instant yeast	17 g	0.6 oz	1 Tbsp plus 1¾ tsp
All-purpose flour	675 g	23.8 oz	4¾ cups plus 1 Tbsp
TOTAL FLOUR	675 g	23.8 oz	4¾ cups plus 1 Tbsp
Fine gray salt	16 g	0.6 oz	2¾ tsp
TOTAL WEIGHT	1,382 g/1.38 kg	48 oz/3 lbs	

Lightly oil or spray a deep 4½- to 5-quart ceramic or glass bread bowl.

✦ Put the biga in the bowl of a stand mixer fitted with the paddle attachment. Add the water and yeast and mix on low speed until the starter is broken up and the mixture appears frothy, about 30 seconds.

✦ In a medium bowl, whisk together the flour and salt. Add to the biga mixture and pulse a few times on the lowest setting (to keep the flour from flying out of the bowl),

then mix on low speed for 3 minutes to combine.

✦ Remove the paddle attachment, scraping any dough from the paddle back into the bowl, and scrape down the sides of the bowl with a plastic bowl scraper. Fit the mixer with the dough hook and mix on low speed for 5 minutes. The dough may try to crawl up the stem of the dough hook; if it does, turn off the machine, scrape the dough down, and continue to mix.

✦ Flour the work surface. Using the bowl scraper, turn out the dough and knead a few times. This is a very sticky dough. Place it in the bread bowl. Cover the bowl with a lightly oiled or sprayed piece of plastic wrap and place in a warm, draft-free spot (see Creating Your Warm Spot, page 17) to proof until the dough is very puffy and has tripled in size, 2½ to 3 hours. The surface will look very bubbly. The dough will still be sticky.

✦ Flour the work surface and turn out the dough, using the bowl scraper. Press out the dough, gather the edges, and roll to pre-shape (see photos, Pre-shaping, page 45). Let sit for 10 minutes.

✦ Dust a 12-inch basket with flour or a mixture of flour and wheat bran (see To Prevent Sticking, Use Flour and Wheat Bran, page 113) or line a large bowl with a floured linen dish towel (see About Proofing Baskets, page 114).

✦ Using your hands and a bench scraper, shape the dough into a boule (see photos, Shaping a Boule, pages 46–47). Dust the top with flour or the flour-bran mixture and place seam side up in the bowl or basket. If using a basket, cover with a clean linen dish towel; if using a linen-lined bowl, fold the linen over the top.

✦ Set in your warm spot to proof until the dough is very puffy but not quite at the top edge of the bowl or basket, about 45 minutes. When the dough is gently pressed with your fingertip, the impression should remain.

✦ Meanwhile, position a rack on the lowest rung of the oven and set a cast-iron skillet on it (see Creating Steam in the Oven, page 108, for more on the steam setup). Position a rack above it, set a baking stone on the rack, and preheat the oven to 450°F.

✦ After the 45-minute proof, using your fingertips, dimple the top of the dough. Let proof for another 15 minutes.

✦ Carefully pull the rack with the stone far enough out that you can invert the bowl or basket directly over the stone. If using an unlined basket, it is best to invert the basket and then, if necessary, use the bowl scraper to gently ease the dough onto the stone. If using a lined bowl, use the linen to ease the dough onto the stone. As soon as the dough is on the stone, quickly dimple the top again and push the rack back in. Then carefully (the handle will be hot) pull the cast-iron skillet out, set the pie plate or steamer basket of ice over or in it, slide it back in, and close the oven door. Reduce the oven temperature to 400°F.

✦ Bake the bread for 40 minutes, or until the top is golden brown. To check for doneness, see Is It Baked?, page 58. The loaf should release easily from the stone, but it will be easier to remove using a peel. Transfer the bread to a cooling rack and let cool completely. For storing options, see How to Store Bread, page 51.

· Variation ·
PANE PUGLIESE BOULE

To make the bread in a cast-iron pot: Follow the steps above through shaping the dough. Once it is shaped, place it seam side down into a fairly generously oiled or sprayed 3½- to 4-quart (9-inch) round cast-iron pot and let it proof as above.

Meanwhile, position a rack in the lower third of the oven, place a baking stone on it, and preheat the oven to 450°F.

After the 45-minute proof, using your fingertips, dimple the dough. Let rise for another 15 minutes.

Dimple the dough again, put the lid on, set on the baking stone, and reduce the oven temperature to 400°F. Bake for 30 minutes.

Take off the lid and bake the bread for about 15 minutes longer, or until the top is golden brown. Carefully remove the loaf from the pot and put it on the baking stone for about 10 minutes to brown the sides and bottom more evenly and ensure that the loaf is baked through. To test for doneness, see Is It Baked?, page 58.

Transfer the bread to a cooling rack and let cool completely.

To make the bread in a clay pot or tagine: Follow the steps above through proofing the dough in the basket or bowl.

Meanwhile, position a rack in the lower third of the oven and set a baking stone on it. Fill a clay pot or the bottom of a tagine with water, place on the stone, and preheat the oven to 450°F.

After the 45-minute proof, using your fingertips, dimple the dough. Let rise for another 15 minutes.

Carefully pour out the water from the clay pot or tagine, dry it, and fairly generously oil or spray it. Dimple the dough again and, using the bench scraper, lift the dough into the clay pot or tagine. (Depending on the width of the boule and the pot, the sides of the boule may need to be gently tucked under to fit in the pot.) Put the lid on and set on the baking stone. Reduce the oven temperature to 400°F and bake for 30 minutes.

Take off the lid and bake the bread for about 10 minutes longer, or until the top is golden brown. Carefully remove the loaf from the pot or tagine and put on the baking stone for about 5 minutes to brown the sides and bottom more evenly and ensure that the bread is baked through. To test for doneness, see Is It Baked?, page 58.

Transfer the bread to a cooling rack and let cool completely.

Taking Liberties: Baking in Other Vessels

Baking in other vessels will show you how the vessel you use can change the shape and interior crumb of the final loaf; see photo, Country Wheat Boule (page 105). Baking a Country Wheat Boule in a smaller clay pot with no lid, for instance, makes for a more mushroomed loaf. (Preheat a 2-quart clay pot, 7 to 8 inches in diameter, as directed on pages 102–103, but leave the pot uncovered.) In addition, baking a Pugliese in a cast-iron pot makes for a taller loaf than one baked in a tagine, which will be wider and slightly flatter or conical, depending on the tagine.

I encourage you to experiment with different baking vessels, because it's actually hard to go wrong. And just as in life, a mistake in baking can teach you more than a success can. I'm aware that this sounds easy for me to say: although flour is inexpensive, your time is precious, and baking is an investment of your time. But it's also true that every time you work with a dough, you're getting a feel for it, a sense memory of it. Every time you try baking bread in a vessel you've never used before, you're gathering more information—and learning to be a better baker.

PANE TOSCANO LOAVES

ⓔ Makes 4 small loaves ⓔ

Pane Toscano, traditionally made without salt, is intended to be served with the salted cured meats and robust foods of Tuscany. I confess that when we traveled to Tuscany I had some trouble getting used to the bread's dense, less colorful appearance. But that was because I was tasting the bread alone, or eating it in the same ways I would other breads. Pane Toscano balances perfectly with the local cuisine. It is always on the table, ready to be served with olive tapenade, fruity young olive oil, and salty salami, such as finocchiona and soppressata.

I couldn't resist adding just a little bit of salt, which gives the bread more color and flavor. Here the dough is divided into four pieces, which yield smaller, flatter loaves. These can be sliced in half and used as the base for open-faced sandwiches or served with a salad of goat cheese, fresh tomatoes, olive oil, fresh basil, salt, and pepper. Or use them as trenchers for a generous ladleful of Kathleen's Pot of Beans (page 123).

Biga (page 100)	100 g	3.5 oz	¼ cup plus 3½ Tbsp
Water at 75° to 80°F/24° to 27°C	320 g	11.2 oz	1¼ cups plus 2 Tbsp
Instant yeast	10 g	0.3 oz	1 Tbsp
All-purpose flour	500 g	17.6 oz	3½ cups plus 1 Tbsp
TOTAL FLOUR	500 g	17.6 oz	3½ cups plus 1 Tbsp
Fine gray salt	1.5 g	0.05 oz	¼ tsp
TOTAL WEIGHT	932 g	32 oz/2 lbs	

Lightly oil or spray a deep 4½- to 5-quart ceramic or glass bread bowl.

+ Put the biga in the bowl of a stand mixer fitted with the paddle attachment. Add the water and yeast and mix on low speed until the starter is broken up and the mixture appears frothy, about 30 seconds.

+ In a medium bowl, whisk together the flour and salt. Add to the biga mixture and pulse a few times on the lowest setting (to keep the flour from flying out of the bowl), then mix on low speed for 3 minutes to combine.

+ Remove the paddle attachment, scraping any dough from the paddle back into the bowl, and scrape down the sides of the bowl with a plastic bowl scraper. Fit the mixer with the dough hook and mix on low speed for 5 minutes. The dough may try to crawl up the stem of the dough hook; if it does, turn off the machine, scrape the dough down, and continue to mix.

+ Flour the work surface. Using the bowl scraper, turn out the dough and knead a few times. This is a fairly stiff dough. Place it in the bread bowl. Cover the bowl with a lightly oiled or sprayed piece of plastic wrap and place in a warm, draft-free spot (see Creating Your Warm Spot, page 17) to proof until the dough is very puffy, 1½ to 2 hours.

• Flour the work surface. Using the bowl scraper, turn the dough onto the work surface. Using a bench scraper, scale (divide) the dough into 4 equal pieces (about 230 grams/8 ounces each). Working with one piece at a time, press out the dough, gather the edges, and roll to pre-shape (see photos, Pre-shaping, page 45). Let sit for 10 minutes.

• Using your hands and a bench scraper, shape each piece of dough into a small boule (see photos, Shaping a Boule, pages 46–47).

• Clean your work surface and sprinkle it again with flour. Place the boules seam side down on the surface, allowing enough room for them to about double in size. Dust the tops of the boules with flour and cover with a clean linen dish towel or a piece of linen (see About Couches or Proofing Linens, page 140). The loaves can also be covered with a Cambro container or a plastic tub. Let proof until very puffy, about 45 minutes. When the dough is gently pressed with your fingertip, the impression should remain.

• Meanwhile, position a rack on the lowest rung of the oven and set a cast-iron skillet on it (see Creating Steam in the Oven, page 108, for more on the steam setup). Position a rack above it, set a baking stone on the rack, and preheat the oven to 450°F.

• After the 45-minute proof, using your fingertips, dimple the top of the dough. Let proof for another 15 minutes.

• Dust a peel with flour or a mixture of flour and wheat bran (see To Prevent Sticking, Use Flour and Wheat Bran, page 113) and, with the help of a bench scraper, carefully lift the dough onto the peel. (Depending on your comfort level and the size of the peel, you may want to move 2 loaves at a time to the stone, rather than all 4 at once. There will be more heat loss from the oven, but getting used to a peel can take a couple of tries.) Carefully (the handle will be hot) pull the cast-iron skillet out, set the pie plate or steamer basket of ice over or in it, and slide it back in. Dimple the top of the loaves again and transfer to the stone. Lower the oven temperature to 400°F.

• Bake the loaves for about 20 minutes, or until golden brown. To test for doneness, see Is It Baked?, page 58. The loaves should release easily from the stone, but it will be easier to remove them using the peel. Transfer the bread to a cooling rack and let cool completely. For storing options, see How to Store Bread, page 51.

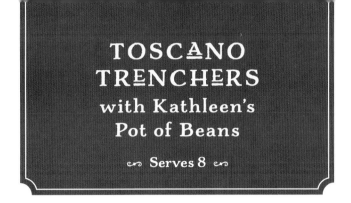

Even with a little bit of salt, Pane Toscano isn't as much a stand-alone bread as the others in this book. But it toasts up firm and crunchy, and it is the perfect trencher for these basic beans, which you can season to your liking with chopped tomatoes, wine, herbs, and/or spices. When you're cooking beans, you may need to add more liquid while they're simmering. I like to keep a pan or kettle of water simmering alongside the beans so I can add warm liquid if it's needed. This way you won't interrupt the cooking process by adding cold water to the pot.

You can use this cooking method for any bean dish, including Jakob's Bean Spread on Meyer Lemon–Rosemary Toast (page 180), which we serve at our café. We like to use white or pale green beans such as cannellini or flageolets. Rancho Gordo's beans are my favorite by far; see Sources, page 270. They offer a tremendous array of heirloom varieties, and they are always fresh.

Kathleen's Pot of Beans (makes about 8 cups)

1 pound (about 2 cups) dried beans, preferably cannellini or flageolets

About 3 tablespoons olive oil

1 small white, yellow, or red onion, cut into ½-inch dice

1 celery rib, cut into ¼-inch dice

1 medium carrot, peeled and cut into ½-inch dice

1 garlic clove, smashed and peeled

1 bay leaf (bay laurel or Turkish bay, not California)

1 dried mild chile

Kosher salt

Toscano Trenchers

4 Pane Toscano Loaves (page 121)

Extra virgin olive oil

recipe continues

For serving (optional)

8 fried or poached eggs

Generous cup of crumbled bacon or cooked lardons

Sliced scallions

Minced herbs, such as parsley or cilantro

For the beans: Spread the beans on a half sheet pan. Check for and remove any small rocks. Rinse the beans under cold water and drain. Put the beans in a large bowl and cover by an inch or two with cold water. Let soak for at least 6 hours or overnight. Do not drain.

‣ Heat a generous film of olive oil in a large cast-iron or flameproof clay pot over medium heat. Add the onion, celery, carrot, and garlic and cook, stirring occasionally, until the vegetables have softened and are fragrant, about 5 minutes. Add the beans and all of the soaking water, then add enough additional water to cover the beans by an inch or two and bring to a slow boil. Turn the heat to the lowest setting and add the bay leaf and chile. (If desired, fill a medium saucepan or a kettle with water and keep at a simmer to add to the pot as needed.) Cook the beans, checking occasionally and adding simmering water if needed to keep them covered, until tender, 2 to 3 hours. (Cooking times can vary significantly depending on the freshness of the beans; see Note.)

‣ The liquor (cooking liquid) will be rich and amazingly flavorful, but you will need to salt it to taste. If making the beans ahead, let

cool, then refrigerate, covered, in the liquor for up to 3 days; reheat slowly to keep the beans from breaking up too much.

‣ Meanwhile, for the trenchers: Cut the loaves of bread lengthwise in half, drizzle with olive oil, and toast under the broiler for a few minutes.

‣ To serve, set a trencher, cut side up, in each serving bowl and scoop a generous ladleful of beans over it, being sure to include plenty of the liquid. Serve as is or topped with fried or poached eggs, bacon, scallions, and herbs.

· Note ·
ON FRESH DRIED BEANS

Have you ever had a pot of dried beans that take hours and hours to become tender? More often than not, it means the beans are old. Unfortunately, it is impossible to pick up a bag of dried beans at the market and know how fresh they are. That is why it is so important to buy beans from a reputable supplier with a good turnover.

THE POWER OF FOOD

When Jakob, our oldest grandson, was born in 2000, our son, Aaron, and our daughter-in-law, Linda, were both working in the bread bakery. A few months after Jakob was born, it was time for Linda to go back to work.

Our lives changed completely and in the most wonderful way. At 3 A.M., Linda would go to the bakery to do the first shaping of the morning. Right before she started work, she'd bring Jakob in to snuggle in bed with Ed and me. It was a fantastic arrangement. The bakery was attached to the house, and there Linda would be, working with a baby monitor tucked into her apron pocket.

Having a new baby in the house was an utter joy, but by the time Jakob was about six months old, we realized if we were to get any work done ourselves, we'd need some help. Enter Michaela, wife of Alejandro, who worked with our daughter, Elisa, at a woodworking studio in Petaluma. Michaela and Alejandro had recently arrived from Oaxaca. Though Michaela was just starting to learn English, it was clear right away that she was fluent in baby. Jakob adored her. It was love at first sight for the rest of us too.

The first thing we noticed about Michaela was her beautiful, open, and trusting face, with deep, dark eyes that are almost black. Compact and strong, she has thick black hair that she always wears pulled back in a ponytail. Her smile is almost beyond description—with it, she could get our little grandson to do anything. Her patience was a constant amazement.

Michaela appeared to be very happy working with us, but one day in late October, I found her crying in the kitchen. Horrified that we might have done something to upset her, I put my arms around her, trying to determine the cause of her tears. It soon became clear that she was feeling a lonely sadness. Between her struggling English

and my bare-bones Spanish, I finally worked out that El Día de los Muertos was coming up, a time when Michaela and her mother used to spend days cooking tamales for family to feast on and to take to the graves of their dead ancestors.

Michaela hadn't been through this holiday without her mother, who had passed away shortly before Michaela and Alejandro left Oaxaca. There are few things sadder than seeing someone you care about absolutely heartbroken. There was no question as to what needed to be done: we needed to make tamales!

I'll tell you now I had no idea what I was getting into. We're talking very traditional, made-from-scratch tamales. Michaela started roasting hot chiles, oregano, cinnamon, and cumin seeds for one sauce, and pumpkin seeds, serranos, and tomatillos for another. I didn't understand why she took the chiles next door to my daughter's house to roast until I went over to check on her. I found her with a bandana tied around her nose and mouth and tears streaming down her face—not the kind of air fit for our little grandson, nor for me. But her eyes were smiling as the tears poured down her cheeks. Who knew that so much work and pain could cause such happiness?

Before long, my friend Kandi and I had joined Michaela for what turned out to be a two-day tamale marathon. We had pork braising in salsa verde, and chicken cooking in a heavenly spiced tomato sauce. We blanched banana leaves and corn husks, and we made the masa dough. Then we learned to roll tamales.

Food has a long tradition of healing, and so it is with bread. Italian women created loaves for every holiday and significant occasion. There were breads for fertility and for birth, breads for death and for resurrection, breads for peace and for war.

One would not think of putting bread into the oven without first praying for it and what it would bring to those who ate it. I know that our tamale-making endeavor provided the same kind of healing ritual for Michaela.

Real-deal tamales are not a simple undertaking, and I have no idea how we pulled this off without the benefit of speaking Spanish, but it didn't matter. When we were done, our faces were shiny with sweat and chile tears, our backs and feet were aching, and every pot in the house was dirty. We were exhausted, but we were happy, and the smile on Michaela's face could have lit up a moonless night. We toasted our tamales with a glass or three of wine and formed a bond that would define our friendship.

OLIVE OIL WREATH

cᴏ Makes 1 large wreath cᴏ

Use good extra virgin olive oil for making this wreath. The amount of oil called for is relatively small, but a delicious fruity oil will have a profound effect on the flavor and texture of the finished bread. Shaping it into a wreath and cutting it like an épi (see page 130) makes it into a gorgeous loaf for the table that's also easy to pull apart into individual pieces. This bread is chewy but tender and a family favorite.

Biga (page 100)	100 g	3.5 oz	¼ cup plus 3½ Tbsp
Water at 75° to 80°F/24° to 27°C	285 g	10 oz	1 cup plus 3½ Tbsp
Extra virgin olive oil	60 g	2 oz	¼ cup plus 2 tsp
Instant yeast	10 g	0.3 oz	1 Tbsp
All-purpose flour	500 g	17.6 oz	3½ cups plus 1 Tbsp
TOTAL FLOUR	500 g	17.6 oz	3½ cups plus 1 Tbsp
Fine gray salt	15 g	0.5 oz	2½ tsp
TOTAL WEIGHT	970 g	34 oz/2.1 lbs	

Lightly oil or spray a deep 4½- to 5-quart ceramic or glass bread bowl.

⁺ Put the biga in the bowl of a stand mixer fitted with the paddle attachment. Add the water, olive oil, and yeast and mix on low speed until the starter is broken up and the mixture appears frothy, about 30 seconds.

⁺ In a medium bowl, whisk together the flour and salt. Add to the biga mixture and pulse a few times on the lowest setting (to keep the flour from flying out of the bowl), then mix on low speed for 3 minutes to combine.

⁺ Remove the paddle attachment, scraping any dough from the paddle back into the bowl, and scrape down the sides of the bowl with a plastic bowl scraper. Fit the mixer with the dough hook and mix on low speed for 5 minutes. The dough may try to crawl up the stem of the dough hook; if it does, turn off the machine, scrape the dough down, and continue to mix.

⁺ Flour the work surface. Using the bowl scraper, turn out the dough and knead a few times. This is a very silky dough. Place it in the bread bowl. Cover the bowl with a lightly oiled or sprayed piece of plastic wrap and place in a warm, draft-free spot (see Creating Your Warm Spot, page 17) to proof until the dough is very puffy, 2 to 2½ hours.

⁺ Flour the work surface. Using the bowl scraper, turn the dough onto the work surface. Press out the dough, gather the edges, and roll to pre-shape (see photos, Pre-shaping, page 45). Let sit for 10 minutes.

⁺ Fairly generously oil or spray a 14-inch cast-iron baking pan, a large cookie sheet, a pizza pan, or the back of a half sheet pan.

· Forming an Olive Oil Wreath ·

Working with a 14-inch cast-iron baking pan helps to make a uniformly round wreath. Results will be a bit more rustic but no less beautiful if you use a cookie sheet.

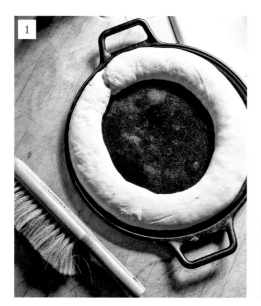

(1) Olive oil dough proofed in a lightly oiled 14-inch cast-iron baking pan. (2) To make the épi, cut the dough with scissors held at a 60-degree angle, leaving the cut dough still attached. Lift and drape the cut piece to one side. (3) Repeat the cuts, alternating the side the pieces are moved to, as you go around the wreath.

+ Using your hands and a bench scraper, rock and push the dough to shape it into a bâtard (see photos, Shaping a Bâtard, pages 52–53), about 1½ by 42 inches. If at any point the dough begins to resist being stretched out to this length, let it rest for 10 minutes, then stretch it again. (If this is too large a piece of dough to comfortably work with, divide it in half and roll each piece to about 22 inches long. Then pinch the ends of the two pieces together to make one long piece. Roll the seam under the palm of your hand to seal and round slightly.)

+ Gently lay the dough along the edge of the prepared pan, bringing the ends together and overlapping slightly, adjusting the dough as necessary to keep the circular shape (see photos, opposite). If you're working on a cookie sheet or on the back of a half sheet pan, the wreath will be more of an oval than a circle. When positioning the dough, keep in mind that you will need some room to cut and separate the pieces (see photos, opposite).

+ Set the pan in your warm spot, cover with a Cambro container or a plastic tub, and let proof until the dough is very puffy, 1 to 1½ hours. When the dough is gently pressed with your fingertip, the impression should remain.

+ Meanwhile, position a rack on the lowest rung of the oven and set a cast-iron skillet on it (see Creating Steam in the Oven, page 108, for more on the steam setup). Position a rack above it, set a baking stone on the rack, and preheat the oven to 450°F.

+ To cut the dough, using scissors held at a 60-degree angle, make a cut, leaving the cut dough still attached (see photos, opposite). Lift the cut piece to one side. Then continue making cuts about every 3 inches, alternating the side the piece is moved to as you go around the wreath.

+ Place the pan on the stone and immediately lower the oven temperature to 400°F. Carefully (the handle will be hot) pull the cast-iron skillet out, set the pie plate or steamer basket of ice over or in it, and slide it back in.

+ Bake the bread until golden brown, 30 to 35 minutes. To test for doneness, see Is It Baked?, page 58. The loaves should release easily from the pan, but it will be easier to remove them using a peel. Transfer the bread to a cooling rack and let cool completely. For storing options, see How to Store Bread, page 51.

PANE DURUM DOUGH

Makes 1.3 kilograms/2.8 pounds

This dough is stiffer than others. If it seems to strain your mixer, turn it out on a floured board and give it a good kneading by hand. You can make this as one large loaf (see Pane Durum Boule, opposite) in a cast-iron pot, so that the baked loaf takes on a sheen, or bake it directly on a stone as two smaller loaves (see Pane Durum Oval Loaves, page 134), for loaves with a soft, dusty look. The bread will be crusty and delicious either way.

Biga (page 100)	300 g	10.5 oz	1¼ cups
Water at 75° to 80°F/24° to 27°C	384 g	13.5 oz	1½ cups plus 2 Tbsp
Instant yeast	7 g	0.2 oz	2 tsp
Durum flour	600 g	21 oz	4 cups plus 2 Tbsp
TOTAL FLOUR	600 g	21 oz	4 cups plus 2 Tbsp
Fine gray salt	15 g	0.5 oz	2½ tsp
TOTAL WEIGHT	1,306 g/1.3 kg	46 oz/2.8 lbs	

Lightly oil or spray a deep 4½- to 5-quart ceramic or glass bread bowl.

 Break the biga into smaller pieces into the bowl of a stand mixer fitted with the paddle attachment. Add the water and yeast and pulse on the lowest setting to break up the biga a bit more; because of the large amount of biga, the water will want to slosh out of the bowl.

⁘ In a medium bowl, whisk together the flour and salt. Add to the biga mixture and pulse a few times on the lowest setting (to keep the flour from flying out of the bowl), then mix on low speed for 3 minutes to combine.

⁘ Remove the paddle attachment, scraping any dough from the paddle back into the bowl, and scrape down the sides of the bowl with a plastic bowl scraper. Fit the mixer with the dough hook and mix on low speed for

6 minutes. The dough may try to crawl up the stem of the dough hook; if it does, turn off the machine, scrape the dough down, and continue to mix. (As mentioned in the headnote, if the mixer is working too hard, finish the kneading by hand on a well-floured board.)

⁘ Flour the work surface. Using the bowl scraper, turn out the dough and knead a few times. The dough will be very smooth and shiny (this is a very easy dough to knead). Place it in the bread bowl. Cover the bowl with a lightly oiled or sprayed piece of plastic wrap and place in a warm, draft-free spot (see Creating Your Warm Spot, page 17) to proof until the dough is very puffy, 1½ to 2 hours.

⁘ The dough is ready to be pre-shaped and shaped into a boule (see opposite) or divided in half, pre-shaped, and shaped into oval loaves (see page 134).

PANE DURUM BOULE

∽ Makes 1 large boule ∽

Golden as candlelight and with a pillowy interior, this bread is beautiful both inside and out. The interior is delicate and has a touch of sweetness from the durum flour. Pane Durum is delicious eaten alone, makes lovely toast, and can soak up any pasta sauce that escapes your fork.

This boule is larger than the others in this book and needs to be proofed and baked in a 6-quart round cast-iron pot.

Pane Durum Dough (opposite)

Flour the work surface. Using a plastic bowl scraper, turn out the dough. Press out the dough, gather the edges, and roll to pre-shape (see photos, Pre-shaping, page 45). Let sit for 10 minutes.

◆ Fairly generously oil or spray the bottom and sides of a 6-quart cast-iron pot. Using your hands and a bench scraper, shape the dough into a boule (see photos, Shaping a Boule, pages 46–47), and place seam side down in the pot. Cover the pot with a lightly oiled or sprayed piece of plastic wrap and place in your warm spot until very puffy again, 1½ to 2 hours. When the dough is gently pressed with your fingertip, the impression should remain.

◆ Meanwhile, position a rack in the lower third of the oven, set a baking stone on it, and preheat the oven to 400°F.

◆ Remove the plastic wrap. Score the dough with an X on the top (see Scoring Dough, page 107), cover the pot with the lid, and bake the boule for 30 minutes. Remove the lid and bake for about 20 minutes longer, or until the bread is golden brown. Carefully remove the loaf from the pot and put on the baking stone for about 10 minutes to brown the sides and bottom more evenly and ensure that the bread is baked through. To test for doneness, see Is It Baked?, page 58. Transfer the bread to a cooling rack and let cool completely. For storing options, see How to Store Bread, page 51.

PANE DURUM OVAL LOAVES

∽ Makes 2 medium oval loaves ∽

Because this dough is so easy to work with, shaping it into ovals is both simple and rewarding. This is the bread to serve to dinner guests with a hearty pasta like pappardelle with a beef, lamb, or wild mushroom ragù. The dusting of all-purpose flour on top of the loaves provides a contrast that sets off the golden glow of the bread.

These loaves are scored using a bench scraper. The scores you initially make will partially close up during proofing, which is why you re-score the dough just before baking.

Pane Durum Dough (page 132)

Flour the work surface. Using a plastic bowl scraper, turn the dough onto the work surface. Using a bench scraper, divide the dough into 2 equal pieces (about 650 grams/22 ounces each). Press out the dough, gather the edges, and roll to pre-shape (see photos, Pre-shaping, page 45). Let sit for 10 minutes.

⁑ Using your hands and a bench scraper, shape each piece of dough into an oval that is high in the center and slopes down the sides.

⁑ Clean a spot on the work surface and sprinkle with flour. Place the ovals seam side down on that spot, allowing room for them to about double in size. Using the bench scraper, make a long, deep score down the center of each loaf, going about halfway through the dough, then turn the loaves cut side down. Cover with a clean linen dish towel or a piece of linen (see About Couches or Proofing Linens, page 140) and then cover with a

Cambro container or a plastic tub. Let proof until very puffy, 45 minutes to 1 hour. When the dough is gently pressed with your fingertip, the impression should remain.

⁑ Meanwhile, position a rack on the lowest rung of the oven and set a cast-iron skillet on it (see Creating Steam in the Oven, page 108, for more on the steam setup). Position a rack above it, set a baking stone on the rack, and preheat the oven to 400°F.

⁑ Flour a peel with some durum flour. Carefully turn both pieces of dough onto the peel and recut the scores with the bench scraper. (Depending on your comfort level and the size of the peel, you may want to move only one loaf at a time into the oven. There will be more heat loss from the oven, but getting used to a peel can take a couple of tries.) Dust the tops generously with all-purpose flour.

+ Carefully (the handle will be hot) pull the cast-iron skillet out, set the pie plate or steamer basket of ice over or in it, and slide it back in. Transfer the loaves to the stone.

+ Bake for about 35 minutes, or until golden brown. To test for doneness, see Is It Baked?, page 58. The loaves should release easily from the stone, but it will be easier to remove them using the peel. Transfer the bread to a cooling rack and let cool completely. For storing options, see How to Store Bread, page 51.

Courage in the Kitchen

❧ MAKING THE MOST OF OVEN RACKS ON CASTERS ❧

Many newer ovens have a rack on casters that slides in and out easily. If you are so lucky, use it to your advantage. Depending on the recipe, you may want the rack with the baking stone on it to be the one that slides in and out easily (think Pane Como Round Loaves, page 110, or the Pane Pugliese Boule, page 117, where the breads are turned out directly onto the stone). If using a peel to transfer the breads to the stone (see Pane Toscano Loaves, page 121), it will probably be more helpful to have the skillet on the sliding rack to make getting the pie plate or steamer basket of ice into the pan quicker.

Because we live on an egg ranch, we always have an abundance of fresh eggs. Hard-boiled fresh eggs can be very difficult to peel; the method given here makes it much easier.

This recipe makes more tapenade and egg salad than you'll need for 8 rusks, but it is great to have extra of both. Yes, you could cut the recipes in half, but who wouldn't want extra in the refrigerator? Spoon the leftover egg salad into Boston or Bibb lettuce cups or even into endive leaves. Try swirling some of the tapenade into tomato sauce, or loosen it with a bit of olive oil and toss with pasta.

At our café, we use anchovy-stuffed olives (see Sources, page 270) in the tapenade. If you can find them, use them as a substitute for the green olives and the anchovies.

Egg Salad (makes 3¾ cups)

12 large eggs, preferably farm-fresh eggs

⅓ cup kosher salt, plus more to season

About 1 cup mayonnaise, preferably homemade

1½ to 2 tablespoons mustard, whatever type you like (spicy brown or even yellow mustard is great for egg salad; if using Dijon, you will probably need less)

Freshly ground black pepper

Sun-dried Tomato–Olive Tapenade (makes 3 cups)

½ cup pine nuts

2 garlic cloves, thinly sliced

1 cup Kalamata olives

1 cup green olives

4 anchovies, well rinsed

1 cup drained sun-dried tomatoes

¾ cup Garlic Oil (page 174)

2 teaspoons freshly squeezed lemon juice

Kosher salt and freshly ground black pepper

recipe continues

Durum Rusks

Eight ⅜-inch-thick slices Pane Durum Oval Loaf
(page 134), or four ⅜-inch-thick slices Pane Durum
Boule (page 132), cut in half

About 1½ tablespoons finely chopped chives

For the egg salad: Place the eggs in a pot that will hold them in a single layer, add the salt and enough water to cover the eggs by 1 inch, bring to a boil, and cook for 8 minutes.

◆ Meanwhile, fill a large bowl with ice and add a small amount of water, just enough to keep the ice moving a bit. (Having large pieces of ice for the eggs to rattle around in will help loosen the eggs from the shells as they cool.)

◆ As soon as they are cooked, drain the eggs and transfer to the bowl of ice; add more ice as needed so that all of the eggs are covered. Let cool completely, occasionally stirring the eggs around a bit in the ice.

◆ Crack and peel the eggs right in the bowl of cold water. Once they are peeled (make sure any pieces of shell stay in the water), dry the eggs and coarsely chop them. Put in a medium bowl and stir in about ½ cup of the mayonnaise and 1 tablespoon of the mustard. Add more mayonnaise and mustard to the desired taste and consistency. Season with salt and pepper to taste. The egg salad can be served at this point, or covered and refrigerated, then served the next day.

◆ For the tapenade: Put the pine nuts, garlic, olives, anchovies, and sun-dried tomatoes in a food processor and process until combined but still chunky (keep in mind that the mixture will continue to be chopped as the oil is added). With the food processor running, add the garlic oil in a steady stream, processing until combined. Transfer to a bowl and stir in the lemon juice. Season to taste with salt and pepper. Like the egg salad, the tapenade will be even better if covered and refrigerated, then served the next day.

◆ For the rusks: Position a rack in the center of the oven and preheat the oven to 350°F.

◆ Arrange the bread on a half sheet pan and bake for 15 minutes. Flip the slices over, rotate the pan from front to back, and bake for another 10 to 15 minutes, until the breads are completely dried out. (The cooled rusks can be stored in an airtight container for a few days.)

◆ To serve, spread about 1 tablespoon of the tapenade on each rusk, followed by about 3 tablespoons of the egg salad. Sprinkle the chives over the top.

· About Couches or Proofing Linens ·

Dough needs to be supported while it's proofing. Baskets are great for round or oval loaves, but when it comes to baguettes and bâtards, at the bakery, we lay the dough out on a board lined with linen that is floured and pleated like an accordion. At home, laying the linen (one piece about 24 by 26 inches or two overlapping linen towels) on a large board or the back of a half sheet pan works well. The loaves should be lined up side by side so they're supporting each other, with a "wall" of floured linen in between them so they don't stick to each other, and then covered with a Cambro container or a plastic tub. This setup of fabric accordioned between the proofing loaves often goes by its French name, *couche*.

Linen is the perfect material for a couche. Flour is used to keep the doughs from sticking to the proofing cloth, but linen's coarse weave and stiffness allow the flour to sit on top of the fabric instead of being absorbed into it. There are plenty of beautiful linen towels on the market; we especially love the ones made by Studiopatró (see Sources, page 270). They are more expensive than regular dish towels, but when you think of them as a tool for your craft, it's a pretty small investment. The towels are handy for more than just proofing bread too. They're lint-free, so they are good for polishing wineglasses and drying dishes.

Another option is to buy proofing linen from a bakery supply house, where linen is sold by the yard and cut to the desired length. Unless the proofing linen gets moldy, don't wash it; just shake it out and store it in an airy, dry location. If blobs of dough get stuck on the linen, hang the cloth out to dry completely, then scrape off the dough clumps and flour with a bench scraper.

If you do need to wash your proofing linen, here's how:

1   Use a bench scraper to remove any clumps of dough and flour.

2   Shake the cloth to remove as much flour as you can.

3   Throw the linen in the washing machine and use unscented laundry soap. This is really important: the fabric will absorb any scent and transfer it to the dough, making for soapy-tasting bread.

4   It's fine to throw your proofing cloth in the dryer. However, letting it air-dry will make it stiffer, which is a good thing—the stiffness helps support the dough.

5   If you wash a piece of cut linen, the edges will fray and can tangle with other items. For that reason, launder it separately and trim the fringe when dry.

TRADITIONAL (SWEET) BAGUETTE & ÉPI

~ Makes 1 baguette or épi or 2 demi-baguettes or demi-épis ~

Because this recipe doesn't use a sourdough starter, we call it a sweet dough. And there's always a place in my kitchen for crusty sweet baguettes. They make great sandwiches and are ideal for a cheese plate. A loaf that's a day or two old can be torn up and tossed with chopped tomatoes and herbs for a bread salad. If you have a hard stale piece sitting around, it can be whizzed in the food processor and transformed into superb bread crumbs to top vegetable gratins or macaroni and cheese.

The baguette may be a French tradition, but it has made its way happily into American culture. However, at Della we like to use a little more dough in our baguettes. The resulting loaf is wider and not quite as long as a traditional baguette. It's a little more challenging to shape uniformly from end to end than some of the other loaves in this book. And depending on the size of your peel and baking stone, it will need to be positioned on the diagonal. If this seems too complicated, the dough can be divided in half and made into demi-baguettes or demi-épis.

FOR DEMI-BAGUETTES AND DEMI-ÉPIS

Biga (page 100)	100 g	3.5 oz	¼ cup plus 3½ Tbsp
Water at 75° to 80°F/24° to 27°C	207 g	7.3 oz	1 cup plus 2 Tbsp
Instant yeast	7 g	0.2 oz	2 tsp
All-purpose flour	288 g	10.2 oz	2 cups plus 1 Tbsp
TOTAL FLOUR	288 g	10.2 oz	2 cups plus 1 Tbsp
Fine gray salt	7 g	0.2 oz	1¼ tsp
TOTAL WEIGHT	609 g	21.5 oz/1.3 lbs	

Lightly oil or spray a deep 4½- to 5-quart ceramic or glass bread bowl.

⁜ Put the biga in the bowl of a stand mixer fitted with the paddle attachment. Add the water and yeast and mix on low speed until the starter is broken up and the mixture appears frothy, about 30 seconds.

⁜ In a medium bowl, whisk together the flour and salt. Add to the biga mixture and pulse a few times on the lowest setting (to keep the flour from flying out of the bowl), then mix on low speed for 3 minutes to combine.

⁜ Remove the paddle attachment, scraping any dough from the paddle back into the bowl, and scrape down the sides of the bowl with a plastic bowl scraper. Fit the mixer with the dough hook and mix on low speed for 6 minutes.

+ Flour the work surface. Using the bowl scraper, turn out the dough and knead a few times. The dough will be very silky but sticky. Place it in the bread bowl. Cover the bowl with a lightly oiled or sprayed piece of plastic wrap and place in a warm, draft-free spot (see Creating Your Warm Spot, page 17) to proof until the dough is very puffy and bubbly, 1½ to 2 hours.

+ Flour the work surface.

+ *For a baguette or épi:* Using the bowl scraper, turn the dough out onto the work surface. Press out the dough, gather the edges, and roll to pre-shape (see photos, Pre-shaping, page 45). Let sit for 10 minutes.

+ Spread a proofing linen (see About Couches or Proofing Linens, page 140) on a large board or on the back of a half sheet pan and dust it generously with flour or a mixture of flour and wheat bran (see To Prevent Sticking, Use Flour and Wheat Bran, page 113).

+ Using your hands and a bench scraper, shape the dough into a baguette (see photos, Shaping a Baguette, page 146), about 2 by 18 inches. If at any point the dough begins to resist being stretched out to this length, let it rest for 10 minutes, then stretch it again. Set the loaf on the linen and gather and lift the linen to create walls on both sides.

+ Set in your warm spot, cover with a Cambro container or a plastic tub, and let proof until very puffy, 45 minutes to 1 hour. When the dough is gently pressed with your fingertip, the impression should remain.

+ Meanwhile, position a rack on the lowest rung of the oven and set a cast-iron skillet on it (see Creating Steam in the Oven, page 108, for more on the steam setup). Position a rack above it, place a baking stone on the rack, and preheat the oven to 450°F.

+ Dust a transfer peel (see Making and Using a Transfer Peel, page 145) and a peel with flour or the flour-bran mixture. Turn the baguette seam side up onto the transfer peel and then turn seam side down onto the peel.

+ If making a baguette, score the top of each by making 4 to 5 parallel cuts down the length of the loaf. Start at the top and make the first cut. Start the second cut about two-thirds down the length of the first. Continue this pattern with subsequent cuts (see Scoring Dough, page 107).

+ If making an épi, holding a pair of scissors at a 60-degree angle, make a cut about 3 inches from one end of the baguette, leaving the cut dough still attached. Lift the cut piece and lay it to one side. Continue down the baguette, making cuts and alternating the side the pieces are moved to (see photos, Forming an Olive Oil Wreath, page 130).

+ Carefully (the handle will be hot) pull the cast-iron skillet out, set the pie plate or steamer basket of ice over or in it, and slide it back in. As noted in the headnote, depending on the size of your stone, the baguette may need to be put diagonally on the stone. Transfer the loaf onto the stone and lower the oven temperature to 400°F. Bake for 25 to 30 minutes, or until golden brown. To test for doneness, see Is It Baked?, page 58. The loaf should release easily from the stone, but it will be easier to remove using the peel. Transfer to a cooling rack and let cool completely. For storing options, see How to Store Bread, page 51.

+ *For demi-baguettes or demi-épis:* Using the bowl scraper, turn the dough onto the work surface. Using a bench scraper divide it into 2 equal pieces (about 300 grams/ 10.5 ounces each). Press out each piece of dough, gather the edges, and roll to pre-shape (see photos, Pre-shaping, page 45). Let sit for 10 minutes.

+ Spread a proofing linen (see About Couches or Proofing Linens, page 140) on a large board or on the back of a half sheet pan and dust it generously with flour or a mixture of flour and wheat bran (see To Prevent Sticking, Use Flour and Wheat Bran, page 113).

+ Using your hands and a bench scraper, shape one piece of dough into a demi-baguette (see photos, Shaping a Baguette, page 146) about 1½ by 14 inches. Set the loaf on the linen and gather and lift the linen to create walls on both sides. Shape the second piece of dough and lay it next to the other so it shares one of the linen walls. Gather the linen on the other side to make a second wall.

+ Set in your warm spot, cover with a Cambro container or a plastic tub, and let proof until very puffy, 1½ to 2 hours. When the dough is gently pressed with your fingertip, the impression should remain.

+ Meanwhile, position a rack on the lowest rung of the oven and set a cast-iron skillet on it (see Creating Steam in the Oven, page 108, for more on the steam setup). Position a rack above it, place a baking stone on the rack, and preheat the oven to 450°F.

+ Dust a transfer peel (see Making and Using a Transfer Peel, opposite) and a peel with flour or the flour-bran mixture. Turn each demi-baguette seam side up onto the transfer peel and then turn seam side down onto the peel; leave plenty of room between them, especially if cutting épis. (Depending on your comfort level and the size of your peel, you may want to do this one at a time. There will be more heat loss from the oven, but getting used to a peel can take a couple of times.)

+ If making baguettes, score the top of each by making 3 parallel cuts down the length of the loaf. Start at the top and make the first cut. Start the second cut about two-thirds down the length of the first. Continue this pattern with the third cut (see Scoring Dough, page 107).

+ If making épis, holding a pair of scissors at a 60-degree angle, make a cut about 3 inches from one end of the baguette, leaving the cut dough still attached. Lift the cut piece and lay it to one side. Continue down the baguette, making cuts and alternating the side the pieces are moved to. Repeat with the second loaf (see Forming an Olive Oil Wreath, page 130).

+ Carefully (the handle will be hot) pull the cast-iron skillet out, set the pie plate or steamer basket of ice over or in it, and slide it back in. Transfer the loaves onto the stone and lower the oven temperature to 400°F. Bake for 20 to 25 minutes, or until golden brown. To test for doneness, see Is It Baked?, page 58. The loaves should release easily from the stone, but they will be easier to remove using the peel. Transfer to a cooling rack and let cool completely. For storing options, see How to Store Bread, page 51.

· Making & Using a Transfer Peel ·

A transfer peel is a vehicle for getting a long loaf from the linen to the peel. It can be a piece of wood, plastic, or melamine, or even a piece of sturdy cardboard. Ideally it should be a rectangle that is slightly longer and wider than your proofed loaf, but look around your house and you'll probably be surprised at what you have that might work. My first transfer peel was the clipboard I had my notes attached to. It did a great job!

When ready to move the loaf, fold down the tented wall of linen next to the bread. Set the edge of the transfer peel up against the side of the dough. Use the other wall of linen to gently turn the dough seam side up onto the transfer peel. Then line the transfer peel up where you want the dough to be on the peel and turn the dough seam side down onto it.

· Shaping a Baguette or Demi-Baguette ·

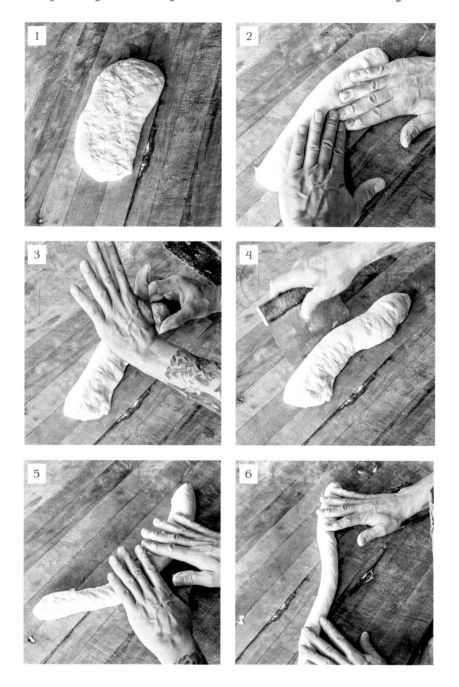

(1) Turn the pre-shaped loaf seam side up. (2) Position your hands under the dough, then fold it over so the ends meet in front of you. (3) Use the heel of your hand to seal the edge. (4) Using a bench scraper, loosen the dough from the work surface, if needed. (5) With the palms of your hands roll and stretch the dough from the center outward to elongate the loaf. (6) Continue rolling until you reach the desired length.

NATURALLY LEAVENED BREADS

CREATING A NATURAL STARTER FOR THE FIRST TIME was a leap of faith for me. Attempting one might feel that way for you too, if it's your first time.

Up until about twenty years ago, my entire understanding of bread baking was based on the belief that the magic of bread came from those little foil packets and jars of yeast bought at the grocery store. The thought that there was enough naturally occurring yeast to create bread living right in my kitchen, and that seemingly inert flour was actually alive, was way out of my comfort zone. But bakers everywhere were talking and writing about natural starters. I had to see for myself if they would really work.

My first try was with the grapes that grow right outside my door, mashed up in cheesecloth by whacking them with a rolling pin. The result was a wonderful, rich starter. But you don't need mashed grapes to make a lively and powerful starter. As you'll learn in this chapter, you can get the same result by just mixing flour and water and leaving it in your kitchen, where it will attract the naturally occurring yeasts and ambient organisms needed to create a starter. At first that bowl of starter may not look or feel much different from a bowl of biscuit dough, but in just a couple of hours, you'll see the starter beginning to puff up. After four hours, it will be twice its original size. Press it with your first three fingers, and it will be like touching a perfectly cooked soufflé, light and airy, but with a definite structure and buoyancy. A well-made starter smells sweet and nutty, with just a hint of sourness.

While naturally leavened breads are often called sourdough, that doesn't mean they have to taste sour. *Sourdough* is simply the term given to naturally leavened breads whose complex flavor comes from long, slow fermentation. Breads leavened with a starter are the heart and soul of our bakery. Making bread this way requires patience and trust. With both, you'll be amply rewarded.

A starter is a living thing that needs to be cared for. In this chapter, you'll learn techniques for the kind of slow fermentation that coaxes the complex flavor out of the flour you're using. You'll taste what a long, slow proof will do for the texture, shape, and flavor of your bread.

The goal in fermenting a mix of flour and water is developing as much flavor as possible. It's not hard work—as you'll see in the Firm Starter recipe on page 156, the flour and water do most of the work for you as they ferment. The only work required on your part will be feeding the starter each day so that it kicks off and blooms into natural leavening. Ten days after the initial mix,

you'll have a starter that you can use to make bread. Depth of flavor will follow in the weeks to come as the starter ripens and takes on the ambient yeasts naturally found where you live.

A starter is, as I said, a living thing, with a life of its own. As you work with one, you'll feel its energy. You'll know when it's well fed and lively, and you'll learn when it has gone too long without food and become lackluster. (When I forget to feed mine, I feel as guilty as I do when I forget to feed my dogs and they give me that sad stare of neglect.) Luckily, your starter is forgiving: as you'll see, once fed, it will revive. Leave it uncared for, though, and it will die—it gets gray, slimy, and stinky. If that happens, you'll have to throw it away and begin the process again.

Once you get into baking naturally leavened breads, you'll see that a starter takes bread to another level. Breads baked on a Sunday will still be edible the following weekend. You can leave your naturally leavened loaf on the counter, covered with linen or a tea towel, and it will never mold. It will certainly dry out, but it can be refreshed in the oven. I actually find that the Pain au Levain (beginning on page 186) and the Pane Integrale Boule (page 209) taste better the second or third day after baking. Though the flavor changes, naturally leavened bread that's a couple of days old never tastes stale.

Naturally leavened bread is more digestible too, because the enzymes and the longer fermentation start to "predigest" the dough before it's baked. Like other fermented products, it contains enzymes our guts need for digestion. There's an Italian toast that says it best: "For your health, today's meat, yesterday's bread, and last year's wine."

An impressive range of styles, shapes, and flavors is possible with naturally leavened breads. Pain de Campagne (beginning on page 159), a simple, rustic loaf made with all-purpose flour, is one of my favorite breads to bake because it's so versatile. It's the base for the Pumpkin Seed, Olive, and Meyer Lemon–Rosemary Campagnes (pages 164, 169, and 176). Pain au Levain Boule (page 198) is my desert island bread. The starter is made with a mix of whole wheat, all-purpose, and pumpernickel flour; the recipe was inspired by bread we had at Poilâne, the celebrated Paris bakery. Levain is the basis for our Walnut-Currant Levain Boule (page 200) and our Grape-Harvest Levain Boule (page 203), as well as for our Potato Levain Bâtards and Sausage-Sage Levain (pages 190 and 195).

Absolutely none of the recipes in this chapter is difficult, but if you haven't ever baked bread, they may feel foreign and even a little awkward at first. You may want to begin with yeasted, enriched, or pre-fermented breads to practice your technique. But if you decide to jump right into naturally leavened breads, all they take is a bit of practice. And if this is your first time baking bread using natural starter instead of commercial yeast, know that you're in for an amazing experience. For me it was like the first time I rode a bicycle, when my father let go of the back fender and I realized I was riding on my own. It felt like magic. After twenty years and thousands of loaves, baking with natural starters still feels that way.

❧ TECHNIQUES ❧

Working with naturally leavened dough is all about sensing the development of the dough at every stage of the process. This chapter introduces a fermentation period where the dough is folded every 30 minutes to help build its structure. You'll see and feel the changes in the dough throughout its development, particularly in the pre-shaping and shaping stages.

Folding dough in a bowl (page 160)
Additional scoring of loaves (see individual recipes)
Free-form baking on a stone (see individual recipes)

❧ EQUIPMENT NEEDED ❧

* Scale
* Stand mixer with paddle and dough hook attachments
* Baking stone
* Thermometer
* Plastic bowl scraper
* Bench scraper
* Plastic wrap
* Liquid measuring cup, preferably with a lid (optional)
* 4½- to 5-quart bread bowl
* Two 9-inch-wide bread baskets (bannetons) or 9-inch bowls
* Two 6-inch-wide bread baskets (bannetons) or 6-inch bowls (optional)

* Two 7¾-by-5½-inch oval baskets (bannetons; optional)
* 12-by-5-inch bread basket (banneton; optional)
* Baker's linen (couche) or linen dish towels
* Quarter sheet pan (9 by 13 by ½ inch)
* Half sheet pan
* Cookie sheet (with no sides; optional)
* 3½- to 4-quart (9-inch) round cast-iron pot
* 3½- to 4-quart round clay pot (about 9 inches in diameter) or 10- to 11-inch tagine
* 3- to 4-quart oval cast-iron pot

* 8-inch cast-iron skillet (optional)
* Cambro container with lid or plastic tub
* Transfer peel
* Peel
* Scissors
* Lame or razor blade
* 10-inch cast-iron skillet
* 9-inch perforated pie plate or collapsible steamer basket
* Ball bearings or a piece of chain link (optional)
* Cooling rack

· Naturally Leavened Breads: A Timetable ·

Making naturally leavened breads brings together all of the skills introduced in the previous chapters and builds upon them. Because these breads involve a bit more of a time commitment than other breads, it's good to know what you're in for. The timetable below will give you a good sense of what to expect. Like most breads, these require a number of resting and proofing periods. It's not all active time, which allows you to go about other business during those intervals.

Most of the steps are the same as for other breads, but here they apply specifically to naturally leavened loaves. All the breads in this chapter follow this model.

1   **Make the starter** (Firm Starter, page 156, or Wet Starter, page 228).

2   **Make the dough:** Combine the starter with the water in the bowl of a stand mixer fitted with the paddle attachment and mix for about 30 seconds to break up the starter. (I like to begin with the starter and the water, because breaking up the starter will give some potency to the water, giving the mixture a head start in its development.) Add the flour(s) and mix for 2 minutes.

Remove the paddle, scraping any dough from the paddle back into the bowl, and let the dough rest for 20 minutes. This will give the dough time for some early development. The starter is active and becoming more so.

Add the salt. The salt is not added earlier because it would inhibit the action of the yeast. Fit the mixer with the dough hook and mix for 6 minutes (in some cases, another ingredient, such as honey, will be added during the last 30 seconds).

3   **Transfer the dough and begin fermentation with folds:** With a plastic bowl scraper, transfer the dough to a lightly oiled or sprayed bowl and cover tightly with a piece of lightly oiled or sprayed plastic wrap. Allow the dough to ferment and develop in the bowl, lifting it to fold it every 30 minutes, for a total of 1½ hours. Folding the dough will increase its strength, and giving it 30 minutes between each fold lets it relax and develop to be ready for the next fold. I love our method of lifting the dough and letting it stretch and hang slightly before folding it underneath itself. It's basically folded the same way you're instructed to do in other chef's bread recipes, like a letter, first from left to right, and then from top to bottom, but here it is all done on the underside of the dough. You'll feel the strength of the dough increasing with each fold.

4   **Give the dough its first proof:** After the last fold, the dough sits until there is bubbling across its surface, 2 to 3 hours; sometimes it can take even longer. (Yes, sometimes it can be shorter, but more often than not, it will be longer.) The dough will show you when it is ready. All doughs will eventually have some bubbling—be patient!

5   **Divide, pre-shape, and shape:** Flour the work surface. How much flour you use will depend on the dough. There needs to be enough flour to keep the dough from sticking but not so much that it could change the makeup of the dough and possibly toughen it.

　　If making more than one loaf, divide the dough.

　　Pre-shape the dough and let it sit for 10 minutes.

　　Shape the dough, transfer it to an oiled cast-iron pot or baking sheet if proofing and baking in (or on) the same vessel, or transfer to a basket or a proofing linen. Cover and set in a warm, draft-free spot (see Creating Your Warm Spot, page 17).

　　Shaping gives you the most options for variation, but it also requires practice. Whether you decide to always proof and bake in cast iron to avoid the need to transfer the proofed dough, or you want to shape the dough, proof, and transfer to the stone to bake, you have options.

6   **Give the dough its second proof:** Proof until when the dough is gently pressed with your fingertip, the impression remains, about 2 hours for most breads, sometimes less.

　　Steps 7 through 9 happen quickly in succession, but it is helpful to view them as individual steps.

7   **Transfer the dough:** For loaves not proofed and baked in cast iron, transfer the dough to a clay pot or other vessel or to the transfer peel and/or peel, if baking on the baking stone.

8   **Score the dough:** Doughs are scored for a variety of reasons. They naturally want to split as they bake, and the shape will dictate that natural split. By scoring, you'll both create a nice aesthetic and help the dough reach its optimum shape. At the bakery, because we bake in production, we often score loaves so we can identify them once they are baked.

9   **Create steam, and transfer the bread to the baking stone:** Create steam for loaves baked directly on the stone and transfer the dough from the peel to the baking stone. Or place the pot on the stone (you won't need to generate steam in the oven—it happens in the pot).

10 **Bake:** Even if you're baking in a pot or on a pan, it's a good idea to turn the loaf out onto the stone for the final 5 to 10 minutes to brown and crisp the sides and bottom more evenly.

11 **Cool:** After the bread is removed from the oven, there will be some carry-over baking. Like a roast, after bread is removed from the oven, it needs to rest. But, unlike a roast, bread needs to cool completely before it is cut. It needs to go through certain natural steps to completely cook and cool. In the process, the crust will soften, then crisp back up again. If the bread is cut into too soon, the exterior may stay on the soft side and the interior can be gummy or undercooked. If left uncut, most loaves will be even better the next day.

FIRM STARTER

⤏ Makes 522 grams/18.3 ounces/about 3½ cups ⤎

Like the biga used in the pre-ferment chapter (page 95), this starter deepens the flavor and develops the texture of the finished loaves. Unlike the biga, though, the firm starter uses all-purpose and whole wheat flours and no commercial yeast.

You'll need to begin making the starter ten days before you plan on using it. Arguably it is usable sooner, but I find ten days to be the minimum required for flavor development. In fact, if you have the time, the starter really should go for three to four weeks before using. But the good news is that once the starter is established, and as long as you feed it, you can keep it ready to go, at room temperature, pretty much indefinitely. If you need to take a break from caring for it, the starter can be refrigerated or frozen; defrost it in the refrigerator. Then take the starter out of the fridge and feed it for three days before using it again.

It's best to weigh the starter to ensure accuracy, but it can be measured by volume if absolutely necessary. If you do have to measure, use damp measuring spoons and cups.

DAY 1

All-purpose flour	190 g	6.7 oz	1¼ cups plus 2 Tbsp
Whole wheat flour	100 g	3.5 oz	½ cup plus 3½ Tbsp
Water at 75° to 80°F/24° to 27°C	290 g	10.2 oz	1¼ cups

In the bowl of a stand mixer fitted with the paddle attachment, mix the flours and water together on the lowest speed for about 1 minute to begin to bring them together. Remove the paddle attachment, scraping any dough from the paddle back into the bowl, and scrape down the sides of the bowl with a plastic bowl scraper.

◆ Fit the mixer with the dough hook and mix on low speed for 2 minutes. The starter will be fairly stiff. Transfer to a very lightly oiled deep liquid measuring cup (one that holds 4 cups or more) or a deep storage container. Cover with the lid or with a lightly oiled or sprayed piece of plastic wrap and let sit at room temperature.

◆ After 24 hours, the starter will be puffier and you will be able to see some bubbles, especially along the sides if it's in a clear container.

Existing starter (from above and then from successive starters each day)	69 g	2.4 oz	¼ cup
Water at 75° to 80°F/24° to 27°C	153 g	5.4 oz	½ cup plus 2½ Tbsp
All-purpose flour	270 g	9.5 oz	1¾ cups plus 3 Tbsp
Whole wheat flour	30 g	1 oz	3½ Tbsp

With damp hands, pinch off a 69-gram (2.4-ounce/¼-cup) piece of starter and put it in the bowl of the stand mixer fitted with the paddle attachment. Discard the remaining starter (or see Note). Add the water and mix on the lowest setting to begin to break up the starter, mixing until it is frothy, about 1 minute. Add the flours and mix on the lowest setting for about 1 minute to begin to bring them together. Remove the paddle attachment, scraping any dough from the paddle back into the bowl, and scrape down the sides of the bowl with the bowl scraper.

+ Fit the mixer with the dough hook and mix on low speed for 2 minutes. The starter will be fairly stiff again. Transfer to a very lightly oiled deep liquid measuring cup or deep storage container. (If using the same container as you did on the first day, make sure it is completely cleaned, dried, and then lightly oiled.) Cover with the lid or with lightly oiled or sprayed piece of plastic wrap and let sit at room temperature for 24 hours.

+ Repeat the process every 24 hours, using the same amounts of starter, water, and flours each day, until the tenth day.

+ On the tenth day, the starter is ready to be used. With damp hands, pinch off the amount needed for the recipe you are making. Then pinch off a 69-gram (2.4-ounce/¼-cup) piece and feed it in the same way, continuing for as long as you want to maintain the starter (see the headnote for information on refrigerating or freezing).

· Note ·
ON WHAT TO DO WITH EXTRA STARTER

So you've put in the effort to make a starter. Now you're supposed to throw away most of it? Unfortunately, yes. It's difficult to make a starter in small amounts. You want to be sure that there's enough of it to really get going and be active. But it won't all go to waste: it's a great idea to store some backup starter. Once the starter is established (after the initial 10 days), pinch off the piece you need and maintain it. Also pinch off a couple of other pieces of the same weight, put each into a small storage container with a lid, and store in the refrigerator or freezer.

· Feeding Your Starter ·

The acidity of your starter can be controlled by temperature and frequent feedings. Basically, the wetter the starter, the faster the bacteria and acid grow, especially at room temperature. At Della Fattoria, our style is more nutty than sour, so we feed our starter in a way that encourages the population of yeast over bacteria and acid. We do this by keeping the starter firm and feeding it on a regular schedule, using only about 15 percent of the old starter for each feeding of flour and water.

PAIN DE CAMPAGNE DOUGH

⁓ Makes 1.35 kilograms/3 pounds ⁓

A request from Thomas Keller right after he reopened The French Laundry in 1995 got me into making pain de campagne. So I asked Thomas lots of questions. (How do you envision serving this bread? Do you like lots of crust? What shape would look best on your bread and butter plate?) In the end, I created the bread he was looking for. For Thomas, I shaped the dough into bâtards. Here we make both a bâtard and a boule.

Firm Starter (page 156)	126 g	4.4 oz	½ cup
Water at 80°F/27°C	506 g	17.8 oz	2 cups plus 2½ Tbsp
All-purpose flour	704 g	24.8 oz	5 cups
TOTAL FLOUR	704 g	24.8 oz	5 cups
Fine gray salt	19 g	0.6 oz	1 Tbsp
TOTAL WEIGHT	1,355 g/1.35 kg	47.6 oz/3 lbs	

Lightly oil or spray a deep 4½- to 5-quart ceramic or glass bread bowl.

+ Put the starter in the bowl of a stand mixer fitted with the paddle attachment. Add the water and mix on low speed until the starter is broken up and the mixture appears frothy, about 30 seconds. Add the flour and pulse a few times on the lowest setting (to keep the flour from flying out of the bowl), then mix on low speed for 2 minutes to combine. Remove the paddle attachment, scraping any dough from the paddle back into the bowl with a plastic bowl scraper, and let sit, uncovered, for 20 minutes.

+ Scrape down the sides of the bowl with the bowl scraper and add the salt. Fit the mixer with the dough hook and mix on low speed for 6 minutes. This is a slightly sticky dough. Using the bowl scraper, turn the dough into the bread bowl. Cover tightly with a lightly oiled or sprayed piece of plastic wrap and let sit for 30 minutes.

+ For the first fold, wet your hands, then loosen the dough from the sides and bottom of the bowl and fold it underneath itself from left to right and then top to bottom (see photos, Folding the Dough, pages 160–161). Cover and let sit for 30 minutes.

+ For the second fold, repeat as for the first fold. Cover and let sit for 30 minutes.

+ For the third and final fold, repeat the folding as before. Cover and let proof in a warm, draft-free spot (see Creating Your Warm Spot, page 17) until there is bubbling on the surface of the dough, 2 to 3 hours.

+ The dough is ready to be pre-shaped and shaped for Pain de Campagne Bâtard (page 163), Pumpkin Seed Campagne Bâtard (page 164), Pain de Campagne Boule (page 166), Olive Campagne Boule (page 169), Chocolate Cherry Campagne Boules (page 170), Garlic Jack Campagne Boule (page 173), or Meyer Lemon–Rosemary Campagne Boule (page 176).

· Folding the Dough ·

Naturally leavened doughs are folded three times during their fermentation process. Allow 30 minutes between each fold. With each fold the dough gains strength, but it needs that time between to relax.

Always start by loosening the dough from the sides and bottom of the bowl with a plastic bowl scraper and/or damp hands.

(1) Position your hands in the middle of the dough and lift it up above the bowl, letting it hang and stretch slightly. (2) As it stretches, move a hand down to one end. (3) Fold and tuck that end under, folding it toward the center. (4) Repeat on the opposite end with the other hand, making a second fold, as if folding a letter. (5) Turn the dough and let it stretch again (it will not be nearly as loose because of the first set of folds). (6) Repeat the folds from top to bottom. The dough will be dramatically tighter. (7) Set the dough back in the bowl.

PAIN DE CAMPAGNE BÂTARD

⌘ Makes 1 large bâtard ⌘

Campagne dough is very versatile and is ideal to work with when beginning to make large free-form loaves, particularly a bâtard.

Pain de Campagne Dough (page 159)

Flour the work surface. Using a plastic bowl scraper, turn out the dough onto the work surface. Press out the dough, gather the edges, and roll to pre-shape (see photos, Pre-shaping, page 45). Let sit for 10 minutes.

✦ Spread a proofing linen (see About Couches or Proofing Linens, page 140) on a large board or on the back of a half sheet pan and dust fairly generously with flour or a mixture of flour and wheat bran (see To Prevent Sticking, Use Flour and Wheat Bran, page 113). Or dust a 12-by-5-inch bread basket fairly generously with flour or a mixture of flour and wheat bran.

✦ Using your hands and a bench scraper, shape the dough into a bâtard (see photos, Shaping a Bâtard, pages 52–53), about 4½ by 10 inches. Set the loaf on the linen and gather and lift the linen to create walls on both sides or place the loaf seam side up in the basket.

✦ Set the loaf in your warm spot, cover with a Cambro container or a plastic tub, and let proof until very puffy, 2 to 3 hours. When the dough is gently pressed with your fingertip, the impression should remain.

✦ Meanwhile, position a rack on the lowest rung of the oven and set a cast-iron skillet on it (see Creating Steam in the Oven, page 108, for more on the steam setup). Position a rack above it, place a baking stone on the rack, and preheat the oven to 450°F.

✦ Dust a transfer peel (if the loaf was proofed on a linen) and a peel fairly generously with flour or the flour-bran mixture. If using a linen, turn the bâtard seam side up onto the transfer peel and then turn seam side down onto the peel. If using the basket, invert the bâtard over the peel. Score the loaf in a diamond pattern (see Scoring Dough, page 107).

✦ Carefully (the handle will be hot) pull the cast-iron skillet out, set the pie plate or steamer basket of ice over or in it, and slide it back in. Transfer the loaf onto the stone and lower the oven temperature to 400°F.

✦ Bake for 50 to 55 minutes, or until the top is golden brown. To test for doneness, see Is It Baked?, page 58. The loaves should release easily from the stone, but it will be easier to remove them using the peel. Transfer the bread to a cooling rack and let cool completely. For storing options, see How to Store Bread, page 51.

PUMPKIN SEED CAMPAGNE BÂTARD

இ Makes 1 large bâtard இ

Food writer Peggy Knickerbocker is a good friend of mine, and this is her favorite bread. With lots of toasted pumpkin seeds inside and a smattering of untoasted seeds on the outside (the seeds toast up as the bread bakes), this is a beautiful loaf with a subtle nutty flavor. The best part is that while the bread's flavor is distinctive, it's also very versatile. I can't think of a thing it wouldn't go with. Toast it for breakfast with jam, slice it up for tuna sandwiches, or serve it with a cheese plate.

¼ cup plus 3½ tablespoons (75 grams/2.6 ounces) pumpkin seeds

Pain de Campagne Dough (page 159), taken through the 6-minute mix and still in the mixer bowl

Preheat the oven to 350°F.

+ Spread ¼ cup plus 2 tablespoons (60 grams/2.1 ounces) of the pumpkin seeds on a quarter sheet pan and toast in the oven until they are a richer brown, about 6 minutes. Spread the seeds on a plate and let cool completely.

+ Add the seeds to the dough and mix on low speed to incorporate, 30 seconds to 1 minute.

+ Follow the remaining steps for Pain de Campagne Bâtard (page 163) through the final proofing. When the bâtard is ready for baking, gently press a damp cloth against the top, remove it, and sprinkle the top with the remaining 1½ tablespoons (15 grams/ 0.5 ounce) pumpkin seeds. Score with 4 diagonal slashes (see Scoring Dough, page 107) and bake as directed.

PAIN DE CAMPAGNE BOULE

⮑ Makes 1 large boule ⮐

Because campagne dough is easy to work with, if you have never made a free-form boule, this is the dough to start with. Regardless, a cast-iron or clay pot will offer amazing results (see Baking Naturally Leavened Breads in Cast-Iron or Clay Pots, page 202).

Pain de Campagne Dough (page 159)

Flour the work surface. Using a plastic bowl scraper, turn out the dough. Press out the dough, gather the edges, and roll to pre-shape (see photos, Pre-shaping, page 45). Let sit for 10 minutes.

⁘ Dust a 9-inch bread basket generously with flour or a mixture of flour and wheat bran (see To Prevent Sticking, Use Flour and Wheat Bran, page 113) or line a large bowl with a generously dusted linen dish towel (see About Proofing Baskets, page 114).

⁘ Using your hands and a bench scraper, shape the dough into a boule (see photos, Shaping a Boule, pages 46–47). Dust with flour or the flour-bran mixture and place seam side up in the basket or bowl. Dust the top. If using a basket, cover it with a clean linen dish towel; if using a linen-lined bowl, fold the linen over the dough.

⁘ Place the dough in your warm spot until it is very puffy again and the top of the dough has reached the top of the bowl or basket, 2 to 3 hours. When the dough is gently pressed with your fingertip, the impression should remain.

⁘ Meanwhile, position a rack on the lowest rung of the oven and set a cast-iron skillet on it (see Creating Steam in the Oven, page 108, for more on the steam setup). Position a rack above it, place a baking stone on it, and preheat the oven to 450°F.

⁘ Dust a peel fairly generously with flour or the flour-bran mixture. If the dough is in an unlined basket, invert the basket over the peel and then, if necessary, use the bowl scraper to gently ease the dough onto the peel. If it's in a lined bowl, use the linen to ease the dough onto the peel. Score the top in a diamond pattern (see Scoring Dough, page 107). Carefully (the handle will be hot) pull the cast-iron skillet out, set the pie plate or steamer basket of ice over or in it, and slide it back in. Transfer the boule to the baking stone and lower the oven temperature to 400°F.

⁘ Bake for 45 to 50 minutes, or until the bread is a rich golden brown. To test for doneness, see Is It Baked?, page 58. Transfer the bread to a cooling rack and let cool completely. For storing options, see How to Store Bread, page 51.

· Note ·

ON MAKING TWO BOULES

Any of the campagne recipes can be used to make 2 smaller boules (but I especially love it for Chocolate Cherry Campagne Boules, page 170). After the dough has had its first proof, flour the work surface, turn out the dough, and divide it into 2 equal pieces (about 675 grams/24 ounces each). Shape each piece into a boule and then put each piece in a floured 9-inch bread basket or lined bowl. (If you have 6-inch baskets or bowls, great; but if you only have 9-inch baskets or bowls, they will work just fine—though the bread won't come up as high and may need a little more coaxing to get out.) Follow the remaining steps (unless you happen to have two small cast-iron or clay pots), score as you would the larger loaf, and bake for 35 to 40 minutes.

Rustic Beauty & Personal Style

The more you work with pre-fermented and naturally leavened doughs, the more comfortable you will be shaping them. Eventually you'll gain more control over these shaggy blobs. But before that happens, you'll surely have some lopsided, unexpected, and uniquely shaped breads. That's great. It's fabulous, in fact. Free-form handmade loaves are always beautiful. Rustic beauty is what Della Fattoria is known for.

Making bread offers many opportunities, particularly when working with pre-fermented and naturally leavened doughs. I really believe the possibilities are endless. A basic dough lends itself to change with simple additions. Add herbs, nuts, or dried fruit, and you have a completely different taste. Experiment with loaf shapes using different-sized baskets, pans, or pots to proof and/or bake in. And then play with designs that go far beyond traditional scores.

At the bakery we make different shapes and sizes of the same dough every day. The recipes here are some of our favorites, but they should be your springboard into developing a personal style. Take the campagne and levain doughs, for example. The basic doughs or any of their variations can be any size you want them to be. I like the Chocolate Cherry Campagne shaped as two small boules, but it could just as easily be a bâtard. Maybe you'd like to make small Pane Integrale boules. Try proofing and baking a large bâtard, like the Levain with sausage and sage in a cast iron or clay-pot. Or perhaps you'd like to make a baguette from the Olive Campagne, the Seeded Wheat, or the Semolina.

Score the loaves with initials, decorate the tops of the loaves with herbs, or use a doily or paper cutout to make a pattern on the dough with flour. Even the random patterns created by the way that the flour from the proofing cloth or basket clings to the finished loaves are pleasing.

OLIVE CAMPAGNE BOULE

⁓ Makes 1 large boule ⁓

What makes pain de campagne so special is the way it seems to bring out the best in just about any ingredient you add to it. I love using big fat Kalamata olives, but any flavorful olive will work. Try serving a slice of this bread drizzled with olive oil, toasted, and then piled with crumbled fresh goat cheese and a bit of chopped sun-dried tomato. It is also delicious eaten alone, or sliced thick and served with lamb roast or stew or tomato soup.

Pain de Campagne dough (page 159), taken through the 6-minute mix

1 cup (150 grams/5.3 ounces) pitted Kalamata olives

Turn the mixed dough out into a lightly oiled bread bowl. Top with the olives and gently press them into the dough. With each fold, the olives will be incorporated and then evenly distributed throughout the dough. (You can also add the olives during the final part of the mix. This will add a little more olive flavor to the dough, but it will also discolor the dough, which I don't like.)

✦ Follow all of the remaining steps through the final proof. Score the dough with an X (see Scoring Dough, page 107) and bake as directed.

Converting a Recipe

Any bread recipe made with commercial yeast can be converted into a naturally leavened one. That's exactly what I did when I first started baking this way. I took my favorite recipes and reworked them by translating the cups and spoons into weights, calculating the percentages of each ingredient, and substituting natural starter (12 percent to start with) for the instant yeast. The natural starter will definitely make a different bread than the yeasted recipe, and you might not like some results as well. I've made many a breadstick with a natural starter, but they've never achieved the same crispness and lightness as yeasted ones. Feel free to use the recipes in this section as a template, or a framework, to experiment with your own recipes.

CHOCOLATE CHERRY CAMPAGNE BOULES

ↄ Makes 2 medium boules ↄ

Once we started baking pain de campagne, I started to imagine how bread and chocolate could make for a winning combo. We began by adding chopped dark chocolate to the dough, and then one of our bakers wanted to try adding rehydrated dried cherries. The result is this bread, which is great for breakfast when toasted and served with mascarpone cheese. It can also be used on a cheese plate with more assertive cheeses, such as a creamy blue cheese or a sharp aged sheep's-milk cheese. Give it a go, and let your imagination have its way.

¾ cup (120 grams/4.2 ounces) dried cherries

½ cup (120 grams/4.2 ounces) brandy or water

¾ cup (about 120 grams/4.2 ounces) ⅜- to ½-inch pieces 70% bittersweet chocolate, preferably Valrhona Guanaja 70%

Pain de Campagne Dough (page 159), taken through the 6-minute mix

Put the dried cherries in a small bowl. Bring the brandy or water to a boil and pour over the cherries. Let sit for at least 30 minutes, or, if using brandy, preferably overnight. Drain.

⁺ To avoid tiny flecks of chocolate that will mar the look of the dough, sift the chocolate to remove any small pieces and chocolate dust.

⁺ Turn the mixed dough out into a lightly oiled bread bowl. Top with the cherries and chocolate pieces and gently press them into the dough. With each fold, the cherries and chocolate will be incorporated and then evenly distributed throughout the dough. (Don't be tempted to incorporate them in the mixer; the cherries will bleed and discolor the dough.)

⁺ Follow all of the remaining steps for making two boules (see Note, page 167) through the final proof. Score with 2 curved parallel cuts across the top (see Scoring Dough, page 107) and bake as directed.

GARLIC JACK CAMPAGNE BOULE

∾ Makes 1 large boule ∾

There was a time in California cuisine when roasted garlic was all the rage. This time may have passed, but roasted garlic remains a great partner with bread. Our original version of this bread was created to showcase an award-winning goat cheese that our goat-farmer friend Barbara Backus made at Goat's Leap Farm in Napa. Her cheese was featured in a gift basket that the Meadowood resort gave to special guests. The chef at that time, Didier Lenders, asked me to bake some small breads using one of Barbara's cheeses. We decided to make a bread that looked like a present. We roasted and pureed the garlic, then spread it on the dough after it was flattened out and topped it with grated aged goat cheese. We wrapped up the bundle like a beggar's purse, sealed it on the bottom, and flipped it over, then poked small garlic heads in the center and placed three or so cilantro leaves with the stems attached in a lacy arrangement around the center. We liked it so much that we increased the size.

Barbara doesn't make cheese anymore, so we eventually switched to Vella Dry Jack, made in Sonoma (see Sources, page 270). Because the bread is so labor-intensive, it's no longer a part of our regular production; we do it now only for special orders. For a home baker, however, this bread is a delightful scene-stealer and well worth a little extra time.

Pain de Campagne Boule (page 166), taken through the pre-shape

¼ cup (90 grams/3.2 ounces) Garlic Puree (recipe follows)

1 cup (100 grams/3.5 ounces) grated hard cheese, preferably dry Jack (Asiago, Grana Padano, or Parmigiano-Reggiano would be great too)

1 small head garlic or 2 or 3 garlic cloves (not peeled)

3 parsley or cilantro leaves with stems (optional)

After the 10-minute rest, turn the dough over (flour side against the work surface) and gently press it into a 9- to 10-inch round. Dimple the top and spread the garlic puree over the dough, leaving a ½-inch border all around. Sprinkle the top with the grated cheese. Fold the sides in, as when forming a boule, enclosing the mixture, then tighten the boule against the work surface until you just begin to see the mixture under the surface of the dough.

◆ Poke a little hole in the center of the dough with a sharp paring knife and push the garlic into the hole. (Don't be tempted to peel the garlic: the "paper" keeps it from drying out and looks like beautiful parchment when baked.) If using, dip the parsley or cilantro leaves in water and press onto the top of the boule.

◆ Generously dust a 9-inch bread basket or linen-lined bowl with flour (for this bread, I prefer to use flour alone, rather than a mixture of flour and wheat bran). Follow the remaining steps for proofing and baking the bread, but dust the peel with the flour only.

GARLIC PUREE & OIL

Makes 360 grams/12.7 ounces/about 1 cup garlic puree and 530 grams/18.7 ounces/2½ cups garlic oil

Making your own garlic puree couldn't be easier. As whole peeled garlic cloves are slowly simmered in olive oil, softening and acquiring a creamy texture, the oil becomes infused with garlic flavor. The oil can be used in the Sun-dried Tomato–Olive Tapenade (page 137), as a dip for bread, or tossed with pasta and roasted vegetables. Unpureed whole cloves can be used in Jakob's Bean Spread (page 180) or added to sauces or dressings for a little garlic richness without a raw garlic bite.

3 cups (450 grams/15.9 ounces) garlic cloves, peeled

2½ cups (530 grams/18.7 ounces) extra virgin olive oil, or to cover

Put the garlic cloves into a medium saucepan and cover with the oil. Bring to a simmer over medium heat and cook, stirring occasionally, for 20 minutes, or until the garlic is tender. Strain the oil into a small storage container. The whole confited cloves can be used at this point or stored in the oil and refrigerated for up to 2 weeks.

To make the garlic puree, process the cloves in a food processor until smooth. For a smoother puree, press through a fine-mesh strainer. Use immediately, or pour into a lidded container, cover with a film of olive oil, and seal tightly. The puree can be refrigerated for up to 2 weeks.

Assembling a
Garlic Jack Campagne Boule

(1) Spread the garlic puree over the dimpled campagne dough, leaving a ½-inch border all the way around.
(2) Sprinkle the grated cheese over the top of the puree.
(3) Fold the sides in to enclose the mixture. Turn the dough seam side down and tighten against the work surface. With your hands, roll the ball against the work surface in a circular motion, gently lifting and lowering as you do, to tighten the seal (see photos, Shaping a Boule, pages 46–47). **(4)** With the tip of a paring knife, poke a small hole in the center and push the small head of garlic into the hole. **(5)** Dip the parsley or cilantro into water and press on the top of the boule.

MEYER LEMON-ROSEMARY CAMPAGNE BOULE

⁓ Makes 1 large boule ⁓

This has become our signature bread. Lemon zest and finely chopped rosemary are mixed with olive oil to make a pesto-like slurry that appears as a bright and delicious swirl along the underside of the crust. But what really sets the bread apart is its raised crown design, studded with large salt crystals.

Ed, my husband, tells everyone to eat this bread toasted with soft-boiled eggs. I love cutting thick slices of the bread and grilling them over low coals, or pulling it apart and eating it just as it is.

1½ tablespoons (8 grams/0.3 ounce) grated lemon zest, preferably from Meyer lemons

1½ tablespoons (6 grams/0.2 ounce) chopped rosemary

About 3 tablespoons (40 grams/1.5 ounces) olive oil

Pain de Campagne Boule (page 166), taken through the pre-shape

1 to 1½ teaspoons (4 to 6 grams/1.4 to 2 ounces) coarse sea salt (see Note)

Combine the lemon zest and rosemary in a small bowl. Add enough olive oil to create a pesto-like slurry.

◆ After the 10-minute rest, turn the dough over (flour side against the work surface) and gently press into a 9- to 10-inch round. Dimple the top, make a well, and add the rosemary mixture to the well. Fold the sides in, as when forming a boule, enclosing the mixture, then tighten the boule against the work surface until you just begin to see the rosemary mixture under the surface of the dough.

◆ Generously dust a 9-inch bread basket or linen-lined bowl with flour or a mixture of flour and wheat bran (see To Prevent Shrinking, Use Flour and Wheat Bran, page 113). Follow the remaining steps for proofing and baking the bread, and when ready to score, score it with a 4-scored asterisk (see Scoring Dough, page 107). It will be because of the slurry underneath that the points raise into a crown as it bakes. Sprinkle the sea salt over the top.

· Note ·
ON COARSE SEA SALT

I prefer La Baleine coarse sea salt (in the red canister). The crystals are clear and shiny like diamonds, and they won't melt.

Assembling a Meyer Lemon–Rosemary Campagne Boule

(1) Make a well in the center of the dimpled campagne dough and spoon the slurry into the well. (2–3) Fold the sides in to enclose the mixture. (4) Turn the dough seam side down and tighten against the work surface. With your hands, roll the ball against the work surface in a circular motion, gently lifting and lowering as you do, to tighten the seal (see photos, Shaping a Boule, pages 46–47).

(5) After proofing, score the loaf with a 4-scored asterisk.

My grandson Jakob and I have done a lot of cooking together. From the time he could walk, he was never much for toys, but instead always wanted to do what the grown-ups were doing. He liked to vacuum, and he liked to cook. I have some adorable photos of him making biscuits. Once he mastered those, we went on to pasta and pizza. Jakob liked his omelet in the morning, and soon he wasn't satisfied just beating the eggs with a fork; he wanted to pour them into the pan of melted butter and cook them. He was eighteen months old, and that's exactly what we did. Apron on, stool next to me in front of the stove, spatula in hand, he cooked his own omelet. It made us both so happy.

Rancho Gordo Beans on Toast has been on the menu from the time the café opened in 2004. Jakob was four years old, and this was his favorite thing to eat. As you will see when you make it, the color of the spread isn't mouthwatering, but a sprinkling of chives makes it beautiful. The flavor and texture are sublime, and when served on slices of toasted or grilled Meyer Lemon–Rosemary Campagne, it is perfection.

Of course, it's best when you cook the beans yourself (see Kathleen's Pot of Beans, page 123), but you can substitute canned white beans.

Bean Spread (makes about 2 cups)

2 cups drained cooked white beans or canned white beans, drained and rinsed

5 whole cloves confited garlic (see Garlic Puree, page 174)

¼ cup extra virgin olive oil, plus additional as needed

⅔ cup crumbled fresh goat cheese (5 ounces)

⅓ cup freshly grated Parmigiano-Reggiano

¼ cup plus 2 tablespoons coarsely chopped pitted Kalamata olives

Kosher salt and freshly ground black pepper

4 thick slices Meyer Lemon–Rosemary Campagne Boule (page 176), cut in half and toasted or grilled

3 tablespoons coarsely chopped chives

For the bean spread: Run the beans through a food mill with the smallest die, or press the beans through a fine-mesh strainer into a bowl, to remove the skins and to finely puree.

✦ Put the beans in a food processor, add the garlic cloves, and pulse to break up the garlic. With the processor running, slowly add the oil, then add the goat cheese and pulse to incorporate.

✦ At this point the spread can be made smooth or chunky. For a smooth puree, add the Parmesan and olives to the food processor and mix until smooth, adding additional oil as needed to loosen. For a chunky puree, transfer the bean mixture to a bowl and mix in the Parmesan and olives, stirring in additional oil as needed. Season to taste with salt and pepper.

✦ The bean spread can be served now, but it will be even better the next day. It can be stored, covered, in the refrigerator for up to 5 days.

✦ To serve, spoon the puree generously onto the toasted bread and top with the chives.

BAGUETTE & ÉPI

◦⌒ Makes 1 baguette or épi or 2 demi-baguettes or demi-épis ⌒◦

A true French baguette is around two feet long, which is too big for most baking stones and home ovens, but it *will* fit into an outdoor brick oven, if you are lucky enough to have one. And as with the Traditional (Sweet) Baguette (page 142), at Della we like to use a little more dough in our baguettes. This recipe makes a baguette that is about six inches shorter and about twice as wide as its French counterpart. It's a little more challenging to shape uniformly from end to end than some of the other loaves in this book. And, depending on the size of your peel and baking stone, it will need to be positioned on the diagonal. Or the dough can be divided in half and made into demi-baguettes or demi-épis.

Either way, you will have loaves with a high crust-to-crumb ratio that are great for sandwiches when sliced in half horizontally, or wonderfully shaped slices when cut crosswise for crostini.

Firm Starter (page 156)	38 g	1.3 oz	2½ Tbsp
Water at 80°F/27°C	235 g	8.3 oz	1 cup
All-purpose flour	342 g	12 oz	2¼ cups plus 3 Tbsp
TOTAL FLOUR	342 g	12 oz	2¼ cups plus 3 Tbsp
Fine gray salt	9 g	0.3 oz	1½ tsp
TOTAL WEIGHT	624 g	22 oz/1.3 lbs	

Lightly oil or spray a deep 4½- to 5-quart ceramic or glass bread bowl.

✦ Put the starter in the bowl of a stand mixer fitted with the paddle attachment. Add the water and mix on low speed until the starter is broken up and the mixture appears frothy, about 30 seconds. Add the flour and pulse a few times on the lowest setting (to keep the flour from flying out of the bowl), then mix on low speed for 2 minutes to combine. Remove the paddle attachment, scraping any dough from the paddle back into the bowl with a plastic bowl scraper, and let sit, uncovered, for 20 minutes.

✦ Scrape down the sides of the bowl with the bowl scraper and add the salt. Fit the mixer with the dough hook and mix on low speed for 6 minutes. This is a very silky dough. Using the bowl scraper, turn the dough into the bread bowl. Cover tightly with a lightly oiled or sprayed piece of plastic wrap and let sit for 30 minutes.

✦ For the first fold, wet your hands, then loosen the dough from the sides and bottom of the bowl and fold it underneath itself from left to right and then top to bottom (see photos, Folding the Dough, pages 160–161). Cover and let rest for 30 minutes.

recipe continues

+ For the second fold, repeat as for the first fold. Cover and let sit for 30 minutes.

+ For the third and final fold, repeat the folding as before. Cover and let proof in a warm, draft-free spot (see Creating Your Warm Spot, page 17) until there is bubbling on the surface, 2 to 3 hours.

+ Flour the work surface.

+ *For a baguette or an épi*: Using a bowl scraper, turn the dough out onto the work surface. Press out the dough, gather the edges, and roll to pre-shape (see photos, Pre-shaping, page 45). Let sit for 10 minutes.

+ Spread a proofing linen (see About Couches or Proofing Linens, page 140) on a large board or on the back of a half sheet pan and dust it generously with flour or a mixture of flour and wheat bran (see To Prevent Sticking, Use Flour and Wheat Bran, page 113).

+ Using your hands and a bench scraper, shape the dough into a baguette (see photos, Shaping a Baguette, page 146) about 2 by 18 inches. If at any point the dough begins to resist being stretched out to this length, let it rest for 10 minutes, then stretch it again. Set the loaf on the linen and gather and lift the linen to create walls on both sides.

+ Set in your warm spot, cover with a Cambro container or a plastic tub, and let proof until very puffy, about 2 hours. When the dough is gently pressed with your fingertip, the impression should remain.

+ Meanwhile, position a rack on the lowest rung of the oven and set a cast-iron skillet on it (see Creating Steam in the Oven, page 108, for more on the steam setup).

Position a rack above it, place a baking stone on the rack, and preheat the oven to 450°F.

+ Dust a transfer peel (see Making and Using a Transfer Peel, page 145) and a peel with flour or the flour-bran mixture. Turn the baguette seam side up onto the transfer peel and then turn seam side down onto the peel.

+ If making baguettes, score the top of each by making 4 to 5 parallel cuts down the length of the loaf. Start at the top and make the first cut. Start the second cut about two-thirds down the length of the first. Continue this pattern with subsequent cuts (see Scoring Dough, page 107).

+ If making an épi, holding a pair of scissors at a 60-degree angle, make a cut in about 3 inches from one end of the baguette, leaving the cut dough still attached. Lift the cut piece and lay it to one side. Continue down the baguette, making cuts and alternating the side the pieces are moved to (see Forming an Olive Oil Wreath, page 130).

+ Carefully (the handle will be hot) pull the cast-iron skillet out, set the pie plate or steamer basket of ice over or in it, and slide it back in. As noted in the headnote, depending on the size of your stone, the baguette may need to be put diagonally on the stone. Transfer the loaf onto the stone and lower the oven temperature to 400°F. Bake for 25 to 30 minutes, or until golden brown. To test for doneness, see Is It Baked?, page 58. The loaf should release easily from the stone, but it will be easier to remove using the peel. Transfer to a cooling rack and let cool completely. For storing options, see How to Store Bread, page 51.

+ *For demi-baguettes and demi-épis*: Using the bowl scraper, turn the dough onto the work surface, divide it into 2 equal pieces (about 310 grams, 11 ounces each), and pre-shape (see photos, Pre-shaping, page 45). Let sit for 10 minutes.

+ Spread a proofing linen (see About Couches or Proofing Linens, page 140) on a large board or on the back of a half sheet pan and dust it generously with flour or a mixture of flour and wheat bran (see To Prevent Sticking, Use Flour and Wheat Bran, page 113).

+ Using your hands and a bench scraper, shape one piece of dough into a demi-baguette (see photos, Shaping a Baguette, page 146), about 1½ by 14 inches (see Note). Set the loaf on the linen and gather and lift the linen to create walls on both sides. Shape the second piece of dough and lay it next to the other so it shares one of the linen walls. Gather the linen on the other side to make a second wall.

+ Set in your warm spot, cover with a Cambro container or a plastic tub, and let proof until very puffy, about 2 hours. When the dough is gently pressed with your fingertip, the impression should remain.

+ Meanwhile, position a rack on the lowest rung of the oven and set a cast-iron skillet over or in it (see Creating Steam in the Oven, page 108, for more on the steam setup). Position a rack above it, place a baking stone on the rack, and preheat the oven to 450°F.

+ Dust a transfer peel (see Making and Using a Transfer Peel, page 145) and a peel with flour or the flour-bran mixture. Turn each demi-baguette seam side up onto the transfer peel and then turn seam side down onto the peel; leave plenty of room between them, especially if cutting épis. (Depending on your comfort level and the size of your peel, you may want to do this one at a time. There will be more heat loss from the oven, but getting used to a peel can take a couple of times.)

+ *If making demi-baguettes*: Score the top of each by making 3 parallel cuts down the length of the loaf. Start at the top and make the first cut. Start the second cut about two-thirds down the length of the first. Continue this pattern with the third cut. (see Scoring Dough, page 107).

+ *If making an épi*: Holding a pair of scissors at a 60-degree angle, make a cut in about 3 inches from one end of the baguette, leaving the cut dough still attached. Lift the cut piece and lay it to one side. Continue down the baguette, making cuts and alternating the side the pieces are moved to. Repeat with the second loaf. (see Forming an Olive Oil Wreath, page 130).

+ Carefully (the handle will be hot) pull the cast-iron skillet out, set the pie plate or steamer basket of ice over or in it, and slide it back in. Transfer the loaves onto the stone and lower the oven temperature to 400°F. Bake for 20 to 25 minutes, or until golden brown. To test for doneness, see Is It Baked?, page 58. The loaves should release easily from the stone, but it will be easier to remove them using the peel. Transfer to a cooling rack and let cool completely. For storing options, see How to Store Bread, page 51.

PAIN AU LEVAIN DOUGH

↷ Makes 1.36 kilograms/3 pounds ↶

Poilâne, the legendary French bakery in Paris, was the inspiration for this rustic bread. It is robust and nutty, with an interior that's bouncy, shiny, and lacy. It goes as well in a picnic basket with a good bottle of wine as it does at an elegant dinner. I never tire of it. Chunks of the bread are delicious just pulled off the loaf and eaten as is or dunked in olive oil. When served with a simple green salad (see page 192) or sliced thick to serve with cheese and pears, it becomes a meal.

The bread's versatility extends to the mixing bowl. There's an almost endless list of what you can add to it: potato, walnuts, currants, sausage, and even wine.

This is a wet dough, so it will feel loose in your hands, and it will require just a bit more flour on the work surface than some of the other breads in the book.

Firm Starter (page 156)	109 g	3.8 oz	¼ cup plus 3 Tbsp
Water at 80°F/27°C	551 g	19.4 oz	2¼ cups plus 1½ Tbsp
All-purpose flour	408 g	14.4 oz	2¾ cups plus 2½ Tbsp
Whole wheat flour	204 g	7.2 oz	1¼ cups plus 2½ Tbsp
Pumpernickel flour	68 g	2.4 oz	½ cup
TOTAL FLOUR	680 g	24 oz	4¾ cups plus 1 Tbsp
Fine gray salt	16 g	0.6 oz	2¾ tsp
TOTAL WEIGHT	1,356 g/1.36 kg	47.8 oz/3 lbs	

Lightly oil or spray a deep 4½- to 5-quart ceramic or glass bread bowl.

✦ Put the starter in the bowl of a stand mixer fitted with the paddle attachment. Add the water and mix on low speed until the starter is broken up and the mixture appears frothy, about 30 seconds. Add the flours and pulse a few times on the lowest setting (to keep the flours from flying out of the bowl), then mix on low speed for 2 minutes to combine. Remove the paddle attachment, scraping any dough from the paddle back into the bowl with a plastic bowl scraper, and let sit, uncovered, for 20 minutes.

✦ Scrape down the sides of the bowl with the bowl scraper and add the salt. Fit the mixer with the dough hook and mix on low speed for 6 minutes. This is a very sticky dough. Using the bowl scraper, turn the dough into the bread bowl. Cover tightly with a lightly oiled or sprayed piece of plastic wrap and let sit for 30 minutes.

✦ For the first fold, wet your hands, then loosen the dough from the sides and bottom of the bowl and fold it underneath itself from left to right and then from top to bottom (see photos, Folding the Dough, pages 160–161). Cover and let sit for 30 minutes.

 ✦ For the second fold, repeat as for the first fold. Cover and let sit for 30 minutes.

 ✦ For the third and final fold, repeat the folding as before. Cover and let proof in a warm, draft-free spot (see Creating Your Warm Spot, page 171) until there is bubbling on the surface, 2 to 3 hours.

 ✦ The dough is ready to be used to make the Pain au Levain Boule (page 198), the Grape-Harvest Levain Boule (page 203), the Potato Levain Bâtards (page 190), or the Sausage-Sage Levain Bâtard (page 195).

PAIN AU LEVAIN BÂTARD

❧ Makes 1 large bâtard ❧

I really like to make large loaves of bread—they are so impressive. However, levain is a little harder to make into one large bâtard because of how slack the dough is, and is best proofed in a 12-by-5-inch bread basket to lend support to it as it proofs.

And while a large loaf is impressive, I also recognize the fact that making one presents a practical limitation. If you aren't feeding a big crowd, it's nice to have the option of making two medium loaves. So keep in mind all of the levain bâtards can be made into either one large or two medium loaves. I find the Potato Levain Bâtards (page 190) and the Walnut Levain Bâtards (page 191) wonderful accompaniments to a weeknight soup or salad, like the Green Salad with Citronette on page 192, so try those as two medium bâtards. But the Sausage-Sage Levain Bâtard (page 195) is especially dramatic as a large bâtard and should be the centerpiece of your next dinner party.

Pain au Levain Dough (page 186)

Flour the work surface. Using a plastic bowl scraper, turn out the dough onto the work surface. Press out the dough, gather the edges, and roll to pre-shape (see photos, Pre-shaping, page 45). Let sit for 10 minutes.

⁕ As mentioned in the headnote, this is a very slack dough, and is best proofed in a basket. Dust a 12-by-5-inch bread basket generously with flour or a mixture of flour and wheat bran (see To Prevent Sticking, Use Flour and Wheat Bran, page 113).

⁕ Using your hands and a bench scraper, shape the dough into a bâtard (see photos, Shaping a Bâtard, pages 52–53) about 4½ by 10 inches. Place the loaf seam side up in the basket.

⁕ Set the loaf in your warm spot, cover with a Cambro container or a plastic tub, and let proof until very puffy, about 2 hours. When

the dough is gently pressed with your fingertip, the impression should remain.

⁕ Meanwhile, position a rack on the lowest rung of the oven and set a cast-iron skillet on it (see Creating Steam in the Oven, page 108, for more on the steam setup). Position a rack above it, place a baking stone on the rack, and preheat the oven to 450°F.

⁕ Dust a peel fairly generously with flour or the flour-bran mixture. Invert the bâtard over the peel and score the loaf with 3 diagonal slashes (see Scoring Dough, page 107).

⁕ Carefully (the handle will be hot) pull the cast-iron skillet out, set the pie plate or steamer basket of ice over or in it, and slide it back in. Transfer the loaf onto the stone and lower the oven temperature to 400°F.

⁕ Bake for 45 to 50 minutes, or until the top is golden brown. To test for doneness, see

Is It Baked?, page 58. The loaf should release easily from the stone, but it will be easier to remove using the peel. Transfer the bread to a cooling rack and let cool completely. For storing options, see How to Store Bread, page 51.

· Note ·
ON MAKING TWO MEDIUM BÂTARDS

As noted in the headnote, any of the levain recipes can be used to make 2 medium bâtards. Because of the smaller size, it will be easier to proof on a linen, unless you have two smaller oval baskets (7¾ by 5½ inch). Also, when the levain dough has additions, it will be even easier to proof on a linen.

Spread a proofing linen (see About Couches or Proofing Linens, page 140) on a large board or on the back of a half sheet pan and dust it generously with flour or a mixture of flour and wheat bran (see To Prevent Sticking, Use Flour and Wheat Bran, page 113). Or dust two 7¾-by-5½-inch oval baskets with flour or the mixture of flour and wheat bran.

After the dough has had its first proof, flour the work surface, turn out the dough, and divide it into 2 equal pieces (about 675 grams/24 ounces each). Press out the dough, gather the edges, and roll to pre-shape (see photos, Pre-shaping, page 45). Let sit for 10 minutes.

Using your hands and a bench scraper, shape one piece of dough into a bâtard (see Shaping a Bâtard, pages 52–53), about 3½ by 9 inches. Set the loaf on the linen and gather and lift the linen to create walls on both sides.

Shape the second piece of dough and lay it next to the other so it shares one of the linen walls. Gather the linen on the other side to make a second wall. Or set the loaves in the baskets seam side up.

Set the loaves in your warm spot, cover with a Cambro container or a plastic tub, and let proof until very puffy, about 2 hours. When the dough is gently pressed with your fingertip, the impression should remain.

Meanwhile, position a rack on the lowest rung of the oven and set a cast-iron skillet on it (see Creating Steam in the Oven, page 108, for more on the steam setup). Position a rack above it, place a baking stone on the rack, and preheat the oven to 450°F.

Dust a transfer peel (if the loaf was proofed on a linen) and a peel fairly generously with flour or the flour-bran mixture. If using a linen, one at a time, turn the bâtards seam side up onto the transfer peel and then turn seam side down onto the peel. If using baskets, turn the bâtards out onto the peel. Score each loaf with 3 diagonal slashes (see Scoring Dough, page 107).

Carefully (the handle will be hot) pull the cast-iron skillet out, set the pie plate or steamer basket of ice over or in it, and slide it back in. Transfer the loaves onto the stone and lower the oven temperature to 400°F.

Bake for about 35 minutes, or until the top is golden brown. To test for doneness, see Is it Baked?, page 58. The loaves should release easily from the stone, but it will be easier to remove using the peel. Transfer the bread to a cooling rack and let cool completely. For storing options, see How to Store Bread, page 51.

POTATO LEVAIN BÂTARDS

Makes 2 medium bâtards

To make this rustic, earthy bread, we keep the skins on the potatoes and cut them into irregular pieces. The recipe will work with most types of potato, but I like russets. They can be cooked just about any way: baked, fried, or boiled. If you boil them, use the cooking water in making the dough: the starch will give a fluffy texture to the finished bread.

The chopped potatoes are pressed onto the dough before it gets pre-shaped. When it comes to a heavy addition like potatoes, you have to give the dough some structure by allowing it to go through the first proof before introducing them.

Pain au Levain Dough (page 186), made with the potato water if you boiled them (see the headnote)

2 cups (320 grams/11.2 ounces) irregular ½- to 1-inch pieces cooked (and cooled) potatoes

Flour the work surface. Using a plastic bowl scraper, turn the dough out onto the work surface. Using a bench scraper, divide the dough into 2 equal pieces (about 675 grams, 23.8 ounces each). Press each piece into a rectangle about 9 by 6 inches. Divide the potatoes between the rectangles (the potatoes will be incorporated as the dough is shaped). Press out each piece of dough, gather the edges, and roll to pre-shape (see photos, Pre-shaping, page 45). Let sit for 10 minutes.

✦ Follow the remaining steps for proofing and baking two levain bâtards (see Note, page 189).

WALNUT LEVAIN BÂTARDS

ᴄᴏ Makes 2 medium bâtards ᴄᴏ

A simple variation on a bread will change it completely. Shaping a loaf into a bâtard versus a boule and adding walnuts rather than walnuts and currants makes for two very different levain loaves. For a cheese plate or a salad, I like a bâtard with walnuts. For a perfect piece of toast, I'll reach for the Walnut Currant Levain Boule (page 200).

Pain au Levain Dough (page 186), taken through the
6-minute mix

1 heaping cup (250 grams/8.8 ounces) walnut halves

Preheat the oven to 350°F.

⁺ Spread the walnuts on a quarter sheet pan and toast until a light golden brown, about 6 minutes. Let cool completely.

⁺ Turn the dough into the lightly oiled bread bowl. Top with the walnuts. With each fold, the walnuts will be incorporated and then evenly distributed throughout the dough.

⁺ Follow the steps for the dough through the first proof. Then follow all steps for two levain bâtards (see Note, page 189).

Courage in the Kitchen
ᴄᴏ MAKING THE MOST OF SLACK DOUGH ᴄᴏ

When the very slack levain dough has something added to it, like any other dough, it becomes much easier to work with. If you don't have the right proofing baskets for levain bâtards, start out with one that has an addition, like the potato, walnut, or sausage. It will be much more forgiving than its plain counterpart. Also, take a look around your kitchen to see what else you might have to proof in. In a pinch, a large bâtard can be shaped in a Pullman pan that has been lined with a couche or dish towels, and smaller ones in loaf pans.

GREEN SALAD
with Citronette

Serves 2 as a main course,
4 as a side salad

I make this salad dressing based on the ingredients I have on hand. It starts with lemons, since we almost always have those. If I feel like herbs, I add them. I might use that nearly forgotten overripe half avocado I always seem to have in the refrigerator. I love goat cheese, but feta is delicious in this salad too—or you can leave the cheese out completely. Bibb is my go-to lettuce, but a mesclun mix, arugula, or a mix of baby kale, tatsoi, and beet greens will all work well with this dressing.

1 lemon, cut in half

¼ teaspoon fine gray or other sea salt, plus more to taste

1 teaspoon Dijon mustard

1 small shallot, coarsely chopped

2 heads Bibb or butter lettuce, any rough outer leaves removed and discarded

½ ripe avocado

About 3 tablespoons extra virgin olive oil

Coarsely cut or torn basil, mint, or oregano leaves (or other herbs or a combination; optional)

About ¼ cup crumbled fresh goat cheese (optional)

Walnut Levain Bâtard (page 191)

Squeeze the lemon (catching any seeds with your other hand) into a large salad bowl. Add the salt, mustard, and shallot. Let sit while you prepare the lettuce.

✦ Separate the heads of lettuce into individual leaves and wash and dry well.

✦ Add the avocado to the lemon juice mixture and use a whisk to break it up. Give everything a turn with the whisk to combine, then slowly whisk in the olive oil until you have an emulsified mixture; the amount of oil you add will depend on the tartness of the lemon. (The dressing will be thick but it should be loose enough to toss with and coat the lettuce leaves.)

✦ Season with additional salt to taste, then add the herbs, if using, and add the greens, tossing to coat. Scatter the cheese over the top, if using, and serve the salad with the sliced bread on the side.

SAUSAGE-SAGE LEVAIN BÂTARD

◈ Makes 1 large bâtard ◈

We originally created this bread for chef Mark Vann of the Sonoma Mission Inn, who wanted a sausage bread similar to one his mother used to make. He used the bread for an olive oil tasting he was doing at B. R. Cohn, a winery and olive oil maker just down the road from the inn. At home, you can use this bread to make great bruschetta or simply eat it by itself—it's not a bread that needs accompaniment.

Pain au Levain Dough (page 186)

226 grams/8 ounces cooked sweet Italian sausage, casings removed if desired, drained well, and coarsely chopped

18 good-sized sage leaves

Flour the work surface. Using a plastic bowl scraper, turn out the dough onto the work surface. Press out the dough, gather the edges, and roll to pre-shape (see photos, Pre-Shaping, page 45). Let sit for 10 minutes

⁺ As mentioned in the headnote for Pain au Levain Bâtard (page 188), this is a very slack dough and is best proofed in a basket. But because of the sausage, it will be easier to work with and can be proofed on a linen.

⁺ Dust a 12-by-5-inch bread basket generously with flour or a mixture of flour and wheat bran (see To Prevent Sticking, Use Flour and Wheat Bran, page 113). Or spread a proofing linen (see About Couches or Proofing Linens, page 140) on a large board or on the back of a half sheet pan and dust generously with flour or a mixture of flour and wheat bran.

⁺ Turn the dough seam side up and press into a rectangle about 12 by 8 inches and top

with the cooked sausage. Coarsely chop 6 of the sage leaves and sprinkle them over the top (the sausage and sage will be incorporated as the dough is shaped).

⁺ Follow the steps for Assembling a Sausage-Sage Levain Bâtard (page 197). Set the loaf in the basket seam side up or on the linen and gather and lift the linen to create walls on both sides.

⁺ Set the loaf in your warm spot, cover with a Cambro container or a plastic tub, and let proof until very puffy, about 2 hours. When the dough is gently pressed with your fingertip, the impression should remain.

⁺ Meanwhile, position a rack on the lowest rung of the oven and set a cast-iron skillet on it (see Creating Steam in the Oven, page 108, for more on the steam setup). Position a rack above it, set a baking stone on the rack, and preheat the oven to 450°F.

recipe continues

+ Dust a transfer peel (if the loaf was proofed on a linen) and a peel fairly generously with flour or the flour-bran mixture. If using a basket, turn the bâtard out onto the peel. If using a linen, turn the bâtard seam side up onto the transfer peel and then turn seam side down onto the peel. Moisten the top of the bâtard with a little water, arrange the remaining 12 sage leaves on the top, and press the leaves gently so they adhere. Sprinkle the top with flour and score with 4 diagonal slashes (see Scoring Dough, page 107).

+ Carefully (the handle will be hot) pull the cast-iron skillet out, set the pie plate or steamer basket of ice over or in it, and slide it back in. Transfer the loaf to the stone and lower the oven temperature to 400°F.

+ Bake for 45 to 50 minutes, or until the top is golden brown. To test for doneness, see Is It Baked?, page 58. The loaf should release easily from the stone, but it will be easier to remove using the peel. Transfer the bread to a cooling rack and let cool completely. For storing options, see How to Store Bread, page 51.

Assembling a Sausage-Sage Levain Bâtard

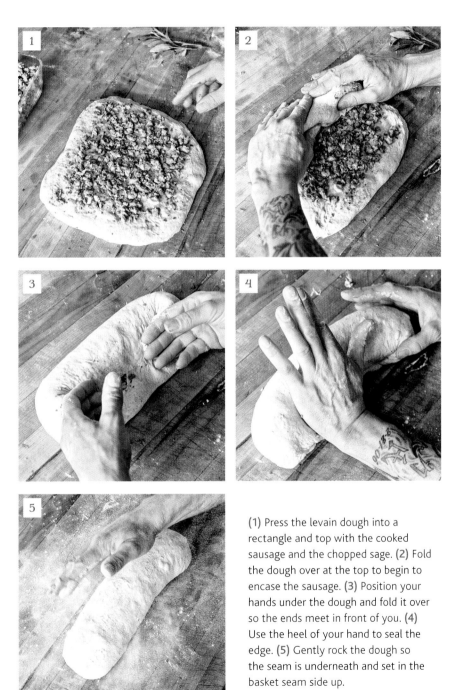

(1) Press the levain dough into a rectangle and top with the cooked sausage and the chopped sage. (2) Fold the dough over at the top to begin to encase the sausage. (3) Position your hands under the dough and fold it over so the ends meet in front of you. (4) Use the heel of your hand to seal the edge. (5) Gently rock the dough so the seam is underneath and set in the basket seam side up.

PAIN AU LEVAIN BOULE

❧ Makes 1 large boule ❧

When Daniel Patterson opened his beloved first restaurant and café, Babette's, in downtown Sonoma in the mid-1990s, he served our Pain au Levain. Our son, Aaron, worked there at the time, and Babette's café was our regular stop almost every Tuesday after selling our breads at the dusk-until-dark Sonoma Farmers' Market. At that time, it wasn't so common to find duck rillettes or cassoulet on a menu, but they were standard at Babette's, along with hamburgers, BLTs, and mouthwatering salads with tart vinaigrettes. Daniel used to request that we bake the levain especially dark. He was one of the few chefs to understand and to want to have his customers appreciate the luscious flavor of sweet butter against almost-burnt crust. The recipe has you bake the boule until it's a rich golden brown, but try it darker if you like. To bake in a cast-iron or clay pot, see Baking Naturally Leavened Breads in Cast-Iron or Clay Pots (page 202).

Pain au Levain Dough (page 186)

Flour the work surface. Using a plastic bowl scraper, turn out the dough. Press out the dough, gather the edges, and roll to pre-shape (see photos, Pre-shaping, page 45). Let sit for 10 minutes.

+ Dust a 9-inch bread basket generously with flour or a mixture of flour and wheat bran (see To Prevent Sticking, Use Flour and Wheat Bran, page 113) or line a large bowl with a generously floured linen dish towel (see About Proofing Baskets, page 114).

+ Using your hands and a bench scraper, shape the dough into a boule (see photos, Shaping a Boule, pages 46–47). Dust the top with flour or the flour-bran mixture and place seam side up in the basket or bowl. If using a basket, cover it with a clean linen dish towel; if using a linen-lined bowl, fold the linen over the dough.

+ Place the dough in your warm spot and let proof until it is very puffy again and the top of the dough has reached the top of the bowl or basket, about 2 hours. When the dough is gently pressed with your fingertip, the impression should remain.

+ Meanwhile, position a rack on the lowest rung of the oven and set a cast-iron skillet on it (see Creating Steam in the Oven, page 108, for more on the steam setup). Position a rack above it, set a baking stone on the rack, and preheat the oven to 450°F.

+ Dust the peel with flour or the flour-bran mixture. If using an unlined basket, invert the basket over the peel and then, if necessary, gently use the bowl scraper to ease the dough onto the peel. If using a lined bowl, use the linen to ease the dough onto the peel. Score the top with 4 parallel commas (see Scoring Dough, page 107).

⁕ Carefully (the handle will be hot) pull the cast-iron skillet out, set the pie plate or steamer basket of ice over or in it, and slide it back in. Transfer the boule to the baking stone and lower the oven temperature to 400°F.

⁕ Bake for 45 to 50 minutes, or until the bread is a rich golden brown. To test for doneness, see Is It Baked?, page 58. Transfer the bread to a cooling rack and let cool completely. For storing options, see How to Store Bread, page 51.

Courage in the Kitchen
∽ HANDLING SLACK DOUGHS ∽

Naturally leavened breads in general, and especially Pain au Levain Bâtard (page 188), are very slack. Don't get discouraged—it's just a question of getting used to handling them. Try making your first one in a cast-iron pot (see Baking Naturally Leavened Breads in Cast-Iron or Clay Pots, page 202). The dough will be proofed in the same vessel it bakes in, so less manipulating is involved in getting a wonderfully shaped boule. Then move on to proofing the bread in a basket and turning it out into a clay pot or tagine (see Baking in a Clay Pot or Tagine, page 102), a method that is also very forgiving. Finally, give free-form baking, where you'll move the dough from proofing basket to peel to baking stone, a go.

WALNUT-CURRANT LEVAIN BOULE

I can't think of a cheese in the world that wouldn't taste great partnered with this walnut-currant boule. Many of our finest restaurant accounts feature this bread on their cheese plates. Chock-full of nuts and fruit, it's not only delicious, but it also keeps longer than most breads—thanks to the fruit and nuts. It makes delicious toast too.

¾ cup plus 1 tablespoon (130 grams/4.6 ounces) currants

1¾ cups (175 grams/6 ounces) walnuts

Pain au Levain Dough (page 186), taken through the 6-minute mix

Preheat the oven to 350°F.

+ To plump the currants, put them in a small bowl. Bring ½ cup (120 grams/4.2 ounces) water to a boil, pour it over the currants, and let sit for at least 30 minutes. Drain.

+ Meanwhile, spread the walnuts on a half sheet pan and toast until a light golden brown, about 6 minutes. Let cool completely.

+ Turn out the mixed dough into the lightly oiled bread bowl. Top with the plumped currants and walnuts and gently press them into the dough. With each fold, the currants and walnuts will be incorporated and then evenly distributed throughout the dough. (Don't be tempted to incorporate them in the mixer; the currants will discolor the dough.)

+ Follow the remaining steps for Pain au Levain Boule (page 198) and bake as directed.

Baking Naturally Leavened Breads in Cast-Iron or Clay Pots

TO BAKE IN A CAST-IRON POT

After the dough has been shaped, place it seam side down in a fairly generously oiled or sprayed cast-iron pot. Cover the pot with a lightly oiled or sprayed piece of plastic wrap. Place in a warm, draft-free spot to proof until the dough is very puffy, 2 to 3 hours.

Meanwhile, position a rack in the lower third of the oven, place a baking stone on it, and preheat the oven to the temperature specified in the recipe.

Score the top of the bread as directed. Put the lid on the pot, lower the oven temperature if directed, and bake for about half the total baking time with the lid on. Remove the lid and bake for an additional 15 to 25 minutes, or until the top of the bread is a rich golden brown. Turn out onto the stone for 5 to 10 minutes to brown and crisp the sides and bottom more evenly and to ensure that the bread is baked through. Transfer the bread to a cooling rack and let cool completely.

Alternately, proof the dough in a basket or lined bowl and set the pot with the lid on the stone during the preheat. Then carefully remove the pot from the oven, fairly generously oil it, transfer the proofed dough to the pot, score, cover, and bake, as directed. Baking times will be less than if the pot hadn't been heated.

TO BAKE IN A CLAY POT OR TAGINE

After the dough has been shaped for a boule, place it seam side up in a generously dusted 9-inch bread basket or a large bowl lined with a generously dusted linen dish towel (see About Proofing Baskets, page 114). Dust the top with flour (or a mixture of flour and wheat bran; see To Prevent Sticking, Use Flour and Wheat Bran, page 113). If using a basket, cover with a clean linen dish towel; or if using a linen-lined bowl, fold the linen over the top.

Place the dough in your warm spot to proof until the dough is very puffy again and the top has reached the top of the bowl or basket, 2 to 3 hours.

Meanwhile, position a rack in the lower third or the bottom of the oven (depending on the height of the pot) and place a baking stone on it. Fill a clay pot or the bottom of a tagine about three-quarters full with water, place it on the stone, and preheat the oven to 450°F. The pot should preheat for at least 1 hour.

If your sink is not close to your oven, set a large pot on the stovetop so there's a place nearby to dump out the hot water. Carefully remove the clay pot or tagine from the oven and pour the water out. Dry the pot and fairly generously oil or spray it.

Transfer the proofed dough to the pot and score the bread as directed. Put the lid on the pot, lower the oven temperature if directed, and bake for about half of the total baking time with the lid on, then remove the lid and bake for an additional 15 to 25 minutes, or until the top of the bread is a rich golden brown. Turn out onto the stone for 5 to 10 minutes to brown and crisp the sides and bottom more evenly to ensure that the bread is baked through. Transfer the bread to a cooling rack and let cool completely.

GRAPE-HARVEST LEVAIN BOULE

ى Makes 1 large boule ص

This beautiful loaf was originally made for the Sonoma Mission Inn's annual auction, which takes place during grape harvest. The first time I tried this, I mixed red wine into the water for the dough, a great destination for the remains of an unfinished bottle. The bakery was thick with the heavenly aroma. For the inn, we made a 2-kilo (almost 4½-pound) boule decorated with tiny Pinot Noir grapes and leaves from the vines at the ranch. For the home version we go a bit smaller, but no less dramatic.

Pain au Levain Dough (page 186), made with half wine and half water (275 grams/9.7 ounces/1 cup plus 3 tablespoons of each, at 75°F/24°C)

A small bunch of small organic grapes or Zante currants (see Note)

3 or 4 organic grape leaves

Flour the work surface. Using a plastic bowl scraper, turn out the dough. Press out the dough, gather the edges, and roll to pre-shape (see photos, Pre-shaping, page 45). Let sit for 10 minutes.

⁕ Dust a 9-inch bread basket generously with flour (for this loaf I prefer to use flour alone, rather than a mixture of flour and wheat bran). The beautiful markings from a basket will elevate this loaf, so I recommend proofing it in an unlined basket rather than a lined bowl. Remove any leaves from the bunch of grapes and trim the tip of the vine (or the currant stem) to about ¼ inch.

⁕ Using your hands and a bench scraper, shape the dough into a boule (see photos, Shaping a Boule, pages 46–47). Cut a small gutter in the top of the loaf and lay in the bunch of grapes. Moisten the top of the boule

with a little water, arrange the leaves around the bunch, and press on the leaves gently so they adhere (see photos, Garnishing a Grape-Harvest Levain Boule, page 204).

⁕ Sprinkle the top of the boule generously with flour and carefully turn, seam side down, into the bread basket.

⁕ Follow the remaining steps for Pain au Levain Boule (page 198) through final proof. Dust the peel with flour and score by cutting a circle about an inch in from the edge (see Scoring Dough, page 107). Bake as directed.

· Note ·
ON ORGANIC INGREDIENTS

It is very important to use organic grapes or currants and leaves in this recipe.

Garnishing a Grape-Harvest Levain Boule

(1) Cut a small gutter in the top of the shaped boule and lay in a bunch of grapes. (2) Moisten the top of the boule with a little water, arrange the leaves around the bunch, and press on the leaves gently so they adhere. (3) Flour the top generously before carefully flipping the boule over and placing it in a generously floured basket to proof.

PUMPERNICKEL RYE BOULE

⁓ Makes 1 large boule ⁓

Many old-style recipes for pumpernickel bread call for the grain drink Postum, which is what makes for the dark-colored bread you may have seen for sale in commercial bakeries. Our version of pumpernickel gets its flavor from a combination of rye and pumpernickel flours, which gives it a dark caramel color, a chewy texture, nuttiness from the rye, and a hearty tanginess.

Rye flour doughs can proof faster than wheat doughs and so require a watchful eye; they can go from just right to overproofed really quickly. To bake in a cast-iron or clay pot, see Baking Naturally Leavened Breads in Cast-Iron or Clay Pots (page 202).

Firm Starter (page 156)	82 g	2.9 oz	¼ cup plus 1 Tbsp
Water at 80°F/27°C	551 g	19.4 oz	2¼ cups plus 1½ Tbsp
All-purpose flour	429 g	15 oz	3 cups plus 1 Tbsp
Rye flour	211 g	7.4 oz	2 cups plus 2 Tbsp
Pumpernickel flour	41 g	1.4 oz	¼ cup plus 1 Tbsp
TOTAL FLOUR	681 g	23.8 oz	5½ cups
Fine gray salt	20 g	0.7 oz	1 Tbsp plus ¼ tsp
Caraway seeds (optional)	5.4 g	0.2 oz	1 Tbsp
TOTAL WEIGHT	1,339 g/1.33 kg	47 oz/3 lbs	

Lightly oil or spray a deep 4½- to 5-quart ceramic or glass bread bowl.

✦ Put the starter in the bowl of a stand mixer fitted with the paddle attachment. Add the water and pulse a few times on low speed until the starter is broken up and the mixture appears frothy, about 30 seconds. Add the flours and pulse a few times on the lowest setting (to keep the flours from flying out of the bowl), then mix on low speed for 2 minutes. Remove the paddle attachment, scraping any dough from the paddle back into the bowl with a plastic bowl scraper, and let sit, uncovered, for 20 minutes.

✦ Scrape down the sides of the bowl with the bowl scraper and add the salt. Fit the mixer with the dough hook, and mix on low speed for 5½ minutes. Add the caraway seeds, if using, and mix for 30 seconds. This is a sticky dough. Using the bowl scraper, turn the dough into the bread bowl. Cover tightly with a lightly oiled or sprayed piece of plastic wrap and let sit for 30 minutes.

✦ For the first fold, wet your hands, then loosen the dough from the sides and bottom of the bowl and fold it underneath itself from left to right and then from top to bottom (see photos, Folding the Dough, pages 160–161). Cover and let sit for 30 minutes.

◆ For the second fold, repeat as for the first fold. Cover and let sit for 30 minutes.

◆ For the third and final fold, repeat the folding as before. Cover and let proof in a warm, draft-free spot (see Creating Your Warm Spot, page 17) until there is bubbling on the surface, 2 to 3 hours.

◆ Flour the work surface. Using the bowl scraper, turn out the dough. Press out the dough, gather the edges, and roll to pre-shape (see photos, Pre-shaping, page 45). Let sit for 10 minutes.

◆ Dust a 9-inch bread basket generously with flour or a mixture of flour and wheat bran (see To Prevent Sticking, Use Flour and Wheat Bran, page 113) or line a large bowl with a generously floured linen dish towel (see About Proofing Baskets, page 114).

◆ Using your hands and a bench scraper, shape the dough into a boule (see photos, Shaping a Boule, pages 46–47). Dust the top with flour or the flour-bran mixture and place seam side up in the basket or bowl. If using a basket, cover it with a clean linen dish towel; if using a linen-lined bowl, fold the linen over the dough.

◆ Place the dough in your warm spot and let proof until it is very puffy again and the top of the dough has reached the top of the bowl or basket, 1 to 1½ hours. When the dough is gently pressed with your fingertip, the impression should remain.

◆ Meanwhile, position a rack on the lowest rung of the oven and set a cast-iron skillet on it (see Creating Steam in the Oven, page 108, for more on the steam setup). Position a rack above it, set a baking stone on the rack, and preheat the oven to 450°F.

◆ Dust the peel with flour or the flour-bran mixture. If using an unlined basket, invert the basket over the peel and then, if necessary, use the bowl scraper to gently ease the dough onto the peel. If using a lined bowl, use the linen to ease the dough onto the peel. Score the top with an S with 2 slashes across the center (see photos, Scoring Dough, page 107).

◆ Carefully (the handle will be hot) pull the cast-iron skillet out, set the pie plate or steamer basket of ice over or in it, and slide it back in. Transfer the boule to the baking stone and lower the oven temperature to 400°F.

◆ Bake for about 45 minutes, or until the bread is a rich golden brown. To test for doneness, see Is It Baked?, page 58. Transfer the bread to a cooling rack and let cool completely. For storing options, see How to Store Bread, page 51.

PANE INTEGRALE
(WHEAT BREAD) BOULE

∽ Makes 1 medium boule ∽

If you or your kids think you don't like whole-grain bread, this loaf will absolutely change your minds. It's chewy, rich, and surprisingly sweet. While the texture is hearty, there will still be air holes in the finished loaf. I recommend toasting slices and topping them with crumbled goat cheese, cured salmon, capers, and pickled onions.

Firm Starter (page 156)	79 g	2.8 oz	¼ cup plus 1 Tbsp
Water at 80°F/27°C	471 g	16.6 oz	2 cups
Whole wheat flour	340 g	12 oz	2¼ cups plus 3 Tbsp
Bread flour	113 g	4 oz	¾ cup plus 3 Tbsp
Pumpernickel flour	57 g	2 oz	¼ cup plus 2½ Tbsp
Cracked wheat	57 g	2 oz	¼ cup
TOTAL FLOUR	567 g	20 oz	3¾ cups plus ½ Tbsp
Fine gray salt	19 g	0.7 oz	1 Tbsp
Honey	40 g	1.4 oz	2 Tbsp
TOTAL WEIGHT	1,176 g/1.17 kg	41.5 oz/2.5 lbs	

Lightly oil or spray a deep 4½- to 5-quart ceramic or glass bread bowl.

⁕ Put the starter in the bowl of a stand mixer fitted with the paddle attachment. Add the water and mix on low speed until the starter is broken up and the mixture appears frothy, about 30 seconds. Add the flours and pulse a few times on the lowest setting (to keep the flours from flying out of the bowl), then mix on low speed for 2 minutes. Remove the paddle attachment, scraping any dough from the paddle back into the bowl with a plastic bowl scraper, and let sit, uncovered, for 20 minutes.

⁕ Scrape down the sides of the bowl with the bowl scraper and add the salt. Fit the mixer with the dough hook and mix on low speed

for 5½ minutes. Add the honey and mix for 30 seconds. This is a loose dough. Using the bowl scraper, turn the dough into the bread bowl. Cover tightly with a lightly oiled or sprayed piece of plastic wrap and let sit for 30 minutes.

⁕ For the first fold, wet your hands, then loosen the dough from the sides and bottom of the bowl and fold it underneath itself from left to right and then from top to bottom (see photos, Folding the Dough, pages 160–161). Cover and let sit for 30 minutes.

⁕ For the second fold, repeat as for the first fold. Cover and let sit for 30 minutes.

⁕ For the third and final fold, repeat the folding as before. Cover and let proof in a warm, draft-free spot (see Creating Your Warm Spot, page 17) until there is bubbling on the surface, 2 to 3 hours.

＊ Flour the work surface. Using the bowl scraper, turn out the dough. Press out the dough, gather the edges, and roll to pre-shape (see photos, Pre-shaping, page 45). Let sit for 10 minutes.

＊ Dust a 9-inch bread basket generously with flour or a mixture of flour and wheat bran (see To Prevent Sticking, Use Flour and Wheat Bran, page 113) or line a large bowl with a generously floured linen dish towel (see About Proofing Baskets, page 114).

＊ Using your hands and a bench scraper, shape the dough into a boule (see photos, Shaping a Boule, pages 46–47). Dust the top with flour or the flour-bran mixture and place it seam side up in the basket or bowl. If using a basket, cover it with a clean linen dish towel; if using a linen-lined bowl, fold the linen over the dough.

＊ Place the dough in your warm spot and let proof until it is very puffy again and the top of the dough has reached the top of the bowl or basket, about 2 hours. When the dough is gently pressed with your fingertip, the impression should remain.

＊ Meanwhile, position a rack on the lowest rung of the oven and set a cast-iron skillet on it (see Creating Steam in the Oven, page 108, for more on the steam setup). Position a rack above it, set a baking stone on the rack, and preheat the oven to 450°F.

＊ Dust the peel with flour or the flour-bran mixture. If using an unlined basket, invert the basket over the peel and, if necessary, use the bowl scraper to gently ease the dough out onto the peel. If using a lined bowl, use the linen to ease the dough onto the peel. Score the top with an asterisk (see Scoring Dough, page 107).

＊ Carefully (the handle will be hot) pull the cast-iron skillet out, set the pie plate or steamer basket of ice over or in it, and slide it back in. Transfer the boule to the baking stone and lower the oven temperature to 400°F.

＊ Bake for about 50 minutes, or until the bread is a rich golden brown. To test for doneness, see Is It Baked?, page 58. Transfer the bread to a cooling rack and let cool completely. For storing options, see How to Store Bread, page 51.

· Note ·
ON BAKING IN A CAST-IRON SKILLET

Because this loaf is smaller than the other boules, it bakes up better in a smaller pan. After it is shaped, set it in a fairly generously oiled or sprayed 8-inch cast-iron skillet, put it in your warm spot, and cover with a Cambro container or a plastic tub. Continue as directed in the recipe.

SEEDED WHEAT BREAD DOUGH

⁓ Makes 1.33 kilograms/3 pounds ⁓

In terms of popularity, our Seeded Wheat is second only to our Meyer Lemon–Rosemary bread. The rustic loaf was originally created for Thomas Keller at The French Laundry to serve as a counterpoint to his rich sauces. The flavor and texture of this bread are very satisfying.

We have many customers for whom this is their everyday bread. One of our very first farmers' market customers on Saturday mornings is always Tom, with his oversized glasses, a hank of light auburn hair that comes slightly over his forehead, and a big smile. A visual artist, he is all about aesthetics, and he prefers a round loaf. So for Tom, every week, we make our seeded wheat boule. I think he's onto something; it does make a very beautiful boule. At the café, we use it untoasted for a vegetarian sandwich, and we serve it toasted and slathered with butter for poached eggs in the morning.

The dough contains almost as much water as it does flour, and there's honey too—this results in a loose dough. Not to worry: the seeds and polenta will absorb the water, so by the time you shape the dough, it will be much firmer and more manageable than when you started. The dough can be shaped into a boule or a bâtard with equally happy results.

Sesame seeds	38 g	1.3 oz	¼ cup
Sunflower seeds	38 g	1.3 oz	¼ cup
Pumpkin seeds	38 g	1.3 oz	¼ cup
Polenta	42 g	1.5 oz	¼ cup
Flaxseeds	40 g	1.4 oz	¼ cup
Firm Starter (page 156)	76 g	2.7 oz	¼ cup plus ½ Tbsp
Water at 80°F/27°C	474 g	16.7 oz	2 cups
Whole wheat flour	408 g	14.4 oz	2¾ cups plus 2½ Tbsp
Bread flour	136 g	4.8 oz	1 cup plus 2 Tbsp
TOTAL FLOUR	544 g	19.2 oz	4 cups plus ½ Tbsp
Fine gray salt	21 g	0.7 oz	1 Tbsp plus ½ tsp
Honey	22 g	0.8 oz	1 Tbsp
TOTAL WEIGHT	1,333 g/1.33 kg	46.9 oz/3 lbs	

recipe continues

Lightly oil or spray a deep 4½- to 5-quart ceramic or glass bread bowl.

* Preheat the oven to 350°F.

* Spread the sesame, sunflower, and pumpkin seeds on a quarter sheet pan and toast until a pale golden brown, 5 to 7 minutes. Transfer to a plate and let cool completely, then combine with the polenta and flaxseeds.

* Put the starter in the bowl of a stand mixer fitted with the paddle attachment. Add the water and mix on low speed until the starter is broken up and the mixture appears frothy, about 30 seconds. Add the flours and pulse a few times on the lowest setting (to keep the flours from flying out of the bowl), then mix on low speed for 2 minutes. Remove the paddle attachment, scraping any dough from the paddle back into the bowl with a plastic bowl scraper, and let sit, uncovered, for 20 minutes.

* Scrape down the sides of the bowl with the bowl scraper and add the salt. Fit the mixer with the dough hook and mix on low speed for 5½ minutes. Add the honey and mix for 30 seconds. Add the seeds and polenta and mix for about 30 seconds, or until incorporated.

* Using the bowl scraper, turn the dough into the bread bowl. Cover tightly with a lightly oiled or sprayed piece of plastic wrap and let sit for 30 minutes.

* For the first fold, wet your hands, then loosen the dough from the sides and bottom of the bowl and fold it underneath itself from left to right and then from top to bottom (see photos, Folding the Dough, pages 160–161). Cover and let sit for 30 minutes.

* For the second fold, repeat as for the first fold. Cover and let sit for 30 minutes.

* For the third and final fold, repeat the folding as before. Cover and let proof in a warm, draft-free spot (see Creating Your Warm Spot, page 17) until there is bubbling on the surface, 2 to 3 hours.

* The dough is ready to be pre-shaped and shaped for the Seeded Wheat Bread Bâtard (page 215) or the Seeded Wheat Bread Boule (page 213).

SEEDED
WHEAT BREAD BOULE

∽ Makes 1 large boule ∽

To bake in a cast-iron or clay pot, see Baking Naturally Leavened Bread in Cast-Iron or Clay Pots (page 202).

Seeded Wheat Bread Dough (page 211)

Flour the work surface. Using a plastic bowl scraper, turn out the dough. Press out the dough, gather the edges, and roll to pre-shape (see photos, Pre-shaping, page 45). Let sit for 10 minutes.

✦ Dust a 9-inch bread basket generously with flour or a mixture of flour and wheat bran (see To Prevent Sticking, Use Flour and Wheat Bran, page 113) or line a large bowl with a generously floured linen dish towel (see About Proofing Baskets, page 114).

✦ Using your hands and a bench scraper, shape the dough into a boule (see photos, Shaping a Boule, pages 46–47). Dust the top with flour or the flour-bran mixture and place seam side up in the basket or bowl. If using a basket, cover it with a clean linen dish towel; if using a linen-lined bowl, fold the linen over the dough.

✦ Place the dough in your warm spot and let proof until it is very puffy and the top of the dough has reached the top of the bowl or basket, 2 to 3 hours. When the dough is gently pressed with your fingertip, the impression should remain.

✦ Meanwhile, position a rack on the lowest rung of the oven and set a cast-iron skillet on it (see Creating Steam in the Oven, page 108, for more on the steam setup). Position a rack above it, set a baking stone on the rack, and preheat the oven to 450°F.

✦ Dust the peel with flour or the flour-bran mixture. If using an unlined basket, invert the basket over the peel and then, if necessary, use the bowl scraper to gently ease the dough onto the peel. If using a lined bowl, use the linen to ease the dough onto the peel. Score the top with 4 diagonal slashes (see photos, Scoring Dough, page 107).

✦ Carefully (the handle will be hot) pull the cast-iron skillet out, set the pie plate or steamer basket of ice over or in it, and slide it back in. Transfer the boule to the baking stone and lower the oven temperature to 400°F.

✦ Bake for about 55 minutes, or until the bread is a rich golden brown. To test for doneness, see Is It Baked?, page 58. Transfer the bread to a cooling rack and let cool completely. For storing options, see How to Store Bread, page 51.

SEEDED WHEAT BREAD BÂTARD

ை Makes 1 large bâtard ை

Once the seeds expand and absorb liquid from this dough, it becomes very malleable, making this an ideal bread with which to perfect your shaping techniques.

Seeded Wheat Bread Dough (page 211)

Flour the work surface. Using a plastic bowl scraper, turn the dough onto the work surface. Press out the dough, gather the edges, and roll to pre-shape (see photos, Pre-shaping, page 45). Let sit for 10 minutes.

✦ Spread a proofing linen (see About Couches or Proofing Linens, page 140) on a large board or on the back of a half sheet pan and dust generously with flour or a mixture of flour and wheat bran (see To Prevent Sticking, Use Flour and Wheat Bran, page 113). Or dust a 12-by-5-inch bread basket fairly generously with flour or a mixture of flour and wheat bran.

✦ Using your hands and a bench scraper, shape the dough into a bâtard (see photos, Shaping a Bâtard, pages 52–53), about 4½ by 10 inches. Set on the linen and gather and lift the linen to create walls on both sides.

✦ Set the loaf in your warm spot, cover with a Cambro container or a plastic tub, and let proof until very puffy, about 2 hours. When the dough is gently pressed with your fingertip, the impression should remain.

✦ Meanwhile, position a rack on the lowest rung of the oven and set a cast-iron skillet on it (see Creating Steam in the Oven, page 108, for more on the steam setup). Position a rack above it, set a baking stone on the rack, and preheat the oven to 450°F.

✦ Dust a transfer peel (if the loaf was proofed on a linen) and a peel with flour or the flour-bran mixture. If using a linen, turn the bâtard seam side up onto the transfer peel and then turn seam side down onto the peel. If using a basket, invert the bâtard over the peel. Score the top with 4 diagonal slashes (see Scoring Dough, page 107).

✦ Carefully (the handle will be hot) pull the cast-iron skillet out, set the pie plate or steamer basket of ice over or in it, and slide it back in. Transfer the loaf to the stone and lower the oven temperature to 400°F.

✦ Bake for about 50 minutes, or until the top is golden brown. To test for doneness, see Is It Baked?, page 58. The loaf should release easily from the stone, but it will be easier to remove using the peel. Transfer the bread to a cooling rack and let cool completely. For storing options, see How to Store Bread, page 51.

MAKING AN ENTRANCE

One day I received a call from Elena Ferretti, senior producer of Martha Stewart's TV show. Elena asked if she could stop by later that day to chat about our possibly being on the show. Since I am a serious Martha fan, this set my heart to thumping. Elena and I hit it off immediately, and she booked us. Filming would start in ten days! Really? Ten days to get ready for prime time.

Were we ready? I should say not. Our old farmhouse was being scraped on the south side, getting prepped for new paint. In fact, not one part of our house or bakery was camera ready, but we weren't about to turn this down. Luckily, it was October, the peak of Indian summer and one of the most beautiful times of the year in Sonoma County. The garden was full of deep-orange French pumpkins, and we had a happy, healthy flock of chickens (any Martha fan knows she loves chickens). The grapes had been harvested, the days were growing shorter, the leaves had turned, and the filtered light created a warm haze over the ranch. We could do it. And we had a crew of bakers, plus family and friends, at the ready to help us pull it together.

So we did what we could to make the place more presentable, and the film crew arrived three days before the shoot to set up the lighting. Their attention to detail was inspiring; they had a warm and friendly sense of fun and an interest in what we were doing that put us right at ease.

All was going well until the day of the shoot, when Elena got a call from Gallo Winery, where Martha was shooting at the time. The Gallo shoot was running over and they wanted to keep her a little longer. It was a warm day, the dough was moving fast, and we were running out of time. Elena was horrified but kept her cool and insisted that the team get Martha here by no later than 2 P.M. The next thing I knew, Ed had maps out and was on the phone with a helicopter pilot lining up coordinates.

We ate lunch without Martha, doing our best to maintain a calm façade. Then, in the distance, there was the unmistakable sound of a helicopter, circling the ranch and beginning its descent into the middle of the field. Suddenly, like in a scene from M*A*S*H, there she was, chopper blades blowing her hair and a big smile on her face (how could you not love this woman?). Then Martha was tromping through our dusty field in her elegant sandals, stopping to admire the chickens.

If I was worried about her judging us, I was wasting my energy. Martha was comfortable here; she stopped to greet the dogs and take a moment to say hello to everyone. She is the real deal, and I was so relieved not to be disappointed. Aaron and Linda showed her how to shape the rosemary bread. She got her hands stuck in the dough only once. When the loaves were ready to go into the oven, Aaron loaded her up, and there she was, maneuvering an eight-foot-long peel piled with six 1½-pound boules into the oven. She impressed all of us with her strength and determination. As Ed said, she is a real trouper, and so far, no one has topped Martha's helicopter arrival at our ranch.

POLENTA BÂTARD

✥ Makes 1 large bâtard ✥

As I do with most of the breads in this chapter, I prefer to make a large loaf of polenta bread. But it can be divided in half and made into two medium bâtards (see Note). It is crispy-crunchy on the outside and buttery and delicate on the inside. Because of that, it makes exceptional French toast and grilled sandwiches. We also use it for our Crouton Rags (page 225). If you've ever grilled cooked polenta, you'll understand how heavenly this bread tastes when it's toasted.

The secret to getting great texture in the finished loaf is cooking (and cooling) the polenta before adding it to the dough, then mixing it in at the last minute so there are golden deposits of polenta throughout the bread.

Years ago, we had an apprentice named Maria, from Colombia, who came to make bread with us. She had just graduated from The Culinary Institute in New York, and she wanted more real-time experience before she went home to open her own bakery. Polenta bread was Maria's favorite. Cooked polenta gets a skin on it as it cools, and we always peel the skin off and save it for the chickens or use it for compost. But Maria peeled off that top layer, rolled it up, and ate it with butter and salt; it was her own special treat. She would say, with a grin, that it reminded her of arepas, Colombian corn cakes.

Firm Starter (page 156)	83 g	2.9 oz	¼ cup plus 1 Tbsp
Water at 80°F/27°C	415 g	14.6 oz	1¾ cups
Bread flour	643 g	22.7 oz	5¼ cups plus 2 Tbsp
All-purpose flour	48 g	1.7 oz	⅓ cup
TOTAL FLOUR	691 g	24.4 oz	5½ cups plus 3⅓ Tbsp
Fine gray salt	21 g	0.7 oz	1 Tbsp plus ½ tsp
Polenta (recipe follows)	152 g	5.4 oz	½ cup plus 2 Tbsp
TOTAL WEIGHT	1,362 g/1.36 kg	48 oz/3 lbs	

140 grams (5 ounces/1 cup) uncooked polenta for coating the top of the bâtard

Lightly oil or spray a deep 4½- to 5-quart ceramic or glass bread bowl.

✦ Put the starter in the bowl of a stand mixer fitted with the paddle attachment. Add the water and mix on low speed until the starter is broken up and the mixture appears frothy, about 30 seconds. Add the flours and pulse a few times on the lowest setting (to keep the flours from flying out of the bowl), then mix on low speed for 2 minutes. Remove the paddle attachment, scraping any dough from the paddle back into the bowl with a plastic bowl scraper, and let sit, uncovered, for 20 minutes.

+ Fit the mixer with the dough hook, add the salt, and pulse a few times to begin to incorporate the salt. Crumble the polenta over the top and mix on low speed for 6 minutes. (Surprisingly, the polenta will actually loosen the mixture.) Using the bowl scraper, turn the dough into the bread bowl. Cover tightly with a lightly oiled or sprayed piece of plastic wrap and let sit for 30 minutes.

+ For the first fold, wet your hands, then loosen the dough from the sides and bottom of the bowl and fold it underneath itself from left to right and then from top to bottom (see photos, Folding the Dough, pages 160–161). Cover and let sit for 30 minutes.

+ For the second fold, repeat as for the first fold. Cover and let sit for 30 minutes.

+ For the third and final fold, repeat the folding as before. Cover and let proof in a warm, draft-free spot (see Creating Your Warm Spot, page 17) until there is bubbling on the surface, 2 to 3 hours.

+ Flour the work surface. Using the bowl scraper, turn the dough out onto the work surface. Press out the dough, gather the edges, and roll to pre-shape (see photos, Pre-shaping, page 45). Let sit for 10 minutes.

+ Spread the uncooked polenta on a small tray. Spread a proofing linen (see About Couches or Proofing Linens, page 140) on a large board or on the back of a half sheet pan and dust the linen generously with flour. Or dust a 12-by-5-inch bread basket fairly generously with flour.

+ Using your hands and a bench scraper, shape the dough into a bâtard (see photos, Shaping a Bâtard, pages 52–53), about 4½ by 10 inches. With a damp towel, moisten the top and sides of the bâtard, then dip into the polenta to coat the top. Set the loaf on the linen and gather and lift the linen to create walls on both sides (see About Couches or Proofing Linens, page 140).

+ Set the loaf in your warm spot, cover with a Cambro container or a plastic tub, and let proof until very puffy, about 2 hours. When the dough is gently pressed with your fingertip, the impression should remain.

+ Meanwhile, position a rack on the lowest rung of the oven and set a cast-iron skillet on it (see Creating Steam in the Oven, page 108, for more on the steam setup). Position a rack above it, set a baking stone on the rack, and preheat the oven to 450°F.

+ Dust a transfer peel (if the loaf was proofed on a linen) and a peel with flour. Turn the bâtard seam side up onto the transfer peel and then turn seam side down onto the peel. If using a basket, invert the bâtard over the peel. Starting about an inch from the end of the loaf, cut a long comma down the side of the loaf. Repeat along the opposite side (see Scoring Dough, page 107).

+ Carefully (the handle will be hot) pull the cast-iron skillet out, set the pie plate or steamer basket of ice over or in it, and slide it back in. Transfer the loaf onto the stone and lower the oven temperature to 400°F.

+ Bake for about 50 minutes, or until the top is golden brown. To test for doneness, see Is It Baked?, page 58. The loaf should release easily from the stone, but it will be easier to remove using the peel. Transfer the bread to a cooling rack and let cool completely. For storing options, see How to Store Bread, page 51.

ON MAKING TWO MEDIUM BÂTARDS

Spread a proofing linen (see About Couches or Proofing Linens, page 140) on a large board or on the back of a half sheet pan and dust it generously with flour. Or dust two 7¾-by-5½-inch oval baskets with flour.

After the dough has had its first proof, flour the work surface, turn out the dough, and divide it into 2 equal pieces (about 675 grams/24 ounces each). Press out the dough, gather the edges, and roll to pre-shape (see photos, Pre-shaping, page 45). Let sit for 10 minutes.

Using your hands and a bench scraper, shape one piece of dough into a bâtard (see photos, Shaping a Bâtard, pages 52–53), about 3 by 10 inches. Set the loaf on the linen and gather and lift the linen to create walls on both sides. Shape the second piece of dough and lay it next to the other so it shares one of the linen walls. Gather the linen on the other side to make a second wall.

Set the loaves in your warm spot, cover with a Cambro container or a plastic tub, and let proof until very puffy, 2 to 3 hours. When the dough is gently pressed with your fingertip, the impression should remain.

Meanwhile, position a rack on the lowest rung of the oven and set a cast-iron skillet on it (see Creating Steam in the Oven, page 108, for more on the steam setup). Position a rack above it, place a baking stone on the rack, and preheat the oven to 450°F.

Dust a transfer peel (if the loaf was proofed on a linen) and a peel fairly generously with flour or the flour-bran mixture. If using a linen, one at a time, turn the bâtards seam side up onto the transfer peel and then turn seam side down onto the peel. If using baskets, turn out the bâtards onto the peel. Starting about an inch from the end, cut a long comma down the side of each loaf. Repeat along the opposite side (see Scoring Dough, page 107).

Carefully (the handle will be hot) pull the cast-iron skillet out, set the pie plate or steamer basket of ice over or in it, and slide it back in. Transfer the loaves onto the stone and lower the oven temperature to 400°F.

Bake for about 40 minutes, or until the top is golden brown. To test for doneness, see Is it Baked?, page 58. The loaves should release easily from the stone, but it will be easier to remove using the peel. Transfer the bread to a cooling rack and let cool completely. For storing options, see How to Store Bread, page 51.

POLENTA

Makes 660 grams/23 ounces/about 2¾ cups

This recipe makes more polenta than is needed for the Polenta Bâtard, but if you are going to the effort, it is worth making extra. Leftover polenta is delicious cut into squares and fried in butter or oil, or brushed with oil or butter and grilled. Top with goat cheese to make an easy canapé.

4 cups (935 grams/33 ounces) water

1 cup (140 grams/5 ounces) polenta

1 teaspoon (6 grams/0.2 ounce) fine gray or kosher salt

About 1 tablespoon unsalted butter, at room temperature, for the plastic wrap

Unsalted butter or oil for cooking polenta squares (optional)

Bring the water to a boil in a large saucepan. Whisk in the polenta and the salt, then continue to whisk until the mixture begins to thicken, about 2 minutes. Adjust the heat as needed to keep it at a low simmer, switch to a wooden spoon, and cook, stirring continuously, until you can see the bottom of the pan when you run the spoon through the polenta, about 12 minutes.

Transfer the ½ cup plus 2 tablespoons (152 grams) of polenta needed for the bread to a small container and let cool. The remaining polenta can be served warm or cooled and cut into squares for frying.

For the squares, line an 8-by-8-inch baking dish with plastic wrap and butter the plastic wrap. Spread the polenta in the pan, being sure to reach the corners. To prevent a skin from forming on top, press a piece of plastic wrap directly against the polenta. Refrigerate for at least a few hours, or for up to 2 days.

To fry the polenta, cut it into 3-inch squares. Fry in melted butter or oil in a nonstick frying pan over medium heat, flipping once, until light golden brown on both sides and heated through, 10 to 12 minutes. Serve hot.

TOMATO BREAD SOUP

❧ Serves 4 to 6 ❧

In the summer, when you have garden tomatoes coming out your ears, this is a soup to rely on. Being bakers, we, of course, always have a lot of bread on hand, so Tomato Bread Soup is one of our go-to meals. Traditionally it's made with stale bread, but we toast the croutons, so you don't need to have stale bread for this recipe. Still, the soup makes brilliant use of a loaf that is a day or two old.

Tomato Bread Soup smells great and looks beautiful, and the flavors are bright and refreshing. Using a combination of tomato varieties and colors makes the soup especially attractive. It's best when at least some of the tomatoes are high-acid varieties, like Early Girl.

2 pounds ripe tomatoes, preferably a mixture, including Early Girls

6 garlic cloves

⅓ cup extra virgin olive oil, plus extra for drizzling

15 medium basil leaves, plus a few more for garnish (optional)

Pinch of red pepper flakes

Kosher salt

4 cups chicken broth or 3 cups broth plus 1 cup red wine

Freshly ground black pepper

Crouton Rags (recipe follows)

Bring a large pot of water to a boil. Blanch the tomatoes in the boiling water until the skins are starting to burst. Remove from the water and let sit until cool enough to handle. Meanwhile, blanch the garlic cloves in the boiling water until tender.

✦ Remove and discard the tomato skins. Halve the tomatoes and squeeze the juice and seeds into a bowl. Set the tomatoes aside. Strain the juice; discard the seeds.

✦ Heat the oil in a large saucepan or small pot over medium-high heat. The oil should be fairly hot—this is more of a stir-fry than a sauté. Add the tomatoes, garlic, basil, pepper flakes, and a generous pinch of salt and stir until the garlic has caramelized, about 6 minutes.

recipe continues

and reserved tomato juice and bring to a simmer. Cook until the liquid has reduced slightly and the raw taste of the tomatoes (and wine) has mellowed, about 10 minutes. Season to taste with pepper and additional salt. Add half the croutons to the soup, remove from the heat, and let stand for 10 minutes.

+ Ladle the soup into wide bowls. Tear a little fresh basil over the top of each bowl, if using, drizzle with olive oil, and top with the remaining croutons.

CROUTON RAGS

Makes a generous 3 cups

I call these Crouton Rags because the bread is torn apart, giving them an appealing tattered texture. I think the croutons are best made with a Polenta Bâtard (page 219), but they're also tasty made with a Pain de Campagne Bâtard (page 163). Don't try to make all the croutons the same size—a range from 1 to 2½ inches across is good. I keep them on the smaller side to use in the Della Panzanella (page 227) or make them slightly larger for the Tomato Bread Soup. Tear the bread into pieces a bit bigger than you want the crouton to be; they shrink up a bit when toasted.

Half a large or 1 medium Polenta Bâtard (page 219), preferably day-old, but fresh is fine

Extra virgin olive oil

Kosher salt and freshly ground black pepper

Use your fingers to tear out irregular tufts of bread.

Heat a generous film of olive oil in a large skillet over medium to medium-high heat. Add a generous pinch of salt and pepper to it, then add the bread in a single layer (toasting in batches if needed). Cook, tossing or stirring the croutons occasionally and adjusting the heat to keep them from getting too dark, until they have a nice golden color, about 5 minutes. Remove from the heat and drain on paper towels.

The croutons are best the day they are made.

DELLA PANZANELLA

⌘ Serves 4 ⌘

Now that you're baking bread like crazy, you need some creative and delicious ideas for using up your leftovers. There are many ways to make this Italian tomato-bread salad; Italians are masters at leftover bread recipes. Tuscans use untoasted stale bread torn into chunks and hydrated with the tomatoes' juices and olive oil. I prefer making it with Crouton Rags (page 225). The croutons offer some extra flavor and, mainly, a little crunch. I like croutons made from a Polenta Bâtard (page 219) for this recipe, but you could use a Pain de Campagne Bâtard (page 163), a Semolina Oval Loaf (page 230), or even a Traditional (Sweet) Baguette (page 142).

This salad should only be made with ripe, full-flavored tomatoes. You can use cherry tomatoes, heirloom tomatoes, or any combination of vine-ripened. If you don't grow tomatoes yourself, head to your local farmers' market.

2 pounds ripe tomatoes, cut into large chunks

Extra virgin olive oil

Kosher salt

2 tablespoons finely chopped shallots

15 to 20 medium basil leaves, torn

An 8-ounce ball of fresh mozzarella

2 cups Crouton Rags (page 225)

Arugula, baby spinach, and baby romaine
(as much or as little as you want)

Freshly ground black pepper

1 to 2 tablespoons red wine vinegar

Place the tomatoes in a wide salad bowl, drizzle generously with olive oil, and sprinkle generously with salt. Toss with your hands to be sure the oil and salt are evenly distributed. Add the shallots and basil, toss again, and let sit for about 5 minutes.

✦ Tear the mozzarella into bite-sized pieces and add to the tomato mixture. Add about two-thirds of the croutons and toss to mix. Scatter the arugula, spinach, and romaine over the top, then sprinkle with (in this order) olive oil, salt and pepper, and the vinegar. Toss well.

✦ Taste for seasoning, scatter the rest of the croutons over the top, and serve. The salad is best when just made; otherwise the croutons start to soften.

WET STARTER

Makes 645 grams/22.6 ounces

The Semolina Oval Loaf (page 230) and the Ciabatta (page 234) use this wet starter. I love the flavor and texture it gives the Ciabatta, and I love the way it helps the Semolina Loaf maintain its scrumptious golden color. Plan on making the starter twenty-four hours in advance. This recipe makes more than is needed, but it is always preferable to make more with a starter, to ensure that it is active. The Firm Starter (page 156) looks like biscuit dough, but this wet starter is actually pourable—think pancake batter. For accurate measurements, it should be weighed. If you insist on measuring by volume, use damp fingers and damp measuring spoons and cups.

This starter is much more volatile than the Firm Starter. It gets sour very quickly because the sugars get eaten up fast. If the starter develops a gray color on top, it is still fine to use, but if it turns pink, it has gone bad and should be discarded.

Although I give instructions here for feeding the starter, I don't recommend keeping it going unless you'll be baking with it every day. Keeping it going involves remembering to feed it every day, and it seems unnecessary when you can so easily create the wet starter overnight using your firm starter. If you do indeed decide to try maintaining one, you'll get the best results when the starter has been fed recently.

Firm Starter (page 156)	69 g	2.4 oz	¼ cup
Water at 75° to 80°F/24° to 27°C	276 g	9.7 oz	1 cup plus 3 Tbsp
All-purpose flour	300 g	10.5 oz	2 cups plus 2 Tbsp

In the bowl of a stand mixer fitted with the paddle attachment, mix the starter and water together on the lowest speed to begin to break up the starter, about 1 minute. Add the flour and mix to begin to bring them together, about 1 minute. This will be a loose mixture. Remove the paddle attachment, scraping any starter from the paddle back into the bowl with a plastic bowl scraper.

 + Fit the mixer with the dough hook and mix on low speed for 2 minutes. Transfer to a very lightly oiled storage container. Cover with the lid or with a lightly oiled or sprayed piece of plastic wrap and let sit at room temperature for 24 hours.

 + The starter is ready to be used.

· Note ·
ON FEEDING THE STARTER

With damp hands, pinch off 105 grams (3.7 ounces/½ cup plus 1 tablespoon) of the starter and put it in the bowl of a stand mixer fitted with the paddle attachment. Add 240 grams (8.5 ounces/1 cup) water and mix on the lowest speed to begin to break up the starter, about 1 minute. Add 300 grams (10.5 ounces/2 cups plus 2 tablespoons) all-purpose flour and mix to begin to bring the mixture together, about 1 minute. Remove the paddle attachment, scraping any starter from the paddle back into the bowl with the bowl scraper.

✦ Fit the mixer with the dough hook and mix on low speed for 2 minutes. Transfer to a very lightly oiled storage container. Cover with the lid or with a lightly oiled or sprayed piece of plastic wrap and let sit at room temperature for 24 hours before using.

SEMOLINA OVAL LOAF

↝ Makes 1 large oval loaf ↜

This is the cakiest of all the breads we make. It has air holes, of course, but they're smaller and the crumb is finer. The dough starts out stiff, but don't be tempted to add more water. It will feel softer after it rests, and by the time you shape the dough, it will have a very springy feel—almost buoyant.

Wet Starter (page 228)	95 g	3.3 oz	½ cup
Water at 80°F/27°C	435 g	15.3 oz	1¾ cups plus 2 Tbsp
Durum flour	245 g	8.6 oz	1½ cups plus 3 Tbsp
Bread flour	245 g	8.6 oz	2 cups plus 1 Tbsp
Semolina flour	16 g	0.6 oz	1½ Tbsp
TOTAL FLOUR	506 g	17.8 oz	3¾ cups plus 1½ Tbsp
Fine gray salt	16 g	0.6 oz	2¾ tsp
TOTAL WEIGHT	1,052 g/1.05 kg	37 oz/2.3 lbs	

148 grams (5.2 ounces/1 cup) sesame seeds for coating the top of the oval

Lightly oil or spray a deep 4½- to 5-quart ceramic or glass bread bowl.

✦ Put the starter in the bowl of a stand mixer fitted with the paddle attachment. Add the water and mix on low speed until the starter is broken up and the mixture appears frothy, about 30 seconds. Add the flours and pulse a few times on the lowest setting (to keep the flours from flying out of the bowl), then mix on low speed for 2 minutes. Remove the paddle attachment, scraping any dough from the paddle back into the bowl with a plastic bowl scraper, and let sit, uncovered, for 20 minutes.

✦ Scrape down the sides of the bowl with the bowl scraper and add the salt. Fit the mixer with the dough hook and mix on low speed for 6 minutes. This is a springy dough. Using the bowl scraper, turn the dough into the bread bowl. Cover tightly with a lightly oiled or sprayed piece of plastic wrap and let sit for 30 minutes.

✦ For the first fold, wet your hands, then loosen the dough from the sides and bottom of the bowl and fold it underneath itself from left to right and then from top to bottom (see photos, Folding the Dough, pages 160–161). Cover and let sit for 30 minutes.

✦ For the second fold, repeat as for the first fold. Cover and let sit for 30 minutes.

✦ For the third and final fold, repeat the folding as before. Cover and let proof in a warm, draft-free spot (see Creating Your Warm Spot, page 17) until there is bubbling on the surface, 2 to 3 hours.

✦ Flour the work surface. Using the bowl scraper, turn out the dough. Press out the dough,

recipe continues

gather the edges, and roll to pre-shape (see Pre-shaping, page 45). Let sit for 10 minutes. Spread the sesame seeds on a small tray.

+ With a damp towel, moisten the top of the boule, then dip it into the sesame seeds. Place the oval, seam side down, in the pot. Fairly generously oil or spray the bottom and sides of a 3- to 4-quart oval cast-iron pot. Using your hands and a bench scraper, shape the dough into an oval (see Shaping a Bâtard, pages 52–53). Place the oval seam side down in the pot. Cover the pot with a lightly oiled or sprayed piece of plastic wrap and place in your warm spot to proof until the dough is very puffy, about 2 hours. When the dough is gently pressed with your fingertip, the impression should remain.

+ Meanwhile, position a rack in the lower third of the oven, set a baking stone on it, and preheat the oven to 450°F.

+ Remove the plastic wrap and score the top with an S with 2 slashes across the center (see Scoring Dough, page 107).

+ Put the lid on the pot, set it on the baking stone, and lower the oven temperature to 400°F. Bake for 30 minutes. Remove the lid and bake for an additional 20 minutes, or until the top of the bread is a rich golden brown. Carefully remove the bread from the pot and set it on the stone to bake for about 5 minutes to brown and crisp the sides and bottom more evenly. To test for doneness, see Is It Baked?, page 58. Transfer the bread to a cooling rack and let cool completely. For storing options, see How to Store Bread, page 51.

· Why Air Holes? ·

The interior structure, or crumb, of a well-crafted loaf of bread should be laced with pockets of carbon dioxide that formed during the process of dough development. These air holes create the lacy interior and shiny string webbing of gluten strands that are the signature of properly made naturally leavened bread. Every step in handling the dough, from mixing and autolyse to careful stretching and folding and, finally, the gentle shaping and proofing, is designed to capture air in the dough. You should even be able to see the sheen of the lace and webbing in the crust where the bread has been scored.

When I cut into a loaf, the crumb is the first thing I look at. If I see a tight crumb, I know there was a problem. Perhaps the bread wasn't proofed long enough, or it was overproofed. It could have been mixed too long or at too high a speed. Or perhaps there was a hydration error and the

dough was too dry. The dough could have missed some folds or been shaped incorrectly, or the oven wasn't hot enough. At the bakery, when there is a problem with a bread, we go over every step of the process to see if we can isolate the cause. Maybe we had a bad batch of flour. In any case, we sure don't want to repeat the mistake the next day.

There is a different kind of hole that can occur in the interior of a loaf of bread, an undesirable hole called a "baker's grave." This type of hole is immediately recognizable and will usually run the length of the loaf. It occurs when flour makes its way inside the loaf during shaping. Just as flour helps keep dough from sticking to your work surface, it can also prevent dough from sticking to itself. See Avoiding Baker's Graves, page 111.

CIABATTA

∾ Makes 1 large slipper-shaped loaf ∾

The word *ciabatta* means "slipper" in Italian, and it refers to the shape of this wide, flat loaf. This bread is in a class of its own, with a thin crust and an interior that's moist and perfumed with olive oil. Its shape and flavor make it a natural for garlic bread or, sliced thick, for dipping into soup or sopping up sauces. With hamburgers, the bread's crusty outside will keep the meat juices inside.

This dough is so wet it makes me laugh when I shape it—unless I'm swearing at it. Until you let it know who's the boss, it will try to run all over the table. A bench scraper is definitely your best friend here.

Wet Starter (page 228)	60 g	2.1 oz	¼ cup plus 1 Tbsp
Firm Starter (page 156)	40 g	1.4 oz	2½ Tbsp
Water at 80°F/27°C	461 g	16.2 oz	1¾ cups plus 3 Tbsp
All-purpose flour	576 g	20.3 oz	4 cups plus 2 Tbsp
TOTAL FLOUR	576 g	20.3 oz	4 cups plus 2 Tbsp
Fine gray salt	15 g	0.5 oz	2½ tsp
Extra virgin olive oil	19 g	0.7 oz	1½ Tbsp
TOTAL WEIGHT	1,171 g/1.17 kg	41.2 oz/2.6 lbs	

Semolina flour for dusting

Lightly oil or spray a deep 4½- to 5-quart ceramic or glass bread bowl.

✦ Put the starters in the bowl of a stand mixer fitted with the paddle attachment. Add the water and mix on low speed until the starters are broken up and the mixture appears frothy, about 30 seconds. Add the flour and pulse a few times on the lowest setting (to keep the flour from flying out of the bowl), then mix on low speed for 2 minutes. Remove the paddle attachment, scraping any dough from the paddle back into the bowl with a plastic bowl scraper, and let sit, uncovered, for 20 minutes.

✦ Scrape down the sides of the bowl with the bowl scraper and add the salt and olive oil. Fit the mixer with the dough hook and mix on low speed for 6 minutes. This is a very wet dough. Using the bowl scraper, turn the dough into the bread bowl. Cover tightly with a lightly oiled or sprayed piece of plastic wrap and let sit for 30 minutes.

✦ For the first fold, wet your hands, then loosen the dough from the sides and bottom of the bowl and fold it underneath itself from left to right and then from top to bottom (see photos, Folding the Dough, pages 160–161). Cover and let sit for 30 minutes.

• For the second fold, repeat as for the first fold. Cover and let sit for 30 minutes.

• For the third and final fold, repeat the folding as before. Cover and let proof in a warm, draft-free spot (see Creating Your Warm Spot, page 17) until there is bubbling on the surface, 2 to 3 hours.

• Flour the work surface. Using the bowl scraper, turn out the dough. Press out the dough, gather the edges, and roll to pre-shape (see photos, Pre-shaping, page 45). Let sit for 10 minutes.

• Lightly oil or spray the back of a half sheet pan or a cookie sheet (with no sides). Sprinkle the area where you will put the dough generously with semolina flour.

• Using your hands and a bench scraper, rock and push the dough into the classic slipper shape. Transfer to the prepared pan.

• Set the loaf in your warm spot, cover with a Cambro container or a plastic tub, and let proof until puffy, 2 to 3 hours. When the dough is gently pressed with your fingertip, the impression should remain.

• Meanwhile, position a rack on the lowest rung of the oven and set a cast-iron skillet on it (see Creating Steam in the Oven, page 108, for more on the steam setup). Position a rack above it, set a baking stone on the rack, and preheat the oven to 450°F.

• Set the sheet pan on the stone. Carefully (the handle will be hot) pull the cast-iron skillet out, set the pie plate or steamer basket of ice over or in it, and slide it back in. Bake the bread until the top is golden brown, about 35 minutes.

• The loaf should release easily from the sheet pan at this point, but it will be easier to remove using a peel. Slide the ciabatta off the pan, and bake it on the stone for about 5 minutes to brown and crisp the bottom more evenly. To test for doneness, see Is It Baked?, page 58. Transfer the bread to a cooling rack and let cool completely. For storing options, see How to Store Bread, page 51.

CRACKERS, BREADSTICKS, PIZZA DOUGHS & FLATBREADS

THE FIRST BREADS WERE FLATBREADS. Every corner of the globe has them, and no matter where on earth they originated, they are more alike than different. Clearly, though, the local grains dictate the breads, and the available food sources influence the cuisine that is served with them. Originally cooked over open fire, or in small tandoori-like ovens, flatbreads were among the foods that were traditionally prepared by women, who gathered to manage the fires and share in meal preparation. When soft, like Chapati (page 263) or Naan (page 257), flatbreads are the perfect utensil for picking up bits of food. When hard, like Swedish Knäckebröd (page 267), the bread becomes an edible plate.

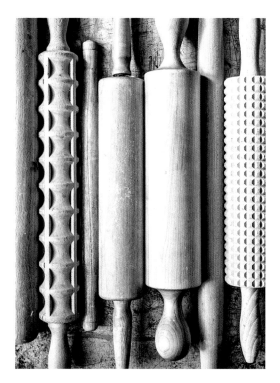

Although we don't usually think of pizza as a flatbread, it is exactly that, and it may be the most favorite food internationally. Everyone loves pizza, and when you make it at home, it's always much better, because you can make it exactly the way you like it. We all have our favorite flavors and styles. I like a thin crust with just a few simple topping ingredients, usually including fresh basil and goat cheese. My daughter likes to pile the ingredients on, the wilder the better—lots of sauce, lots of meat, and lots of cheese. So in our family, we each make our own small pizzas, and it becomes a friendly competition to see who will create the most beautiful and delicious one. This chapter also includes a recipe for the thin Italian flatbread known as *piadina*. We've included the recipe for our favorite filling, a tuna salad with peperoncini, but you should know that a piadina is just as versatile as a pizza, limited only by your imagination.

Few people think of making crackers at home. There are so many varieties available at grocery stores or gourmet shops—so why bother? Although I often share that sentiment, would you rather have a homemade cookie or a store-bought one? If you prefer homemade, consider that making crackers is no more trouble than baking cookies, and the difference is just as profound. Add to that the fun you'll have making them, and the opportunity it affords you to play with shapes, sizes, and flavors to customize and create the perfect cracker for your menu. A bunch of tall Breadsticks (page 246) or long crispy Durum Crackers (page 243) to serve with drinks is a delightful and mouthwatering start to a dinner party. A crystal bowl mounded with Spicy Cheddar Crackers (page 240)—the perfect combo of crunch and flavor—is so irresistible that it should be served with a warning label. Next time you have a dinner party, don't make just the dessert, make the crackers too.

❧ TECHNIQUES ☙

Rolling out cracker dough (pages 240 and 243)
Rolling out breadsticks (page 247)
Shaping a pizza (page 250)

Shaping naan (page 248)
Shaping chapati (page 263)
Rolling out knäckebröd (page 267)

❧ EQUIPMENT NEEDED ☙

* Scale
* Stand mixer with whisk, paddle, and dough hook attachments
* Food processor
* Baking stone
* Thermometer
* Plastic bowl scraper
* Bench scraper
* Plastic wrap
* 3-quart bread bowl (optional)

* 4½- to 5-quart bread bowl
* Half sheet pans or cookie sheets (with no sides)
* Grill or grill pan
* 10-inch cast-iron skillet
* Parchment paper or 2 silicone baking mats
* Rolling pin
* Knäckebröd rolling pin (optional; see the pin on the far right in the photo opposite)

* Chapati rolling pin and board (optional)
* Spatula and/or palette knife
* Pastry brush
* Spray bottle
* Peel
* Pizza cutter
* Fluted pastry wheel
* Cooling racks
* Bottle screw top or 1-inch round cookie cutter

SPICY CHEDDAR CRACKERS

Makes 384 small crackers

Don't be put off by the large yield of this recipe: the crackers are tiny, and you will eat a handful before you know it—and then go back for more. The crackers can, of course, be cut larger, and if you do that, you'll need to bake them a few minutes longer. They can also be cut into different shapes. If tightly wrapped, the dough can be refrigerated for up to two days, or it can be frozen for up to a month. When I make a batch, I like to freeze half the dough to save for last-minute drop-ins. We eat these so fast that there are rarely leftovers, but sealed airtight and stored at room temperature, the crackers will keep for four or five days.

Red pepper flakes give the crackers a definite and delicious kick, but they can be left out if you'll be serving the crackers to young children.

All-purpose flour	280 g	9.8 oz	2 cups
Fine gray salt	9 g	0.3 oz	1½ tsp
Red pepper flakes	4.5 g	0.16 oz	2 tsp
Unsalted butter, cut into ½-inch cubes, cold	112 g	4 oz	8 Tbsp
Cheddar cheese (preferably half white and half yellow), grated	450 g	16 oz	
Cold water	about 30 g	1 oz	2 Tbsp

Put the flour, salt, and red pepper flakes into a food processor and pulse to combine. Add the butter and mix until you have a crumbly mixture. Add the cheese and mix until the cheese is broken down and completely incorporated. With the processor running, stream in the water, processing until the dough comes together.

+ Position the racks in the upper and lower thirds of the oven and preheat the oven to 350°F. Line two half sheet pans with parchment paper or silicone baking mats.

+ Divide the dough in half. (The dough can be worked with right away or wrapped individually in plastic wrap and refrigerated for up to 2 days or frozen for up to 1 month; if frozen, defrost completely in the refrigerator before using.)

+ Dust the work surface with flour. Use a rolling pin to roll one piece of dough into a rectangle, slightly larger than 12 by 16 inches, adding flour as needed to the work surface and rolling pin to keep the dough from sticking. Turn the dough as you roll to keep it at an even thickness. Dock the dough with a fork. Using a pizza cutter, or a sharp knife, trim the edges to form a 12-by-16-inch rectangle. Cut the dough into 1-inch-wide squares. Using a spatula or

a palette knife, transfer the squares to one of the lined sheet pans. Repeat with the second piece of dough and the second pan. (The pieces will all fit on the sheet pans, but they will be close together. You can also spread them farther apart on the pans, and bake in batches as needed.)

＋ Bake for about 15 minutes, rotating the pans once from top to bottom and front to back midway through baking. The crackers will puff up as they bake, but you will know they're done when you smell the cheese. The crackers will look more golden brown, but they will not be firm at this point. Remove from the oven and let cool on the sheet pans. If the crackers are not completely crisp once cool, they can be popped back in the oven for a few minutes.

＋ Store in an airtight container for up to 5 days. (If the crackers soften, they can be popped back into the oven to crisp them up.)

DURUM CRACKERS

~ Makes sixty-four 10-by-1-inch crackers ~

If you like your crackers on the crispy side, these are for you. The thinner you roll the dough, the crisper the cracker will be. You can cut the crackers into any shape that suits your fancy. I like to roll the dough into large rectangles and cut it into long strips with a pizza cutter or a fluted pastry wheel. The herbs you use will add not only flavor but also beauty, as the crackers are so thin you can almost see through them, and the herbs create a dramatic visual impact.

Durum flour	300 g	10.6 oz	2 cups plus 1 Tbsp
Fine gray salt	6 g	0.2 oz	1 tsp
Warm water (90° to 100°F/32° to 38°C)	240 g	8.5 g	1 cup
Extra virgin olive oil (plus additional for brushing the top; optional)	30 g	1 oz	2 Tbsp plus 1 tsp
Finely chopped basil or parsley, or combination	16 g	0.6 oz	¼ cup
Ground sumac, red pepper flakes, or sweet or smoked paprika (optional)	1.5 g	0.05 oz	½ tsp

Flaky sea salt or fleur de sel for sprinkling

In the bowl of a stand mixer fitted with the paddle attachment, combine the flour and salt. With the mixer running on the lowest speed, add the water and then the oil and mix until the dough just comes together, about 30 seconds. Add the basil and sumac, if using (or whatever herb and spice you choose), and mix to incorporate evenly, about 30 seconds.

+ Flour the work surface. The dough will be very sticky. Using a plastic bowl scraper, turn the dough out onto the work surface. Knead it a few times, then wrap in plastic wrap. Let sit at room temperature for at least 30 minutes, or up to 4 hours.

+ Position a rack in the center of the oven and preheat the oven to 450°F. Line a half sheet pan with parchment paper or a silicone baking mat.

+ Divide the dough into quarters. (The pieces can be wrapped individually in plastic wrap and refrigerated for up to 2 days; they will come to room temperature very quickly when you are ready to use them.) Wrap 3 of the pieces and keep refrigerated while you make the first batch.

+ Dust the work surface with flour. Use a rolling pin to roll one piece of dough into a large, thin rectangle, adding flour as needed to the work surface and rolling pin to keep the dough from sticking. Turn the dough as you roll to keep it at an even thickness, until it is about 12 by 18 inches. If at any time the dough offers resistance, cover it with plastic wrap and let it rest for 5 to 10 minutes, then begin again; you can roll out another piece while the dough rests. Each time you return to the dough, you will be able to roll it a little thinner.

+ Use a knife to trim the dough to a rectangle about 10 by 16 inches. Brush off the excess flour and set the dough on the lined sheet pan. Using a pizza cutter or a fluted pastry wheel, cut the dough crosswise into 1-inch strips. (Be careful not to press too hard if using the pizza cutter; you only want to cut through the dough, not the mat!) The dough should be cut all the way through, but if there are a few areas that are only scored (which can happen closer to the edges of the pan, where it is more difficult to roll all the way to the edge of the dough), that's OK. Don't try to separate the crackers; you will break them apart after they bake. Sprinkle with sea salt.

+ Spritz the top of the dough lightly with water. Bake, staying close to the oven and watching very carefully: the thinnest parts of the crackers will start to brown in 2 to 3 minutes, and the crackers should be done in 4 to 6 minutes. (Because of the thinness of the dough and the quick baking time, it is best to bake only one pan at a time.)

+ Let the pan sit on a cooling rack for about 5 minutes, then break the crackers apart, set them directly on the cooling rack, and let cool completely.

+ Repeat with the remaining dough.

+ Store the crackers in a covered container at room temperature for up to 3 days.

Breadsticks (page 246) and Durum Crackers (cut using a fluted pastry wheel)

BREADSTICKS
(KNOBBY WITCHES' FINGERS)

ↄ Makes 32 breadsticks ↄ

I love the crunch of breadsticks, and I like the drama of really long sticks. Once I start rolling them out, oftentimes I end up getting them longer than the pan. One day when I got carried away, instead of pinching the ends off, I just put a few bends in the breadsticks and baked them like that. The result looked just like the knobby fingers of the witch I remember seeing in my illustrated version of the childhood fairy tale, or, rather, horror story *Hansel and Gretel*. So I named them Knobby Witches' Fingers. Of course, you have the option of making these sticks straight and elegant. Either way, put them in a tall glass, serve with wine or sherry, and watch them disappear.

Adding finely chopped fresh herbs to the dough makes the breadsticks look really beautiful, and I like playing with the flavors, but they are still delicious without the herbs.

All-purpose flour	350 g	12.3 oz	2½ cups
Instant yeast	12 g	0.4 oz	1 Tbsp plus ½ tsp
Fine gray salt	6 g	0.2 oz	1 tsp
Finely ground black pepper	2.5 g	0.08 oz	1 tsp
Grated Parmigiano-Reggiano or Grana Padana cheese	40 g	1.4 oz	¼ cup plus 2 Tbsp
Mix of finely chopped herbs, such as chives, parsley, and thyme (optional)	8 g	0.3 oz	2 Tbsp
Hot sauce, such as Cholula	2.5 g	0.08 oz	½ tsp
Warm water (80° to 90°F/27° to 32°C)	240 g	8.4 oz	1 cup

Olive oil for brushing

Flaky salt or fleur de sel and freshly ground black pepper (for sprinkling)

Sesame seeds for sprinkling (optional)

For the dough: Lightly oil a deep 4½- to 5-quart ceramic or glass bread bowl.

+ Put the flour, yeast, salt, pepper, cheese, herbs, and hot sauce in the bowl of a stand mixer fitted with the whisk attachment and mix to combine. Switch to the dough hook and, with the mixer running on low speed, add the water and mix until the mixture comes away from the sides and gathers around the hook, about 2 minutes.

+ Dust the work surface with flour. Using a plastic bowl scraper, turn the dough out and knead for a few minutes until it's no longer sticky. Put the dough into the bread bowl and turn it so it's oiled all over. Cover tightly with a lightly oiled or sprayed piece of plastic wrap, set in a warm, draft-free spot (see Creating Your Warm Spot, page 17), and let proof until doubled, about 1½ hours.

+ Meanwhile, position the racks in the upper and lower thirds of the oven and preheat the oven to 425°F. Line the backs of two half sheet pans or cookie sheets with parchment paper or silicone baking mats.

+ Lightly flour the work surface and turn out the dough again. Pat it out into a rectangle about 12 by 9 inches. Divide the dough into 4 pieces. Work with one piece at a time, keeping the others covered with a linen dish towel.

+ Using your index finger as a guide, cut one piece of dough into 8 equal pieces, about the width and length of your finger. Roll each piece under your palms until it is the length of a half sheet pan and set the strips on one of the pans, leaving space between them (about as wide as the breadsticks). You can leave the strips straight, but I like to let them bend as I put them on the pans, or even pinch them in a few spots to make them really knobby.

+ Repeat with a second piece of dough, putting the strips on the second pan. Brush the breadsticks with olive oil. Sprinkle with salt and pepper, and with sesame seeds, if you like.

+ Bake the breadsticks for 15 to 20 minutes, or until golden and firm. Transfer to a cooling rack and let cool completely.

+ Repeat with the remaining dough.

+ The breadsticks are best the day they are made, but they will keep in an airtight container (you may need to break them in half to fit) for up to 3 days.

HURRY-UP PIZZA DOUGH

Makes about 1 kilogram/2.2 pounds, enough for 2 large (12-inch), 4 medium (10-inch), or 8 small (8-inch) pizzas

Throw this dough together, let it proof for as little as 60 minutes, and you're ready to go. In the time you might spend waiting for a pizza delivery, you can make your very own crust—and it will taste so much better. The dough is sticky when it first comes off the mixer but becomes more manageable as you work with it. Though dough made the night before and allowed to proof for a day will have more complex flavor, this quick dough is also excellent.

Pizza dough freezes well: any extra can be sealed in plastic and stored in the freezer for a month. Leftover dough can also be used to make Tuna Melt Piadina (page 255).

All-purpose flour	550 g	19.4 oz	3¾ cups plus 3 Tbsp
Fine gray salt	10 g	0.3 oz	1¾ tsp
Instant yeast	6 g	0.2 oz	1¾ tsp
Water, at room temperature (65° to 70°F/18° to 21°C)	400 g	14 oz	1½ cups plus 3½ Tbsp
Extra virgin olive oil	60 g	2 oz	¼ cup plus ½ tsp

Lightly oil or spray a deep 4½- to 5-quart ceramic or glass bread bowl.

⁜ Combine the flour, salt, and yeast in the bowl of a stand mixer fitted with the paddle attachment. Add the water and oil and pulse a few times on the lowest setting to begin to incorporate them, then mix on low speed to combine, about 2 minutes. Remove the paddle attachment, scraping any dough from the paddle back into the bowl, and scrape down the sides of the bowl with a plastic bowl scraper.

⁜ Fit the mixer with the dough hook and mix on low speed for 6 minutes.

⁜ Flour the work surface. Using the bowl scraper, turn the dough out onto the work surface. The dough will be sticky and loose at this point. Knead for a few minutes, until it feels silky to the touch.

⁜ Transfer it to the prepared bowl, cover the bowl with a lightly oiled or sprayed piece of plastic wrap, and set in a warm, draft-free spot (see Creating Your Warm Spot, page 17) to proof until puffy and about doubled, 45 minutes to 1 hour.

⁜ The dough is ready to be shaped for pizzas (see Weber Family Pizza, page 250).

OVERNIGHT PIZZA DOUGH

Makes 1.4 kilograms/3 pounds, enough for 3 large (12-inch),
6 medium (10-inch), or 12 small (8-inch) pizzas

The basic steps for this recipe are the same as for the Hurry-Up Pizza Dough (opposite), but this dough gets an overnight fermentation in the fridge. The wait is worth it: you'll have a dough with a superior texture and a deeper flavor. To make the dough, use the largest bowl you have—about three times the volume of the dough.

All-purpose flour	750 g	26 oz	5¼ cups plus 2 Tbsp
Fine gray salt	10 g	0.3 oz	1¾ tsp
Instant yeast	6 g	0.2 oz	1¾ tsp
Water, at room temperature (65° to 70°F/18° to 21°C)	540 g	19 oz	2¼ cups plus 1 Tbsp
Extra virgin olive oil	90 g	3.2 oz	¼ cup plus 2½ Tbsp
Honey	30 g	1 oz	1½ Tbsp

Lightly oil or spray a deep 4½- to 5-quart ceramic or glass bread bowl.

+ Combine the flour, salt, and yeast in the bowl of a stand mixer fitted with the paddle attachment. Add the water, oil, and honey and pulse a few times on the lowest setting to begin to incorporate them, then mix on low speed to combine, about 2 minutes. Remove the paddle attachment, scraping any dough from the paddle back into the bowl, and scrape down the sides of the bowl with a plastic bowl scraper.

+ Fit the mixer with the dough hook and mix on low speed for 6 minutes.

+ Using the bowl scraper, transfer the dough to the prepared bowl. The dough will be sticky and loose. Cover the bowl with a lightly oiled or sprayed piece of plastic wrap. Refrigerate for at least 10 hours, or, preferably, up to 24 hours.

+ The dough is ready to be shaped (see Weber Family Pizza, page 250).

WEBER FAMILY PIZZA

Makes 2 or 3 large, 4 to 6 medium, or 8 to 12 small pizzas depending on the dough used

The beauty of pizza is that the dough is just waiting for you to customize it into your own favorite creation. In that spirit, I keep a few different toppings on hand. We start out with either the Hurry-Up Pizza Dough or the Overnight Pizza Dough and a simple tomato sauce, then we add whatever strikes our fancy that day.

Tomato Sauce (makes about 2⅔ cups)

Two 28-ounce cans whole San Marzano or plum tomatoes

¼ cup plus 2 tablespoons extra virgin olive oil

6 medium garlic cloves

Kosher salt

8 basil leaves, torn

½ teaspoon red pepper flakes

2 tablespoons unsalted butter

All-purpose flour for dusting

Overnight or Hurry-Up Pizza Dough (page 248 or 249)

Semolina flour or medium-ground cornmeal for dusting the peel

Assorted toppings: fresh mozzarella, basil leaves, grated Parmigiano-Reggiano, crumbled fresh goat cheese, thinly sliced Fontina, Kalamata olives, and/or thinly sliced salami, pepperoni, or prosciutto

Position a rack in the lower third of the oven, set a baking stone on it, and preheat the oven to 425°F. The oven should preheat for at least 30 minutes before you start to make the pizzas.

+ For the tomato sauce: Drain the tomatoes in a sieve set over a bowl; reserve the juice. Then halve the tomatoes, remove and discard the seeds, and tear into large pieces.

+ Heat the olive oil in a large sauté pan over medium heat. Add the garlic, reduce the heat to medium-low, and cook, turning occasionally, until the garlic begins to color, about 5 minutes. Remove the garlic and discard.

recipe continues

+ Add the tomatoes to the garlic oil, along with a generous pinch of salt, the basil, and red pepper flakes. Cook, stirring occasionally, until the tomatoes caramelize, about 7 minutes. Add the reserved juice, lower the heat, and simmer until the mixture has thickened, 25 to 30 minutes.

+ Stir in the butter and season to taste with additional salt. Remove from the heat. (The sauce can be made up to 3 days ahead and refrigerated, covered.)

+ Flour the work surface. Using a plastic bowl scraper, turn out the dough. Using a bench scraper, divide the dough into the desired number of pieces: 3 for large pizzas, 4 for medium, or 8 for small. Shape into balls: shape larger ones as if shaping a boule (see photos, Shaping a Boule, pages 46–47), medium and smaller ones as if forming rolls (see photos, Shaping Rolls, page 77). Dust the tops lightly with flour, cover with a linen dish towel, and let rest for 10 minutes.

+ Work with one piece of dough at a time, keeping the remaining dough covered. Dust the work surface with flour. You want to stretch the dough as thin as possible— about 12 inches for large pizzas, 10 inches for medium, and 8 inches for small. Using your fingertips or knuckles, press the dough out from the center to begin to flatten it into shape. Then roll it out with a rolling pin, or drape it over your fists to stretch it as you rotate it. If the dough resists and bounces back, cover it and let rest for a few minutes before continuing, then continue to roll or stretch to the desired size. Pinch the edges to make them a little bit thicker.

+ Dust a pizza peel with semolina or cornmeal and move the dough to the peel (once you become proficient using a peel, depending on its size and the size of your baking stone, you may be able to do 2 medium or 3 small pizzas at the same time). Spread some sauce and sprinkle some toppings and cheese over the dough, keeping in mind that the heavier the topping, the harder it can be to transfer the pizza from the peel to the stone.

+ Slide the pizza onto the stone and bake until golden brown: 15 to 17 minutes for a large pizza, 12 to 15 minutes for medium, and about 10 minutes for small. Slide onto a cutting board and cut into wedges to serve.

+ Repeat with the remaining dough and toppings.

TUNA-MELT PIADINA

Makes 2 large piadinas, serving 2 to 4

I was in the café recently when one of our old customers stopped by to tell me he had moved out of town. He wanted me to know that when friends asked what he missed the most about Petaluma, he always said, "Della's Tuna Melt Piadina."

The thing is, I never even liked tuna melts. So when Aaron came up with this concept for the menu, I was less than enthusiastic. In fact, I wouldn't even taste it until Elisa insisted, and, wow, was I surprised! The lively peperoncini and peppery arugula perfectly set off the richness of the tuna and cheese, and the flavor and texture of the pizza crust creates the perfect package.

It's essential to use good-quality tuna, as any "off" taste will become more pronounced on heating. And I recommend using tomatoes only when they are in season; otherwise, leave them out. Once you have all the ingredients ready, the sandwiches will come together quickly. Make these for supper and serve with a crisp Sauvignon Blanc.

Tuna Salad (makes 2⅓ cups)

Two 5-ounce cans chunk white tuna, drained (see Note)

2 tablespoons extra virgin olive oil

1 to 1½ tablespoons freshly squeezed lemon juice (to taste)

½ cup mayonnaise, preferably homemade

½ cup finely chopped red onion

Kosher salt and freshly ground black pepper

1 pound Overnight or Hurry-Up Pizza Dough (page 248 or 249), divided in half

1½ cups arugula

½ lemon

Kosher salt and freshly ground black pepper

About 2 tablespoons extra virgin olive oil

About ¾ cup grated cheddar cheese

½ cup chopped ripe tomatoes (optional)

2 tablespoons sliced jarred peperoncini

recipe continues

Position a rack in the center of the oven and preheat the oven to 375°F.

   ✦ For the tuna salad: In a medium bowl, combine the tuna, olive oil, lemon juice, mayonnaise, and red onion. Add salt and pepper to taste. Set aside.

   ✦ Cover one piece of dough and set aside. Roll or stretch out the other piece of dough into a 10-inch-round: Start by using your fingertips or knuckles to press it out from the center, then roll it out with a rolling pin or drape it over your fists to stretch it as you rotate it. If the dough resists and bounces back, cover it and let rest for a few minutes before continuing.

   ✦ In a small bowl, toss the arugula with the juice of the lemon and season with salt and pepper.

   ✦ Heat a 10-inch cast-iron skillet over medium heat. Add a generous film of oil and heat it for a few minutes, then place the dough in the pan. Cook for about 2 minutes, until it begins to brown in spots, then flip and cook on the second side for about 2 minutes.

   ✦ Remove from the heat and sprinkle about ¼ cup of the cheese over half of the piadina. Spread some tuna salad over the cheese (I use a generous serving, ¾ to 1 cup). Top with a little more cheese, half the arugula, half the tomatoes, if using, and half the peperoncini. Fold the dough over and place in the oven for 1 to 2 minutes to melt the cheese.

   ✦ Be careful when you remove the pan from the oven; the handle will be hot. Remove the piadina from the pan, wipe it out, and repeat with the second piece of dough.

   ✦ Slice the piadinas in half and serve. Leftover tuna salad can be covered and refrigerated for 2 to 3 days.

· Note ·
ON TUNA

The oil-packed tuna from Italy and Spain that comes in jars tastes great, but because you can't tell how it's been fished (often in nets that trap other fish besides tuna), I don't buy it. Instead, I use a fancy grade of large-chunk white tuna that's packed in water and labeled "dolphin safe." My favorite brand is Wild Planet (see Sources, page 270). The tuna is pole- and line-caught, which is the dolphin-safe part of it, and it is also significantly lower in mercury.

NАAN

Naan, a South Asian flatbread, can be baked outside on a grill or indoors on a stovetop grill pan. You brush the bread with melted butter before grilling. Then keep it simple with seasonings—nothing fancier than salt and pepper, maybe some chopped herbs. I like this naan best made with our Firm Starter (page 156), but if you don't have any starter ready to go, just make a sponge the night before (see Note). The dough will be a little stickier to work with, but the result will still be delicious.

All-purpose flour	340 g	12 oz	2¼ cups plus 3 Tbsp
Whole wheat flour	21 g	0.7 oz	2½ Tbsp
Instant yeast	7 g	0.2 oz	2 tsp
Fine gray salt	7 g	0.2 oz	1¼ tsp
Water, at room temperature (65° to 70°F/18° to 21°C)	184 g	6.5 oz	¾ cup plus ½ Tbsp
Plain yogurt, preferably whole-milk	117 g	4 oz	½ cup
Extra virgin olive oil	11 g	0.4 oz	2½ tsp
Firm Starter (page 156)	206 g	7.3 oz	¾ cup plus 1 Tbsp
Unsalted butter, melted	85 g	3 oz	6 Tbsp
Kosher salt and freshly ground black pepper			
Chopped herbs (optional)			

Lightly oil or spray a deep 4½- to 5-quart ceramic or glass bread bowl. (The amount of dough for this bread will work well in a 3-quart bread bowl, if you have one.)

✦ In the bowl of a stand mixer fitted with the paddle attachment, mix together the flours, yeast, and salt on low speed. Add the water, yogurt, and oil and mix for about 1 minute to combine. Add the starter and mix for 2 minutes to combine. Remove the paddle attachment, scraping any dough on the paddle back into the bowl, and scrape down the sides of the bowl with a plastic bowl scraper.

✦ Fit the mixer with the dough hook and mix on low speed for 6 minutes.

✦ Using the bowl scraper, transfer the dough to the prepared bowl. The dough will be sticky and loose. Cover the bowl with a lightly oiled or sprayed piece of plastic wrap and place in a warm, draft-free spot (see Creating Your Warm Spot, page 17) to proof until very puffy, 1 to 1½ hours.

✦ Flour the work surface. Turn out the dough, using the bowl scraper. Using a bench scraper, scale (divide) the dough into 12 equal pieces (74 grams/2.6 ounces each). Shape each one into a ball (see photos, Shaping Rolls, page 77). Dust the tops lightly with flour, cover with a linen dish towel, and let rest on the work surface for 1 hour. The dough can be stored in a tightly sealed container in the refrigerator for up to 3 days.)

+ Prepare a fire in a charcoal grill or preheat a gas grill to medium-high heat. Or heat a grill pan over medium-high heat. Oil or spray the grill grate or grill pan. If your grill is small or you are using a grill pan, you'll have to make the naan in batches.

+ The naan can easily be stretched with your fingertips or you can roll it out with a rolling pin. If you have them, a chapati board and rolling pin (see Note, page 264) work well for naan too. Lightly flour the work surface and stretch or roll each piece into a 5- to 6-inch circle. The dough can all be shaped at once, keeping the pieces dusted with flour and covered with a linen towel, or it can be shaped a few pieces at a time and grilled in batches. If you're very fast and a good multitasker, you can roll and cook simultaneously.

+ Just before cooking, brush one side of each piece of stretched dough with melted butter and sprinkle with salt and pepper, and with herbs, if using. Place brushed side down on the grill (or place one naan in the grill pan). Brush the top with butter, and season if desired. Grill, adjusting the heat if needed, until the dough is well marked, 2 to 3 minutes. Flip over and grill on the second side until well marked, 2 to 3 minutes. Remove from the grill and transfer to a towel-lined serving bowl to keep warm while you grill the remaining breads. Naan is best the day it is made.

· Note ·
ON MAKING NAAN WITH A SPONGE

In the bowl of a stand mixer fitted with the paddle attachment, combine 128 grams (4.5 ounces/¾ cup plus 2½ tablespoons) all-purpose flour, 77 grams (2.7 ounces/¼ cup plus 1 tablespoon) room-temperature water (65° to 70°F/18° to 21°C), and 1.5 grams (0.05 ounce/½ teaspoon) instant yeast and mix for 2 minutes. Scrape down the paddle and the sides of the bowl and pulse to combine. Cover the bowl with lightly oiled or sprayed plastic wrap and let sit at room temperature for 10 to 15 hours. Substitute the sponge for the Firm Starter.

LAMB TAGINE

Serves 4

I always like recipes that look more complicated and difficult than they are.

My friend David Shalleck is one of the best chefs I know, and a true artist when it comes to food styling. I asked him for some help with a tagine that would be easy to make, beautiful, and delicious. One of the most important methods I learned from him is to rub the spice mixture directly onto the meat and let it sit for an hour before browning. The spices infuse themselves into the meat, creating a wonderful depth of flavor. Then, while the oil is heating, the lamb is lightly dusted with flour. In the past I mixed the spices and flour together, but never again!

One of the delights of tagine cooking is that you will be working in a beautiful vessel that is the ultimate "slow cooker"—everything is done in one pot, and when you present it at the table it adds a touch of exotic drama. The amounts in this recipe fit our go-to 10- to 11-inch tagine (see Baking in a Clay Pot or Tagine, page 102), but another size will work equally well. Just don't overcrowd the base; use only enough meat and onion to fill the base in an even layer. And keep the meat covered with stock, but leave some room at the top so it doesn't bubble over. You can always add a little more as it cooks.

Spice Blend

½ teaspoon saffron threads

½ teaspoon ground turmeric

½ teaspoon ground ginger

1 teaspoon ground cumin

1½ teaspoons Spanish pimentón or paprika

1 teaspoon freshly ground black pepper

2 pounds leg of lamb, trimmed of excess fat and any silver skin, cut into 2-inch pieces (see Note)

Fine sea salt

About ¼ cup all-purpose flour, for dredging

2 tablespoons canola or pure olive oil

½ large yellow onion, cut into 1-inch pieces (about 1 cup)

¾ cup dry white wine

2 cups low-sodium chicken stock, warm

recipe continues

2 bay leaves (bay laurel or Turkish bay, not California)

2 to 3 strips orange zest (use only 2 if the orange is particularly fragrant)

⅔ cup dried apricots

¼ cup golden raisins

⅓ cup fresh pomegranate seeds

3 cups cooked rice

Naan (page 257) or Chapati (page 263)

Crush the saffron threads and blend with the remaining spices.

⁺ Rub the blend into all sides of the lamb. Lightly cover with plastic wrap and let rest at room temperature for an hour.

⁺ Season the lamb with the salt and lightly dredge in the flour. Heat the oil in the base of a 10- to 11-inch tagine starting with very low heat and raising it to medium-high heat. Brown the meat in batches and set aside.

⁺ Add the onions to the tagine and cook until lightly browned, 3 to 5 minutes. Add the wine and cook, scraping any browned bits from the bottom and the sides of the tagine, until the wine has reduced and about 3 tablespoons remain.

⁺ Add the lamb to the onions in an even layer in the bottom. It is OK if the pieces touch a bit, but they should not overlap or be too snug. Pour in enough of the stock to cover the meat, but keep below the rim of the tagine. Add the bay leaves and the orange zest, place the cover on the tagine, and bring the liquid to a boil. Lower the heat to keep the liquid at a slow, even simmer. During the cooking, from time to time, keeping the lid off for as little time as possible, check the level of the

stock and the rate of the simmer, adding stock as needed to come to the top of the meat and for the simmer to be slow and steady. After 2 hours, add the apricots and the raisins, gently pushing them just below the surface of the liquid and between the pieces of meat. Continue to cook until the meat is very tender when pierced with a fork, about 1 hour more.

⁺ Remove the bay leaves and zest. Scatter the pomegranate seeds across the top and bring to the table in the tagine.

⁺ Serve with white rice and bread on the side.

· Note ·
ON LAMB

Not all lamb is the same. We are lucky to eat lamb raised on our ranch. It really is night and day from store-bought lamb, which can have a strong flavor. Some would call it gamy. If you have lamb that tends this way, another great tip from David is to rub a little distilled white vinegar on the meat a few minutes before it gets the spice mixture. This will help to neutralize some of the gaminess.

CHAPATI

⤷ Makes 10 chapatis ⤶

Chapati, sometimes called roti, is different from naan in that it calls for whole wheat flour, and serves as more of the daily bread in an Indian household. I love these best with lamb curry or other Indian food, a torn-off piece substituting for an eating utensil. Chapati can also be filled with rice and vegetables and rolled up like a burrito or other wrap.

Whole wheat flour	130 g	4.6 oz	¾ cup plus 3 Tbsp
All-purpose flour	125 g	4.4 oz	¾ cup plus 2½ Tbsp
Fine gray salt	6 g	0.2 oz	1 tsp
Extra virgin olive oil	30 g	1 oz	2 Tbsp plus 1 tsp
Hot water (112° to 120°F/44° to 49°C)	180 g	6.3 oz	¾ cup
Vegetable oil (optional)			
Unsalted butter, melted	57 g	2 oz	4 Tbsp

Lightly oil or spray a 4½- to 5-quart ceramic or glass bread bowl. (The amount of dough for this bread will work well in a 3-quart bread bowl, if you have one. But the larger 4½- to 5-quart bowl that is needed for all the other doughs will work just fine too.)

✦ In a large, shallow bowl, use your hands to combine the flours and salt. Add the olive oil and then the hot water and mix with your hands until you can gather the dough into a ball.

✦ Lightly flour the work surface. Using a plastic bowl scraper, turn out the dough and knead until you have a smooth ball, about 5 minutes. Put the dough in the prepared bowl, cover with a lightly oiled or sprayed piece of plastic wrap, and let rest for at least 30 minutes, or up to 6 hours.

✦ Scale (divide) the dough into 10 equal pieces (47 grams/1.6 ounces each). Roll the dough into balls. Dust the tops lightly with flour, cover with a linen dish towel, and let rest on the work surface for 30 minutes. This rest will make the dough easy to roll out. (The balls can be stored in a tightly sealed container in the refrigerator for up to 3 days.)

✦ Lightly flour a chapati board, if using (see Note), or the work surface. Dip your hands into a little flour and use your fingertips to pat each ball into a round. Then work with one piece at a time, keeping the remaining rounds covered. Using a rolling pin made for chapati (see Note) or a traditional rolling pin, roll each piece into a thin 6- to 7-inch round (see photos, Making Chapati, page 265). The rounds can all be rolled out at once, keeping them dusted with flour and covered with a linen towel, or they can be rolled out a few at a time and cooked in batches. If you're very fast and a good multitasker, you can roll and cook simultaneously.

✦ Heat a 10-inch cast-iron skillet over medium-high heat. If your pan is not well seasoned, add a very thin film of oil. When the pan is hot, gently set a chapati in the pan and watch for it to start bubbling and browning a little on the underside, about 30 seconds (see photos, Making Chapati, opposite). Brush with melted butter, flip it over, and brown on the other side, about 30 seconds. Brush again with melted butter, and flip back to the first side. With a spatula, gently press on the edges and rotate it in the pan, cooking until in bubbles up, 15 to 30 seconds. (Do not be discouraged if it doesn't puff up—if there are any tiny holes in the surface, air will escape and it will not puff, but that does not mean it will be any less delicious.) Remove from the pan (it will deflate) and place in a towel-lined serving bowl to keep warm. Carefully wipe out any flour in the pan, heat a little more oil, only as needed to keep the chapati from sticking, and cook the remaining chapatis.

✦ Chapatis are best eaten while they are still warm.

· Note ·
ON CHAPATI PIN AND BOARD

Although not essential, a traditional board and pin (see Sources, page 270) are great for making chapati. The small round board will serve as a guide to rolling out even rounds.

Courage in the Kitchen
❧ TAKE A BREATHER ❧

When making quick-cooking flatbreads like naan and chapati in batches, cooking them can get away from you. If that happens, resist the urge to try to plow through them: finish the batch you're working on, stop, and take a breath. This is especially important if you're working on other parts of your dinner at the same time.

If you think the pan is getting too hot, it probably is. Lower the heat before you continue. If you tried to flip the dough too soon and it stuck, give the bits of dough a minute to burn off, then scrape the pan clean, re-oil it, and continue.

The same holds true for pizzas. Handling a peel takes practice, and some of your toppings may end up on the stone, on the bottom of the oven, or even against the back of the oven. Your kitchen might get a little smoky, but resist the urge to clean up the mess right away. Give whatever you're working on the time to cook, then clean up stray bits.

If the pizza flops off the peel onto the stone, you still might be able to save most of it. If it can't be saved, let the stuck-on mess cook for a few minutes, then carefully scrape it off. Give the stone a few minutes to reheat, and try again.

Making Chapati

Chapati dough comes together very quickly, making it a great bread to make at the last minute. But the dough can sit at room temperature for up to 6 hours.

(1) Mix the dough by hand. (2) Roll into balls. (3) Flatten with your fingertips. (4–5) Roll into a thin round. (6) Cook until it puffs and browns in spots.

KNÄCKEBRÖD

Makes 16 large crackers

There are some nights when Ed and I aren't in the mood for a big dinner. In fact, left to my own devices, most nights supper would be small plates, hors d'oeuvres, little nibbles, or grazing food. Swedish hardtack, or knäckebröd, is the best cracker for piling on multiple ingredients such as cream cheese, smoked fish, pickled onions, and capers. These sturdy guys will stand up to just about anything, and although they never last long in our household, I'm told they will keep for weeks. Historically they were used by sailors to survive long sea journeys.

In the days when people routinely had to deal with pesky rodents, they needed to find clever ways to keep their precious goods out of harm's way. Most solutions involved hanging the items on some sort of contraption that the mice couldn't climb. The clever Swedes did this by putting a hole in the center of their crackers so they could be threaded onto a stick or broom handle and suspended. I make my holes with bottle tops and thread them onto drumsticks. I tie a piece of kitchen twine to each end of the drumsticks and hang them from a hook, or even a pot handle.

The first time I made these, I rolled them out with a regular rolling pin and docked (pricked) them with a fork. It worked, but then I found a traditional notched rolling pin online for about $20 (see photo, page 238). Of course I had to try it, and it made a magnificent product. That rolling pin flattened out the circles in no time, and it left the traditional dents you find in RyKrisps and similar products. I recommend you try docking them with a fork the first time and then, if you love these crackers as much as I do, invest in the special rolling pin (see Sources, page 270).

Warm water (80° to 90°F/27° to 32°C)	275 g	9.7 oz	1 cup plus 3 Tbsp
Instant yeast	12 g	0.4 oz	1 Tbsp plus ½ tsp
Cumin seeds	7 g	0.25 oz	1 Tbsp
All-purpose flour	270 g	9.5 oz	1¾ cups plus 3 Tbsp
Rye flour	82 g	2.9 oz	¾ cup plus 1 Tbsp
Whole wheat flour	72 g	2.5 oz	½ cup
Mixed seeds (see Note)	145 g	5 oz	1 cup
Fine gray salt	7 g	0.3 oz	1¼ tsp

recipe continues

In the bowl of a stand mixer fitted with the whisk attachment, combine the water, yeast, and cumin seeds and whisk to blend. Remove the whisk and fit with the dough hook.

✦ In a medium bowl, whisk together all the remaining ingredients. Add the dry ingredients to the wet and mix for 7 minutes, or until the dough comes together around the dough hook. Remove the dough hook and, using damp hands, scrape any dough from the hook back into the bowl. Cover the bowl with a lightly oiled or sprayed piece of plastic wrap and let sit until puffy and about doubled, 45 minutes to 1 hour.

✦ Meanwhile, position the racks in the upper and lower thirds of the oven and preheat the oven to 425°F. Line two half sheet pans with parchment paper or silicone baking mats.

✦ Lightly flour the work surface. Using a plastic bowl scraper, turn out the dough. Pat it out into a rectangle about 1 inch thick. Scale (divide) the dough into 16 equal pieces (55 grams/1.9 ounces each). Shape each one into a ball (see photos, Shaping Rolls, page 77). Dust the tops lightly with flour and cover with a linen dish towel.

✦ Since these crackers are rolled out very thin, only 3 will fit on each pan at a time, so this will need to be done in batches. Work with one piece of dough at a time, keeping the remaining dough dusted with flour and covered with the linen towel. Using your palm and flattened fingers, flatten and press one piece into a disk about 5 inches across. Then, with a rolling pin made for knäckebröd or a traditional rolling pin, roll the dough until it won't stretch any

further and is about 7 inches across. It is OK if these are not perfect rounds; in fact, it's better if they aren't. With a bottle screw top or a 1-inch round cookie cutter, punch a hole in the center. Transfer to one of the prepared pans and go on to the next one, putting 3 crackers on each pan. If using a traditional rolling pin, prick the surface of each with a fork.

✦ Bake for 5 to 6 minutes, then rotate the pans from top to bottom and front to back (you can also flip the crackers over if you like for more even browning). Bake for 5 to 6 minutes more, keeping a watchful eye on the crackers. You want them to have some nice color (it won't be even) but not be burned. They need to be crisp and strong before you remove them from the oven. Think of the first bake as your observation bake, and figure out your hot spots and time and techniques from there.

✦ Transfer the crackers to cooling racks, and bake the remaining crackers.

✦ When the crackers are cool, thread them onto drumsticks, chopsticks, or whatever works in your kitchen and then, as written in the headnote, this is where they will live until you eat them. No amount of money could buy a better decoration for your kitchen.

· Note ·
ON SEEDS

I use a mixture of flax, black and natural sesame, and fennel seeds, but I have seen recipes with sunflower, anise, and pumpkin seeds, and even with minced fresh rosemary. Use your favorites.

SOME PARTING WORDS

Home bakers are a passionate lot. Many have sent me photos that amaze me and make me say, "I wish I'd baked that!" Really, these are pictures of masterpieces, and in them I see the time that it took, the skills that were developed, and, most of all, the pride of the baker's accomplishment. I encourage you to take pictures and document your creations—the real thing will be gone before you know it.

My friend David Sheff is a devoted home baker and an accomplished author. He wrote *Beautiful Boy* and, more recently, *Clean,* and in 1980 he did the last in-depth interview with John Lennon and Yoko Ono, for *Playboy.* David generously let me quote an excerpt from it.

He started the interview by asking John what he'd been doing.

LENNON: I've been baking bread.
PLAYBOY: Bread?
LENNON: After I had made the loaves, I felt like I had conquered something. But as I watched the bread being eaten, I thought, "Well, Jesus! Don't I get a gold record or knighted or nothing?"

That pretty much sums it up. No matter what we do with the rest of our lives, how large or small our paychecks, how famous or modest our talents, pulling a heavenly scented crusty loaf of bread out of the oven ranks right up there with being knighted or winning an Academy Award. And for that kind of thrill, wouldn't you just want to do it over and over again? I'll answer for myself: Yes, I do—every day.

SOURCES

*Here's a list of my favorite purveyors. Many of these items
likely can be found in your own local stores—I'm a big
believer in supporting local businesses; seek them out.*

Ingredients

BAY STATE MILLING
Tel: 530-666-6565

Flours and grains
(for professionals only)

CENTRAL MILLING
centralmilling.com

Many flours and grains,
including durum wheat, cracked
wheat, rye, pumpernickel, and
wheat bran

GIUSTO'S
giustos.com

Flours and grains, including
whole wheat, semolina, and
polenta

KING ARTHUR FLOUR
kingarthurflour.com

SAF red instant yeast; many
flours and grains, including
diastatic malt powder

L'EPICERIE
lepicerie.com

Chocolate, including Valrhona
Guanaja 70%

MOTHER'S
mothersnatural.com

Instant barley

RANCHO GORDO
ranchogordo.com

Dried beans

THE SPANISH TABLE
spanishtable.com

Anchovy-stuffed olives,
pimentón, and piquillo peppers

VELLA CHEESE COMPANY
vellacheese.com

Vella Dry Jack

WILD PLANET
wildplanetfoods.com

Tuna

Equipment

AMAZON
amazon.com

Cambro storage containers,
chapati board and rolling pin,
perforated pie pans, baking
mats, and other baking
equipment

BASKETS OF AFRICA
basketsofafrica.com

Fair-trade baskets

BRAM
bramcookware.com

Clay pots and tagines

EMILE HENRY
emilehenryusa.com

Cookware and bakeware,
including Flame clay pots and
tagines

HEMSLÖDJ
hemslodj.com

Knäckebröd rolling pin

ILEONI
ileoni.com

Bread bowls and other
kitchenware

JB PRINCE
jbprince.com

Pullman pans and other baking
equipment

LA TIENDA
tienda.com

Cazuelas

LE CREUSET
cookware.lecreuset.com

Cookware and bakeware,
including round and oval cast-
iron pots

LODGE
lodgemfg.com

14-inch baking pans, cast-iron
skillets, and grill pans

MY WEIGH
myweigh.com

Assorted scales, including the
iBalance 2600 and 5500 models

OXO

oxo.com

Digital scales, silicone sink strainer, pop-up steamer basket, and liquid measuring cups

SAN FRANCISCO BAKING INSTITUTE

sfbi.com

Bread baskets (bannetons), lame and blades, wooden boards and peels, linens (couches), plastic bowl scrapers, and bench scrapers

THE SPANISH TABLE

spanishtable.com

Cazuelas

STUDIOPATRÓ

studiopatro.com

Linen dish towels and aprons

SUR LA TABLE

surlatable.com

Baking stones, cookie sheets (with no sides), quarter sheet pans, half sheet pans, KitchenAid Artisan stand mixers (and extra bowls), fluted pastry wheels,

pastry brushes, 8-inch cake rounds

THERMOWORKS

thermoworks.com

Thermapen thermometers

WILLIAMS-SONOMA

williams-sonoma.com

Silicone baking mats, cooling racks, La Chamba cookware, loaf pans, food processors, palette knives (icing spatulas), rolling pins, and pizza cutters

ACKNOWLEDGMENTS

Thank you to all of the bakers at Della Fattoria.
These dear hardworking and talented people have caught the magic
and spend their days baking the bread of my dreams.

Thank you to my editor at Artisan, Judy Pray. I couldn't ask for a more perfect match; from the moment we met, I knew I would love her. She and her team at Artisan worked so hard to sculpt and craft this book.

Thank you to my agent, Kitty Cowles; she has an eye and ear for stories that need to be told and the persuasive abilities of a snake charmer! Looking back, I realize she knew the road to completion would be long and arduous, but she just smiled and cheered me on, allowing me to do things I would have thought impossible.

Thank you to Amy Albert for helping me find the words, and for performing the daunting task of trying to keep me on schedule, a bit like herding cats. We met years ago when she did a story on us for *Fine Cooking*; we have been friends ever since.

Thank you to Amy Vogler for making sense of my recipes, for the countless hours she spent testing and writing them, and for being the precise (but compassionate) brain that I lack. I thought I was getting a recipe tester and instead found my right hand, the most meticulous proofreader ever, and a new dear friend and collaborator.

Thank you to Ed Anderson, photographer extraordinaire. I would say he makes everything more beautiful, but he would hate that. His aesthetic is more about honesty and finding the beauty in our scars and wrinkles. I love what he does.

Thank you to Michel Suas for believing in me and helping me set up my first ever baking space, and for loaning me a little fork mixer while I waited for the big spiral to come from Italy. I have never understood how it took six months to get the bill for that first spiral mixer, but I have always remembered the kindness.

Thank you to my lifelong friend Stuart Sutton, who introduced me to my husband, Ed, in 1963, taught me how to make "survival stew" in our starving student days, and bought me my first potato peeler. In 1990 he gave me the copy of *The Italian Baker* that would forever change our lives. He was a "first reader" on this manuscript, and he and his partner, Jon Paul, are forever part of the Weber family.

Thank you to Steven Barclay and Garth Bixler, dear friends, for support, encouragement, and reminding me to just tell the story. And thank you for giving Ed and me a place to stay in Paris. It opened our eyes to the tradition of fine bakeries and cafés that was so essential in creating our own café.

Thank you to Peggy Knickerbocker, who took us under her wing and opened door after door for us. Having a friend who just happens to be a cookbook author and food writer is invaluable to a first-time writer.

Thank you to Jan Rodd for calling her customers whenever I baked to announce there would be a basket of bread arriving at her nail salon at 3 P.M. She was my original sales manager, and I will always remember the day she looked me square in the eyes and said, "You're going to make it you know." It made me believe.

Thank you to my friend and office mate Kandi Figone, who sat next to me trying to run the business side of things while I was trying to find these words. She endured my fits of frustration and covered for me in my absence while I was writing this book.

Thank you to all who stepped up and kept Della going strong over this past year. I would especially like to thank my kids, Elisa and Aaron, and our dynamite café manager, Kim Bourdet. And finally, thank you to my husband, Ed, who lent his support, ate mountains of bread, and distracted and recharged my batteries with beautiful Sunday drives.

INDEX

A

Aaron's Spicy Slaw, 78, 79
air holes, 233, *233*
anchovies: Sun-dried Tomato–Olive Tapenade, 137, 139
Arborio Rice Bread, *36*, 37–38
Aunt Clara's Wheat, White, and Pumpernickel Bread, 64–65
autolyse, 26
avocado: Green Salad, 192, *193*

B

Backus, Barbara, 173
baguettes, 26, *147*
    Baguette and Épi, 182, *183*, 184–85
    shaping, *146*
    Traditional (Sweet) Baguette, 142–44
baker's box, 28–29
baker's grave, 111, 233
baker's percentages, 28–29
baker's terms, 26–28
baking:
    in cast-iron pot, 106, 202
    in cast-iron skillet, 210
    in clay pot or tagine, 102–3, *103*, 202
    in other vessels, 119
    process, 26
    in two standard loaf pans, 86
    in two traditional loaf pans, 50–51
baking stone, 16, 18
barley:
    instant (note), 67
    Wheat and Barley Pullman Loaf, 66–67

basil:
    Della Panzanella, *226*, 227
    Durum Crackers, *242*, 243–44, *245*
    Tomato Bread Soup, 223, *224*, 225
    Tomato Sauce, 250, 253
bâtards, 26
    Crouton Rags, 225
    making two (medium), 189, 221
    Pain au Levain Bâtard, 188–89
    Pain de Campagne Bâtard, *162*, 163
    Polenta Bâtard, *218*, 219–20
    Potato Levain Bâtards, 190
    Pumpkin Seed Campagne Bâtard, 164, *165*
    Sausage-Sage Levain Bâtard, *194*, 195–96, *197*
    Seeded Wheat Bread Bâtard, *214*, 215
    shaping, *52–53*
    Walnut Levain Bâtards, 191, *193*
beans:
    fresh dried beans (note), 125
    Jakob's Bean Spread, 180–81
    Kathleen's Pot of Beans, 123, *124*, 125
bench scraper, 21, *21*, 44
Beranbaum, Rose Levy, 80
biga, 26, 96
    Biga, 100–101
    Country Wheat Boule, 104, *105*, *106*
    Free-Form Pane Pugliese, *116*, 117–19
    Olive Oil Wreath, 128, *129*, *130*, 131
    Pane Durum Dough, 132
    Pane Pugliese Boule, 118–19
    Pane Toscano Loaves, *120*, 121–22
    Traditional (Sweet) Baguette and Épi, 142–44
boules, 27
    Chocolate Cherry Campagne Boules, 170, *171*
    Country Wheat Boule, 104, *105*, *106*
    Garlic Jack Campagne Boule, *172*, 173–74

D

David, Elizabeth, 37

de-gas, 27

Della Panzanella, *226*, 227

Della's Roll Dough, 73

    Dinner Rolls, 76, *77*

    Hamburger or Hot Dog Rolls, 74–75, *75*

demi-baguettes, *see* baguettes

dimpling, 27

Dinner Rolls, 76, *77*

doneness, checking, 58

dough:

    buttery/sticky, and flour on work surface, 82

    getting the feel of, 41, *84*

    prevention of sticking, 113

    ready for baking, 39

    scoring, 107, *179*

    slack, handling, 199

    slack, making the most of, 191

    sticking to hands, 101

dough cutter, 21, *21*

Durum Crackers, *242*, 243–44, *245*

Durum Rusks, 139

E

eggs:

    Egg Salad, *136*, 137, 139

    Toscano Trenchers, 123, *124*, 125

    weighing, 83

enriched breads, 69–93

    brushing doughs before and after proofing, 86

    Della's Roll Dough, 73

    equipment needed, 72

    flour on work surface, 82

    Rose's Overnight Brioche Dough, 80–82, *84*

    techniques, 72

épis, 27

    Baguette and Épi, 182, *183*, 184–85

    Traditional (Sweet) Baguette and Épi, 142–44

equipment, 14–21

    sources, 270–71

F

fermentation, 25, 26, 150

Ferretti, Elena, 216

Field, Carol, *The Italian Baker,* 96, 97

finger test, 39

Firm Starter, 156–57

    Baguette and Épi, 182, *183*, 184–85

    Ciabatta, 234–35, *235*

    feeding, 150–51, *158*

    Naan, 257–58

    Pain au Levain Dough, 186–87, *187*

    Pain de Campagne Dough, 159

    Pane Integrale (Wheat Bread) Boule, *208*, 209–10

    Polenta Bâtard, *218*, 219–20

    Pumpernickel Rye Boule, 206–7

    Seeded Wheat Bread Dough, 211–12

first proof, 25

flatbreads, 237–68

    Breadsticks (Knobby Witches' Fingers), *245*, 246–47

    Chapati, *262*, 263–64, *265*

    Durum Crackers, *242*, 243–44, *245*

    equipment needed, 239

    Hurry-Up Pizza Dough, 248

    Knäckebröd, *266*, 267–68

    Naan, 257–58

    Overnight Pizza Dough, 249

    Spicy Cheddar Crackers, 240–41, *241*

    techniques, 239

flour, 9–12

    all-purpose, 10

    bread, 10

    durum, 12

    pumpernickel, 12

    rye, 10

    semolina, 12

    storing, 12

S

salads:
    Aaron's Spicy Slaw, *78*, 79
    Della Panzanella, *226*, 227
    Egg Salad, *136*, 137, 139
    Green Salad, 192, *193*
    Tuna Salad, 255–56
salt, 13
    coarse sea salt (note), 176
Sam's After-School Bread, 48–51, *48*
Sauce, Tomato, 250, 253
Sausage-Sage Levain Bâtard, *194*, 195–96, *197*
scale (noun), 14, 16
scale (verb), 28
scoring dough, 107, *179*
Scott, Alan, 96–97
second fermentation, 25
second proof, 26
Seeded Wheat Bread Dough, 211–12
    Seeded Wheat Bread Bâtard, *214*, 215
    Seeded Wheat Bread Boule, 213
seeds, note, 268
Semolina Oval Loaf, 230, *231*, 232
Shalleck, David, 259
shaping, 25
    baguettes or demi-baguettes, *146*
    bâtards, *52–53*
    boules, *46–47*
    naturally leavened dough, 167
    pre-fermented doughs, 167
    pre-shaping, 44, *45*
    rolls, *77*
Sheff, David, 269
soup: Tomato Bread Soup, 223, *224*, 225
sources, 270–71
Spice Blend, 259–60
Spicy Cheddar Crackers, 240–41, *241*
Spicy Slaw, *78*, 79

sponge, 28, 33
    making Naan with, 258
    Sponge for Brioche, 80–81
starter (pre-ferment), 28, 96, 150
    extra, 157
    feeding, 150–51, *158*, 232–33
    Firm Starter, 156–57
    Milk Starter, 110–11
steam, creating, 108–9, *109*
Stewart, Martha, 216, *217*
stews: Lamb Tagine, 259–60, *261*
sticking, prevention of, 113
Sticky Buns, *88*, 89–90
storing bread, 51
sugar, 13
Sun-dried Tomato–Olive Tapenade, 137, 139

T

tagine:
    baking in, 102–3, 202
    Lamb, 259–60, *261*
tapenade: Sun-dried Tomato–Olive Tapenade, 137, 139
thermometer, 21
timer, 21
tomatoes:
    Della Panzanella, *226*, 227
    Sun-dried Tomato–Olive Tapenade, 137, 139
    Tomato Bread Soup, 223, *224*, 225
    Tomato Sauce, 250, 253
    Tuna-Melt Piadina, *254*, 255–56
Toscano Trenchers, 123, *124*, 125
Traditional (Sweet) Baguette, 142–44
transfer peel, 145, *145*, *152*
tuna:
    note, 256
    Tuna-Melt Piadina, *254*, 255–56
    Tuna Salad, 255–56

CONVERSION CHARTS

Here are rounded-off equivalents between the metric system and the traditional systems used in the United States to measure weight and volume.

WEIGHTS		VOLUME			OVEN TEMPERATURE			
US/UK	METRIC	AMERICAN	IMPERIAL	METRIC		°F	°C	GAS MARK
¼ oz	7 G	¼ TSP		1.25 ML	VERY COOL	250–275	130–140	½–1
½ oz	15 G	½ TSP		2.5 ML	COOL	300	148	2
1 oz	30 G	1 TSP		5 ML	WARM	325	163	3
2 oz	55 G	½ TBSP (1½ TSP)		7.5 ML	MEDIUM	350	177	4
3 oz	85 G	1 TBSP (3 TSP)		15 ML	MEDIUM HOT	375–400	190–204	5–6
4 oz	115 G	¼ CUP (4 TBSP)	2 FL OZ	60 ML	HOT	425	218	7
5 oz	140 G	⅓ CUP (5 TBSP)	2½ FL OZ	75 ML	VERY HOT	450–475	232–245	8–9
6 oz	170 G	½ CUP (8 TBSP)	4 FL OZ	125 ML				
7 oz	200 G	⅓ CUP (10 TBSP)	5 FL OZ	150 ML				
8 oz (½ LB)	225 G	¾ CUP (12 TBSP)	6 FL OZ	175 ML				
9 oz	255 G	1 CUP (16 TBSP)	8 FL OZ	250 ML				
10 oz	285 G	1¼ CUPS	10 FL OZ	300 ML				
11 oz	310 G	1½ CUPS	12 FL OZ	350 ML				
12 oz	340 G	1 PINT (2 CUPS)	16 FL OZ	500 ML				
13 oz	370 G	2½ CUPS	20 FL OZ (1 PINT)	625 ML				
14 oz	400 G	5 CUPS	40 FL OZ (1 QT)	1.25 L				
15 oz	425 G							
16 oz (1 LB)	450 G